Truisms II

Other Books by Alexander Theroux

FICTION
Three Wogs
Darconville's Cat
An Adultery
Laura Warholic; or, The Sexual Intellectual

FABLES
The Schinocephalic Waif
The Great Wheadle Tragedy
Master Snickup's Cloak
Fables

SHORT FICTION
Early Stories
Later Stories
Cape Cod Tales

POETRY
The Lollipop Trollops and Other Poems
Collected Poems
Truisms
Godfather Drosselmeier's Tears and Other Poems

NONFICTION
The Primary Colors
The Secondary Colors
The Enigma of Al Capp
The Strange Case of Edward Gorey
Estonia: A Ramble Through the Periphery
The Grammar of Rock: Art and Artlessness in 20th Century Pop Lyrics
Einstein's Beets: An Examination of Food Phobias
Artists Who Kill and Other Essays on Art

Alexander Theroux

§

Truisms II

TOUGH POETS PRESS
ARLINGTON, MASSACHUSETTS

Copyright © 2024 by Alexander Theroux.

Cover artwork by Edward Sorel.

ISBN 979-8-218-54517-8

Tough Poets Press
Arlington, Massachusetts 02476
U.S.A.

www.toughpoets.com

For Sarah,
Shiloh and Shenandoah,
sun, moon, stars

"*Volu ut sis.*"
(I want you to be what you are.)
—St. Augustine

"Vision is the art of seeing what is invisible to others."
—Jonathan Swift

Prologue

I would like to offer this second volume of truisms to readers of mine as an added allowance to those who, being familiar with the collection of my book *Truisms*, might wish to see more. Putting together this selection, I have continued to think of it as a repeated visit to a land where information comes in the kind of capsule form that makes truth not only easy to see but also corroborates a manifest reality that we all recognize, know, and share. As an assemblage, this book comprises all new work and extricates nothing whatsoever from the previous one.

A truism simulates proverbs, each one a repository of what arguably suggests the inevitability or, say, irresistibility, of an ever-fixed mark. There are Mafia adages—"You never get no back talk from no corpse"—and African proverbs such as "You must be a friend to get a friend"—and *Poor Richards Almanac*-isms: "We do not inherit the earth from our ancestors, we borrow it from our children." "The eye never forgets what the heart has seen"—and no end of Chinese adages, mainly corrective, often negatives like "A fierce dog bankrupts a liquor store" and "There is no road, the road is made as you walk" and "He who hides his faults plans to make more." And "Want a thing long enough, and you don't." A truism involves a disclosure, can sound a headline, calls upon the rude inexorable, the inescapable, the undeniable, and, in that each is a declaration that states or even approaches a general truth, seems sweeping—comprehensive, daringly all-inclusive, unrestrictive, even usurpative—and so as an Absolute can be disquieting. A universal assertion is being made, after all. The principal notion is *always* a force which can be either a comfort or a burden.

Evermore is complicated—continuous infinitive. The perpetual, the lasting, the persistent. While a truism remains abiding by dint of its insistent authenticity, that it can approach dogma may invite scorn. A vigorous truth, in a sense, bullies us to believe by its display and in a very real way, confronts an individual to challenge or contest it as a fact. What compels, tyrannizes. One can hear or discern in a truism an imperative mood that makes a direct command in asking belief. Yet that certainty can serve as an anodyne, as well. Has not the poet Jalal Ad-Din Rumi told us with assuring calmness, "The wound is the place where the light enters you"? "What you seek is seeking you," he says. "Sell your cleverness and buy bewilderment." "Lovers don't finally meet somewhere. They're in each other all along." To go without models was the great Sage of Concord's plea to us, an exhortation that we be original. Did this idea lie behind American cynic Ambrose Bierce's *infra dig* definition of an aphorism, what he referred to as "Predigested wisdom"—which he also called "driblets"!

The poetry of Alexander Pope glitters with epigrams, which is also the case with Henry Fielding in his novels. Mark Twain's *Pudd'nhead Wilson* is replete with adages. Cyril Connolly's *The Unquiet Grave* is an assembly of French maxims. Sun

Tzu's *The Art of War* is a catch basin of axioms. Reading the works of Tolstoy, Jane Austen, and George Eliot, one comes across no end of bywords, precepts, maxims, and memorable brocards. Dr. Samuel Johnson lived to pontificate and very rarely without concise, succinct, and compendious pronouncement: "All theory is against the freedom of the will; all experience for it." "Patriotism is the last refuge of a scoundrel." "Where grief is fresh, any attempt to divert it only irritates." "The chief glory of every people arises from its authors." "Nothing is more hopeless than a scheme of merriment." "No man was ever great by imitation."

Law in all nations down through history is a parade of legal maxims: "*Actus dei nemini facit injuriam*" (The act of God causes injury to no one.) "*Volens non fit injuria*" (No injury can be done to a willing person) "*Ubi jus ibi remedium*" (There is no wrong without a remedy, or where there is a legal right, there is a remedy. "*Fraus et jus nunquam cohabitant*" (Fraud and justice never dwell together)

It is the same with Wall Street and the stock market. "I got rich by selling too soon" (Bernard Baruch.) "A paper loss is a very real loss." (Jim Rogers) "A bull market is like sex. It feels best just before it ends." (Barton Biggs). "The four most dangerous words in investing are 'This time it's different'." (John Templeton). Risk, alone, is a subject spawning no end of truisms. "I am cautious about going against the herd; I am liable to be trampled on." (George Soros) "If you stick around when the market is severely against you, sooner or later they are going to carry you out." (Randy McKay). Other's I have heard—"Never catch a falling knife" and "Bull markets climb a wall of worry" and "Leverage should never expire."

There is a long tradition in spiritual writings of the aphorism. The manuscript of the "Sayings of Jesus" in the fragments of the Oxyrhynchus Papyri, found in 1897 in Egypt, constitute such precepts, for example, along with, say, the *Apophthegmata Patrum*, a collect of adages of Egyptian monks, dating from both the 4th and 5th centuries, and the Marcionite Prologues, found in many manuscripts of the Vulgate, to say nothing of the Scriptural Book of Proverbs. I am thinking, as well, of special works on the interior life such as the *Cautelas* and *Avisos* of St. John of the Cross; the works of the 12th-century Guigo II the Carthusian, sometimes referred to as Guy or by the moniker the "Angelic" —his most famous book is most commonly known today as *Scala Claustralium* (*The Ladder of Monks*), although it has also been known as the *Scala paradisi* (*The Ladder of Paradise*)—*The Ladder of Divine Ascent*, the ascetical treatise for monasticism in Eastern Christianity, written by John Climacus in c. 600 A.D., and, indeed, the *Imitation of Christ*, the 15th-century devotional written by the German-Dutch canon regular Thomas a Kempis, and which, according to the martyr St. Thomas More, is one of the three books everybody ought to own.

"We are all debts owed to death," "Dancing is silent poetry," "I have often regretted my speech, never my silence" are some of the truisms or epigrams of Simonides of Ceos, (c. 556–468 B.C.), Greek lyric poet and a well-known writer of encomia, whom the philosopher Xenophenes, out of some ancient pique, used to describe as a "*kimbix*," some sort of annoying insect, gnat, or midge.

Along with the *Analects of Confucius* and the book of Ecclesiastes, pithy aphorisms,—often mere scraps of thought— are found everywhere. The Cambodian revolutionary leader, dictator, and politician Pol Pot Cambodia who ruled as Prime

Minister of Democratic Kampuchea between 1976 and 1979 had a penchant for coming up with them, a mindless of spate of grim sloganeering chants—brainlessly cruel and savage—repeated by the fanatical Khmer Rouge, such as "To spare you is no profit, to destroy you is no loss," "No gain in keeping, no loss in weeding out," "He who protests is an enemy; he who opposes is a corpse," "Hunger is the most effective disease, "Better to kill an innocent by mistake than spare an enemy by mistake." The bloodthirsty and often frankly inhuman remarks which are compiled in Henri Locard's *Pol Pot's Little Red Book: The Sayings of Angkar*, remain, despite the ghastly portentousness of the evil and brutish words, a valuable contribution to the study of Cambodian history and to the study of genocide in general. Locard examines the nature of the extensive collection of such commonly repeated sayings from this barbaric period, and the picture they paint is chilling. The mindset of the Pot regime was a volatile mixture of savagery, cunning, and unyielding extremism: a government of sociopaths, with not a smidgen of concern for the welfare of its own people. Few phrases illustrate this more vividly, memorably, than their most widely known sayings.

Racism flourishes with sleazy apothegmata. James Baldwin: "The only way to police a ghetto is to be oppressive," "To be a Negro in this country and to be relatively conscious is to be in a state of rage almost all of the time." Louis Farrakhan: "When you want something in this world, the Jew holds the door." Joseph Smith: "Had I anything to do with the Negro, I would confine them by strict law to their own species." Brigham Young: "You must not think, from what I say, that I am opposed to slavery. No! The Negro is damned and is to serve his master 'till God chooses to remove the curse of Ham." The late Prince Philip of England loved them. "If it has four legs and is not a chair, has wings and is not an airplane, or swims and is not a submarine, the Cantonese will eat it," he said. In 1988 he declared: "I don't think a prostitute is more moral than a wife, but they are doing the same thing."

Many a truism, solid as gold, however, goes straight to the heart of fact and validates human behavior. Truisms ride on conviction. "Anything that consoles is fake," pronounced novelist Iris Murdoch, who also memorably declared, "Between saying and doing, many a pair of shoes is worn out" and "Love is the difficult realization that something other than oneself is real." Thomas "Stonewall" Jackson was a studious aphorist—"Never take counsel of your fears," "I sweat my men tonight, that I may save their blood tomorrow," and "Shoot the brave officers, and the cowards will run away." The sagacious rhetorician G. K. Chesterton wrote "Impartiality is a pompous name for indifference, which is an elegant name for ignorance," "An inconvenience is only adventure wrongly considered" and "The true soldier fights not because he hates what is in front of him, but because he loves what is behind him." He also wittily declared, "Poets have been mysteriously silent on the subject of cheese" and "The traveler sees what he sees. The tourist sees what he has come to see," and "Do not be so open-minded that your brains fall out."

Among other random favorites of mine are "There is something monstrous about a woman who writes." (Anita Loos) "To know all is not to forgive all. It is to despise everybody." "Music is the shorthand of emotion" and "The more you care, the more you fear." (Wayne Gerard Trotman). "Heretics are the only bitter remedy against the entropy of human thought." (Yevgeny Zamyatin). The original is one who returns to the origins." (St. John of Damascus). "Peace comes from within. Do not seek it without" and "We are shaped by our thoughts, we become what we think." (Buddha). "We become what we repeatedly do." (William James). "Never confuse motion with action" (Benjamin Franklin). "There is another world, but it is this one." (Paul Eluard, on the plight of the poor.) "The secret of a successful restaurant is sharp knives." (George Orwell) "All wine tastes like cider to me." (Gene Fowler) "Never put anything really hot in your stomach." (Diana Vreeland) "If we are not self-created, we are answerable to a truth we don't produce." (Rowan Williams, Archbishop of Canterbury). "A dinner ending without cheese is like a beautiful woman with only one eye." (Brillat-Savarin) "The God who made New Hampshire/taunted the lofty land with little men." (Robert Frost) "The writer is the one that does not look away." (Akira Kurosawa) "O have never known anyone worth a damn who wasn't irascible." (Ezra Pound) "Truth is tarter than taradiddles and nothing is tarter, terser, than truth on the track of tired trash in a trance." (Frederick Rolfe, Baron Corvo)

Love is a common—if, indeed, not the most recurrent—epigrammatic topic. "The most exclusive love for a person is always a love of something else." (Marcel Proust) "The homosexual world is a world of spinsters." (Quentin Crisp) "It is death that lends spice to our kisses." (Jan Greshoff) "Loving—is that not one person making a present of his own loneliness to another? It is the ultimate thing that one can give of oneself." (Clarice Lispector) "You will find love the day you can show your own weakness without the other person using it to affirm his strength." (Cesare Pavese) "The first duty of love is to listen." (Paul Tillich) "In matters of the heart, nothing is true except the improbable." (Madame de Stael) "A man can be happy with any woman, as long as he does not love her." (Oscar Wilde)

A bunch of anonymous truisms occur to me, as well: "A falling knife has no handle." "Hurt people hurt people." "Holding a grudge is like drinking poison and waiting for the other person to die." "If your neighbor has wind chimes, you have wind chimes." "Perfect is the enemy of good enough." And what about the state of Texas? "Pigs get fat, hogs get slaughtered." "Never sign anything by neon." "No real Texan ever squats on his spurs." "Never approach a bull from the front, a horse from the rear, or a fool from any direction." "Life is simpler when you plough around the stump." "Never miss a good chance to shut up."

Surely Charles Dickens may be numbered among quondam aphorists, having notably written, among other things,

> "It was the best of times, it was the worst of times, it was the age of wisdom, it was the age of foolishness, it was the epoch of belief, it was the epoch of incredulity, it was the season of Light, it was the season of Darkness, it was the spring of hope, it was the winter of despair."

and, of course, Shakespeare, author of a good many of them, far, far too many possibly to begin to list. One example in *Hamlet*, Act I, Scene 3, has the sententious Polonius, a windbag to some and a rambler of wisdom to others, although it has also been suggested that he only acts like a "foolish prating knave" in order to keep his position and popularity safe as well as to keep any nosy individuals from discovering his plots for social advancement speak the following lines to Laertes:

> "Neither a borrower nor a lender be,
> For loan oft loses both itself and friend,
> And borrowing dulls the edge of husbandry.
> This above all: to thine own self be true,
> And it must follow, as the night the day,
> Thou canst not then be false to any man."

So, praise the truism. Its gift is its concision, a metaphorical schema, so to speak, its framework its model, empowering itself by way of its blunt yet enormous economy and allowing value judgments to be made without any—never mind heavy—rhetorical assertion. A truism is an exhortation, in that it calls upon a reader for belief, a nod of agreement. "Not believing in force is the same as not believing in gravity," said Leon Trotsky, not only an individual who knew a good deal about force, arguably the ultimate exhortation, but who was something of an aphorist, as well. "Revolutions are always verbose," he declared. "Fascism is nothing but capitalist reaction." "Insurrection is an art, and like all arts has its own laws." "The end may justify the means as long as there is something that justifies the end." "Technique is noticed most markedly in the case of those who have not mastered it."

A great prose epigram, curiously, can often function—indeed, serve quite well—as a line of verse. "Give me liberty of give me death" (Patrick Henry), "No man has a good enough memory to be a successful liar" (Abraham Lincoln), "The creation of a thousand forests is in one acorn" (Ralph Waldo Emerson), "All faults may be forgiven of him who has perfect candor." The weak can never forgive. Forgiveness is the attribute of the strong" (Mahatma Gandhi) On consideration, you will find, I believe, that it proves true more often than not.

One needs to hear for comfort—to have verified—what ultimately seems to be perpetually the case. History repeatedly shows the universality in the nature of our behavior. The profound ascetic, radical political activist, uncompromising philosopher, intellectual, and French mystic, Simone Weil, than whom, zealous for God, no one was more passionately spiritual, stated, "The future is made of the same stuff as the present." This brave Christian was both in her piety and social commitment a mistress of the apothegm: "All sins are attempts to fill voids." "The destruction of the past is perhaps the greatest of all crimes." "To be a hero or a heroine, one must give an order to oneself." "The love of God is pure when joy and suffering inspire in us equal gratitude." "God withdrew from his creation because only love and not force, however well-intentioned, could serve both His and man's true purpose." "Everything beautiful has a mark of eternity." "Mercy is a specifically divine attribute. There is no human mercy." "Every sin is an attempt to fly from emptiness."

Ralph Waldo Emerson, who desired all Americans to be poets and mystic, brought a perpetual newness to the truism. "In the thought of genius, there is always a surprise," he wrote in "Experience," his most carefully wrought essay. Nothing he ever wrote was wanting in what could legitimately called a memorable adage. "The American Scholar," the oration he delivered at Harvard on August 31, 1837—a manifesto of insight and erudition that the great scholar Harold Bloom called "the central meditation upon American literary originality"—is replete with gnomic brilliance: "The one thing in the world, of value, is the active soul," "One must be an inventor to read well." It was the same a year later in his "Divinity School Address:" "Let me admonish you, first of all, to go alone: to refuse the good models," "The child amidst his baubles, is learning the action of light," "He who does a mean deed, is by the action itself contracted," "Every man is a divinity in disguise, a god playing the fool," "Life is as journey, not a destination."

One truism simply but powerfully follows another in Emerson's "Self-Reliance," a speech published in *Essays—First Series* (1841): "In every work of genius, we recognize our own rejected thoughts: they come back to us with a certain alienated majesty . . . I shun father and mother and wife and brother, when my genius calls me." Reading for us, he insists—thinking—should be taking back what is ours! "When good is near you, when you have life in yourself, it is not by any known or accustomed way: you shall not discern the foot-prints of any other."

So, here I am again. The truisms in this grouping—analects, I propose—are more than anything salvageable observations. I did not pluck arbitrary ideas from popular notions and pin them to paper, capsule-wise. History, inevitably as it rolls, breaks like crashing waves onto a rude shore, leaving as it recedes shards and shells, scraps and fragments to be picked up by any curious and questing beachcomber with a wandering interest and a scrap bag. I can say I have found, felt, and learned these truths from wide if indiscriminate reading, as well as from my own repeated—and often feverish—thoughts. How else indeed are they born? Francis Bacon, Pascal, Erasmus, Friedrich Nietzsche, Oscar Wilde, among others who favored the medium, would surely agree—even going back to Pythagoras, Hesiod, Epictetus.

I have always also been struck by the gnomic utterances of the brilliant Ludwig Wittgenstein, as much a poet as a philosopher, and not only in his pithy and astonishing *Tractatus Log-*

ico-Philosophicus but in much of his other writings: "What can be shown, cannot be said." "Language disguises thought." "The limits of my language mean the limits of my world." "Philosophy is not a theory but an activity." " If a lion could talk, we could not understand him." "It is love that believes the Resurrection." "Nothing is so difficult as not deceiving oneself." "A serious and good philosophical work could be written consisting entirely of jokes."

Leo Tolstoy, in his religious writings, specifically in his *A Confession* and his *The Gospel in Brief,* the latter which by the way had an immense effect of Wittgenstein—asserted that the book "essentially kept him alive" during World War I—was often aphoristic and breviloquent. Some examples: "The true life is outside time; it is in the present." "It is impossible to prove the truth. The truth itself proves all the rest." "Moses gave us a law, but we received the true faith through Jesus Christ." "No one has seen God or will ever see God, only his son, who is in the Father, has shown us the path of life." "Do not make any distinction among men as to nationality, and love strangers like your own people."

Religion can often breed sanctimonious cant, and frankly some aphorists are dullards. Peter Deunov, a nature mystic who lived in Bulgaria from 1864 to 1944, who, in his preaching developed a form of Esoteric Christianity known as the Universal White Brotherhood—he was white bearded and benevolent and looked like everyone's idea of St. Peter—was of just such a theosophical bent, a moralizing, pietistic sentimentalist of the "Half of what I say is meaningless, but I say it so that the other half may reach you" ilk, the sort of figure puffed by the likes of swami-inclined Wayne Dyer, the facile self-help and motivational speaker who launched about 40 dim-witted books with titles like *Wishes*

Fulfilled and *Pulling Your Own Strings*.

Deunov's spiritual name was "Beinsa Douno," and several of his unmemorable but quirky exhortations are: "People are free only when they think," "You will come to resemble the food you eat"—he hated meat, insisted fasting got rid of fear, and declared that all food should penetrate the tongue ("So food should remain longer in the mouth")—and "Gossiping is a form of impurity."

Any observer in a social world inevitably sees trends. Assertion in abrupt form can seem rude—even personally chauvinistic. In 1927, the journalist and satirist Karl Krause published his *Epigramme*, which includes such gems as "Solitude would be an ideal state if one were able to pick the people one avoids," "Psychology is as useless as directions for using poison," "The secret of the demagogue is to make himself as stupid as his audience, so they believe they are as clever as he." "An aphorism can never be the whole truth; it is either a half-truth or a truth-and-a-half," "There is no more unfortunate creature under the sun than a fetishist who yearns for a woman's shoe and has to settle for the whole woman." "Politics is what a man does on order to conceal what he is and what he himself does not know."

"It is more comfortable for me, in the long run, to be rude than polite," declared the painter/writer Wyndham Lewis, a master of the adage, the epigram, the philosophical brocard. "The Modern World is due almost entirely to Anglo-Saxon genius," Lewis insisted on saying. "You should be emotional about everything, rather than sensitive." "Laughter is the wild body's song of triumph." "As a result of the feminist revolution, 'feminine' becomes an abusive epithet." And witty P.G. Wodehouse in the course of having written over a hundred books was a fund of sharp truisms, as only he in his many memorable literary moments could come up with them: "Red hair, sir, in my opinion, is dangerous," "All the unhappy marriages come from the husband having brains," "Musical comedy is the Irish stew of drama," "You would not enjoy Nietzsche, sir. He is fundamentally unsound," "'There are moments, Jeeves, when one asks oneself, 'Do trousers matter?'"

What I am presenting here in fine, then, is a continuation of subject matter by way of new aphoristic additions not yet seen before, but ones that I wish to preserve, in spite of the fact that we are told by none other than Vincent van Gogh, "Do not become the slave of your model." Bumptious as it may sound, I only wish to declare here, by way of underlining if not reinforcing it, that I am well in contact with myself. Creativity has no off-season. I carry around thoughts not unlike the way the bumbling, but earnest and uninspired President Millard Fillmore humped a dictionary along with him at all times in order to improve his vocabulary.

I was and am reminded in the making of this compilation of the sage advice, quoted in Matthew 9:17, against putting new wine in old wine bottles, or as the English journalist, political philosopher, novelist, and irrepressible radical William Godwin—a zealous promoter himself of many lucid truisms ("Justice is the sum of all moral duty," "Superior virtue must be the fruit of superior intelligence," "God himself has no right to be a tyrant," "Human depravity originates in the vices of political constitution," "Act up to the magnitude of your destiny," "There is reverence that we owe to everything in human shape," etc.)—has duly warned us, "No one can display or can cultivate a fervent zeal in the mere repetition of a form."

I wholeheartedly agree. I wholeheartedly agree. Let me add that in my every attempt at putting a poem to passage I have come to understand fully what Dr. Samuel Johnson meant when, out of stressful experience, he declared, "Of the caution necessary in adjusting narratives, there is no end." Therefore, I plead, let the content absolve the form—and wish my reader blessings.

Truisms II

Victorian children mainly drank beer at lunch.
As many as seven states all border Kentucky.
High interest rates invariably cause a credit crunch.
Italians consider the number seventeen unlucky.

No woman has ever become the world's richest person.
Jesus created fish and bread for breakfast (John 6:1–13).
Criminologists believe that sexual problems link to arson.
Many prudes consider the "Song of Solomon" obscene.

Clouds drawn by kids all have the shape of France.
All quack products hawked on TV sell for $19.95.
Any horse has suffered who's been taught to prance.
Leather tanners breathe deadly toxins as they skive.

Sexist—the role's to groom his wife!—is the word *groom*.
A drowned man mainly floats on his face, not on his back.
The fly agaric cep, a conspicuous but harmless mushroom,
beloved of all gnomes, fairies, looks like a fatal death cap!

Marble is by far the best work surface for pastry.
Only the shiny side of foil reflects heat: use it face down,
A tectonic valley bottom is swallowing the Dead Sea.
One's natural teeth are less durable than a dental crown.

The sport of high jumping constantly ends in failure.
Yeast breads need gluten for strong elastic structure.
Prostitution is fully legal throughout all of Australia.
The sole preoccupation of Millenarians is the Rapture.

Not one scene of whipping/bodily torture can be found
in *Uncle Tom's Cabin*—Stowe purposely omitted them.
Mainly because early foods were stews, plates are round.
Heart failure is often co-indicated by red or pink phlegm.

Any charge is, somehow, always proven once it is made.
Flattering an audience is classic show business pandering.
Young girls, not a bride's pals, in the UK are bridesmaids.
Turkey least accepts extra-marital affairs or philandering.

Pope John Paul condemned any and all armed conflict.
Visitors to Verona rub the Juliet statue's right breast for love.
The tallest flowering plant on Earth is the eucalypt.
No rule in boxing requires that combatants first touch gloves.

Scale—in all instances—is everything.
Jesus—Matthew 5:34—warned that no one take an oath.
Everyday, all day, all things on the planet are eating.
Nitrogen in saltwater controls the amount of plant growth.

Baked beans are as full of starch as any dress shirt.
The length of a dash in code is equivalent to three dots.
No piety exceeds that of a newly religious concert.
As able for work on logic as hymns was Isaac Watts.

Succès d'estime ultimately butters no parsnips.
A woman cannot literally *testify* when taking an oath.
Nitrogen gas is what puffs bags of potato chips.
Agathokakological means one is good and evil, both.

It is a chilled *palate* that causes ice-cream headache—
sphenopalatine ganglionneuralgia, i. e, brain freeze.
While cooking does not, one needs an oven to bake.
Every panda on the planet belongs to the Chinese.

Protestants are completely indifferent to Mariology.
Boundaries work to liberate as well as confine limits.
Scallops, whose muscle we eat, can't close their shells tightly.
Thomas the Apostle was also known as Didymus.

Franz Kafka burned more than 90% of what he wrote.
All cruciferous vegetables taste much better buttered.
"Kidding" it's called when birth is being given by a goat.
Restaurants serving sharkskin soup should be shuttered.

Moses is in fact not a Hebrew but an Egyptian name—
and it shares the same root as kings named "Rameses."
A name with a dactyl and a spondee guarantees fame.
Political hacks and hangers-on all live on their knees.

No agreed image of Jesus Christ's face exists.
Eggs are not once mentioned in the New Testament.
Encyclopedic novelists love to make long lists.
Architect Stanford White was master of the pediment.

Brigham Young, who had 72 wives, always slept alone.
Observing the unsaid is a key to reading autobiographies,
The past is both a stepping-stone as well as a millstone.
Child performances on film are not acting, but mimicries.

Rowers see where they've been, not where they're going.
The bigger the truck, the smaller the head of the man driving it.
Sow traditionally choose middle of the night for farrowing.
A $100 bill's 3D security ribbon make it tough to counterfeit.

Islam rejects idea of a Trinity (cf. *Qur'ān*, Maryam, 16:35):
"It beseems not Allah that He should take to Himself a son."
A "frozen rope" is old baseball slang for a hard line-drive.
Cotton candy can only be made centrifugally by being spun.

In Canada, glass eels are the most valuable seafood.
Reductive exegesis is exactly what a work of art opposes.
No extended motorcycle ride does not cause lippitude.
Stuttering was a speech condition suffered by Moses.

A true sailor is able to smell a boat from its ball of twine.
European children wear socks with sandals, a U.S. fashion crime.
Broad Australian English is humorously denoted "strine."
Automobile drivers between 45 and 55 have the best reaction time.

TRUISMS II

Al Capp's Li'l Abner was perennially 19 years old.
Lobster heads used in bisque serve just as good as tails.
Bart Simpson stays 10 years old, any growth on hold.
Everything is water, according to philosopher Thales.

Curnonsky insisted all food should taste of what it is.
A white burgundy is Chardonnay; red burgundy, Pinot Noir.
A specific modified heart muscle is the Bundle of His.
Port Salut is the superb mild cheese of the Pays de la Loire.

The 1911 *Encyclopedia Britannica* set is the nonpareil.
If red wine soils a white dress, white wine poured on de-stains it.
A death knell is three times rung of a church bell's peal.
Adverse possession grants full ownership to whomever claims it.

Pure greed is what wakes a lawyer up every morning.
Interpretation is to literature is what improv is to music.
Meat gets added iron but also fat and sodium by corning
Literally untranslatable is the Russian word "*мужик*."

Wind always conveys in it the tentativeness of life.
Podiatrists occupy steerage in the medical profession.
The decency of a man shows in the health of his wife.
As a cabbie runs a meter, a psychiatrist runs a session.

Carson McCullers called the voices of Negroes "brown rivers."
Christ crucified was, notably, pierced by a lance on his *left* side.
On every Vincent Van Gogh canvas, the subject matter quivers.
He is in fact Dr. Jekyll *transformed*—there *is* no Edward Hyde!

The Chinese translation for AIDS is *aisibing*, which conveniently
also happens to be a homophone "the sickness of loving capitalism."
Singapore, with a low crime rate, deals with no offenders leniently.
Mary Baker Eddy's pet aversion was the use of animal magnetism.

There is no mention of Jerusalem in the *Qur'an*.
Dr., to be pedantically correct, should be abbreviated "D.r."
Mountaineering is completely banned in Bhutan.
No exam taken isn't made unnerving by a walking proctor.

It is never once said in the Bible that we have a soul.
A grasshopper's favorite food is other grasshoppers.
Euphemisms to UK upperclasses are considered prole.
American women are fanatical recreational shoppers.

Anyone's long reach constitutes a jurisdiction.
Showbusiness wives are unwelcome in Vegas casinos.
A Buddhist mind is stretched by contradiction.
Using a mouth to point is common among Filipinos.

An author's hastily scribbled autograph implies disdain,
airs, loftiness, condescension, vanity: "I'm a busy man."
The Commonwealth of Massachusetts once included Maine.
Revealed over a period of 23 years was the Holy *Qur'ān*.

Diderot blamed the potato as the cause of all flatulence.
Wyoming in the United States produces the most coal.
Pernod anise liqueur is a timorous imitation of absinthe.
The pathogens of most human parasites are protozoal.

TRUISMS II

Pat Kennedy Lawford, who alone had a bad relationship
with her father, unlike all the rest of her siblings—she felt
ignored and, enjoying the long distance—rarely took a trip
to the family compound, dealing with what she was dealt.

"Yankee," a British term for GIs during World War II,
was never used for Union soldiers during the Civil War.
Back in ancient Rome, all servants wore the color blue.
In bowling, the 7 pin is often called the "mother-in-law."

Both God and Man, Jesus is one Christ, not two—
one, not by his divinity turned into flesh, rather
by God's taking humanity to himself, created new
in the unity of one person, begotten of the Father.

The Sinatra "Rat Pack" all read at a seventh-grade level.
PTSD, vague, is kingpin of reified psychiatric behaviors.
Not one of the 50 United States is met at an even bevel.
Every dictator gulls the public as bringing them saviors.

A rule of thumb sailing from England to the Caribbean:
go south 'til the ship butter melts, then head directly west.
No plots are more sinister than found in drama Jacobean.
A three day visit is the polite and civil limit for any guest.

The central thesis of Freud fixed on repressed wishes'
substitute forms: memories, slips of the tongue, jokes.
With more than one species, the correct plural is *fishes*.
Only a dominant and submissive animals can be yoked.

Rapists believe a body's gratified, even if the will resists.
Justice Sandra O'Connor hugely disliked Antonin Scalia.
Christ crucified hung by the "Destots space" (the wrists).
No female Dane (cf. *Hamlet*) was ever named Ophelia.

No date is ever stated on any 45 r.p.m. records.
Rahab, the scarlet harlot, was an ancestress of Jesus Christ.
Showbusiness people alone are rabid for awards.
No commodity more than perfume is thievingly overpriced.

"Sir" virtually opened Dr. Samuel Johnson's every remark.
The scent of lemon is the chemical isobutoprochlosniffazine.
Intuition is a driving insistence to fight for light in the dark.
The #1 medium of engagement in her U.S. is the magazine.

Every fear is, at bottom, the fear of loss.
Jesus never once performed a miracle in order to help himself.
No woman has ever won the Victoria Cross.
Catholics say "bless oneself," Protestants say "cross oneself."

Humans are born with two kidneys yet need only one.
Balanchine felt Wagner's music inappropriate for ballet.
Double-entendres alone impart humor and style to a pun.
Pushed to left—the "French pull"—is the military beret.

The word for corn in Chilean Spanish is *choclo*.
A marinara sauce traditionally has no tomatoes.
(A *true* red tomato sauce is *salsa di pomidoro*.)
For mashing, avoid high-starch russet potatoes.

TRUISMS II

Mayflower people called themselves neither Pilgrims
nor Puritans, a term of reproach that they disavowed;
they identified as "Separatists," a term distilled from
choosing to follow doctrines they were not allowed.

Of books beside one's bed, the top alone tend to be read.
Locust trees are first to flower, last to lose their leaves.
*Be*head means to endow one; an execution is to *de*head.
What lost love disregards, jealousy always retrieves.

Ciribiribin in song is a *girl's name*, so are Frenesi,
Amapola, Rama Lama Ding Dong, Be Bop a Lula,
Cracklin' Rosie, Sloopy, Poinciana, Boni Moronie,
Margorine, Macarena, Misirlou, and Malagueña.

James Brown would not go on stage until he was paid.
Fitzgerald's portrait of Gatsby as a bootlegger rings false.
Joan of Arc was a *pucelle*, that is, a virgin, so a maid.
Elvis Presley's "Are You Lonesome Tonight?" is a waltz.

It is impossible to identify a person's gender by hair.
Any person's past in a relationship needs to be solved.
Joan Crawford's shoulders were terrifyingly square.
Human morality and decency have never quite evolved.

If one man can be called Jesus's assassin, that man is Caiaphas.
An *Egyptian*, Thermouthis, raised Moses, gave the baby his name.
No tub-thumping American evangelist is not also a rabid chiliast.
Matisse found an outside/inside link in painting a window frame.

A porthole that cannot be opened is a *deadlight*.
Emily Dickinson had a crush on Henry David Thoreau.
A neurotic's car leaves on a perpetual headlight.
Chionophobia is the name for an intense fear of snow.

Losing a knife overboard on any ship is bad luck,
as is the act of wearing red mittens in a shipyard;
by painting a hatch-cover blue you will go amuck
and by coiling rope counterclockwise also scarred.

Gandhi objected not to Jesus, but to Christians.
Mozzarella made of buffalo milk (not cow's) tastes best.
Herbiverous dinosaurs were all ornithischians.
No English noun exists for a perpetrator of incest.

Knocks on a table to a waiter in China means *thank you*.
First artist in Rock 'n Roll Hall of Fame: Jerry Lee Lewis.
By family wealth, prep school students always rank you.
Although a Moabite princess, Ruth was never a Jewess.

Sechuan and Hunan are the spiciest Chinese cuisines.
The Russell Trust is code name for Yale's Skull & Bones.
Most Muslim nations' flags display a variation of greens.
The fifth of the seven canonical hours (3 p.m.) is *nones*.

Slugger Ted Williams always used a thirty-two-ounce bat.
The Goldman Sachs firm never advised on hostile takeovers.
There were 9 different sites for pioneers to cross the Platte.
The cheapest tickets cost one penny for Jacobean playgoers.

TRUISMS II

The name Wendy was created by W. E. Henley's daughter,
Margaret, who meeting J. M. Barrie, to say "My Friendly,"
being unable to pronounce the letter R—no annunciator—
gave the *Peter Pan* author the lovely new name, "Wendy."

Mice, for safety, consistently travel along baseboards.
"Langley" is via insider code a metonym for the C.I.A.
Not brushing one's tongue fosters bacteria called sordes.
In Tanzania, Gabon, and Gambia, one is punished if gay.

Israel racist Golda Meir declared of all Palestinians
—coldly—"I don't even consider them human beings."
No rivalry for Rome exceeded hatred for Carthaginians.
Bumping noses in Oman is a joyful method of greetings.

Häagen-Dazs ice cream is an utterly concocted name.
All three of Jesus' replies to Satan were taken from Deuteronomy.
Dying scorned is almost always the true legacy of fame.
Half of any Italian chat or conversation involves dactylonomy.

Poncy rock bands, named to appear tough, use umlauts.
The Bethlehem Magi—the "Three Kings"—were all Gentiles.
Cancer risk are lessened by sulforaphane in Brussels sprouts.
Fraud, via inaccuracy, is the beating heart of dating profiles.

Only wind coming out of the west is called a *zephyr*.
No lineal descendants of Shakespeare were alive after 1670.
A pianist in a bar or a café is called in slang "professor."
The highest risk of a sex-offender is designated "level three."

Start cutting peat only when yellow flag irises flower,
because by then all the oils in the bog will have risen.
It is *both* lime or lemon juice that makes a whisky sour.
Catholic baptism calls for oil and balsam as a chrism.

John Wesley believed children were "natural atheists"
because, over the Lord, they enjoyed nature's leisure,
so, withholding tasty food defeated that spirit's laziest
sin by preventing the expectation of natural pleasure.

A full 80% of the southern hemisphere is only water.
9 (!) to 14 are the ages of a Vladimir Nabokov nymphet.
Mothers let their sons grow up but *raise* a daughter.
Being born, said Samuel Beckett, was his one regret.

Just as the destruction of Jewry provided the necessary
rise and expansion of Nazism, so the ethnic cleansing
of Germans was a precondition—collateral accessory—
for the Stalinization of Poland, the parallel depending.

Old New Englanders ate 3 kinds of pie for breakfast.
Hitler loved Disney's *Snow White & the Seven Dwarfs*.
Queen Alexandra always wore a choker or necklace.
High school bullies constantly torment ectomorphs.

John Philip Sousa's favorite march was "Semper Fidelis."
Nothing is fiercer than a mother's advocacy for her child.
No opprobrium can surpass that of Annas and Caiaphas.
Al-Aqsa mosque entered by a Jew is considered defiled.

TRUISMS II

One of the two oxen in a team is always the lead.
Romans 7:15–25 presages *Notes from the Underground*.
Brown algae is the most commonly eaten seaweed.
Great Britain's most endangered dog is the otterhound.

Paperbacks in the 1940s were seen as lewd.
Queen Elizabeth II never gave an interview.
Piercings may cause belly buttons to obtrude.
The oldest boat in history was a plain canoe.

No boxer hits equally hard with both hands.
Morel and matsutake mushrooms fight cultivation.
Whatever an individual focuses on, expands.
E. A. Poe's "Weir" existed only in his imagination.

The painter "Master of the Embroidered Foliage,"
based in 15th-century Brussels, leaving not a mark
—being anonymous—of any personal knowledge,
we know only by the dainty shrubbery of his work.

Due to the perilous crisis of global warming,
all English gardens move south, climatically
speaking, sixty-six feet per day, conforming
to all official danger signs, symptomatically.

Male friends all desert Chandler's Philip Marlowe.
Only 1/6 of an eyeball is exposed to the outside world.
Monagasques are banned from Casino Monte Carlo.
A lobster tail, properly cooked, is always curled.

In late-19th-century, condoms were known
(wink) as "a little something for the weekends."
a phrase used in England (smile, undertone)
in barbershops, the key retailer, for dividends.

White rum is a must ingredient in true Indian Pudding.
All Lewis & Clark explorers received 1600 acres of land.
The Israeli Mossad cruelly invented criminal hooding.
Not one muscle exists in the fingers of the human hand.

Expectation—wish—is life's greatest impediment.
Molnar's *Liliom* was banned in England for blasphemy.
Sentimentality is the direct enemy of true sentiment.
The pillar of French cuisine are the foods of Gascony.

Lizzie Borden's hated stepmother caught her
naked with maid Bridget, and, fearing she'd tell,
Liz killed her to keep the secret but saw in a blur
that she then had to murder her father, as well.

Abby Borden suffered nineteen mortal gashes,
Andrew, her husband, only ten. So, the rhyme
of Lizzie's forty whacks in those fatal clashes,
same with forty-one, misrepresents the crime.

Petulant opera divas are enormously revered by gays.
Simone Weil found the Gospels warped by the Old Testament.
Psychics see ominous links between Mars and Tuesdays.
Both parents must be recognized in matters of bilateral descent.

Longitude circles going N-S tell E-W distances.
Racing pigeons is the primary sport in Yemen.
Latitude circles going E-W tell N-S distances.
Vitamin C has its highest content in the lemon.

Greenland is a region as bright as white with ice,
which is right by Iceland which is green with flora.
Choose only kidney beans for red beans and rice.
Lack of hospitality was the prime sin of Gomorrah.

A chalky soil bestows in wine the taste of apples.
Serve always from a guest's left, using your left hand.
No pastors nor congregations typify Welsh chapels.
The 27th alphabet letter used to be the ampersand.

Mark Twain insisted that he would rather be damned to
John Bunyan's heaven than read James's *The Bostonians*.
A bothy is a hut is a whare is a shiel is a hok is a lean-to.
A fast or easy smile does not come naturally to Estonians.

Norman Mailer on May 10, 1997, told the *Washington Post*
he'd do a "better job" writing of Christ than the Evangelists.
Clover-eating groundhogs makes the most delicious pot roast.
Ireland still sounds—nine strikes—the bells of the Angelus.

Tibet's Potala, built with no steel, has no elevators.
The CIA has always been Yale-dominated and influenced.
Nile crocodiles are the most aggressive alligators.
Kidney stones can result from thirsts randomly quenched.

Comfort your despair, so as quickly to remove it.
French citizens eat burgers and pizza with cutlery.
Toddlers misbehave to check if adults approve it.
To an anchorite, comfort by definition is a luxury.

H. G. Wells despised the writer Upton Sinclair.
Hedda would appear together, Louella always declined.
It is a fatal challenge among animals to stare.
The nine planets will never, ever, be perfectly aligned.

Seven stands out as the sacred number of infinity.
Women will warp morally if nervously ill too long.
The Korean (Hangul) vowel *I* is pronounced *ee*.
St. Augustine believed that prayer exists in song.

Jesus actually appears rude and biased in Matthew 15: 21–28.
George Eliot based her novel *Middlemarch* on real people.
A French braid crosses *under*, whereas *over* is a Dutch plait.
No corpse nor anything dead is eaten by an American eagle.

"Aeolus" alone in *Ulysses* is "suitable for recital." (Joyce.)
Americans always use *anxious* for *eager*, incorrectly.
The RR logo never spins on the wheels of a Rolls-Royce.
War, a political slant, is always entered into indirectly.

Overweight people are now called "gravity enhanced."
Peter Pan, a boy, is customarily played by a grown woman.
Morals, in retrograde, prove to have never advanced.
Scandalizing a child is the definition of being inhuman.

Natalie Clifford Barney never read anything but poetry.
Pusillanimous Richard Nixon turned critics into enemies.
High fees, claim psychiatrists, *aid* cures in psychiatry!
Voodoo, with its cradle Benin, is a faith of the Beninese.

No predicate contradictory of a thing can belong to it.
People consume more of a product, if/when its price rises.
To obey the "ignore all rules" rule, it's necessary to ignore it.
All professional US sports teams are considered franchises.

Wisteria, a legume, creates its own (nitrogen) fertilizer.
Saints Peter and Paul never really understood each other.
Two tests must be taken by police for the breathalyzer.
Frosting on perfect butter cream cakes must fully smother.

Puss—a quick, brief peck—means to "kiss" in Swedish.
TV's Fred Rogers answered every letter he ever received.
In Israel, banned are most cultural activities in Yiddish.
Most philosophy deals with how experience is perceived.

Bret Harte's poem of 1870, "The Heathen Chinee"
went a long way in inciting cries of "yellow peril."
All their villages were permanent among the Pawnee.
Donkeys can reproduce but mules are always sterile.

Chopsticks, in China are called 筷子—*kuàizi*,
which may be translated as "quick little boys."
The Supreme Court is an entity impossible to sue.
An ongoing *shhh* is audible under white noise.

A few quick courses can make you an official mohel.
Quakerism for R.W. Emerson was perfect Protestantism.
Highbrow girls tend to consider their kisses a bestowal.
Dyslexics are given in speech to the habit of spoonerism.

Thoreau only really felt himself when in opposition,
with an error to correct, a flaw to expose, a fault to fix.
China, Cuba, Ecuador, and Venezuela refuse extradition.
Native Thais and Cambodians avoid using chopsticks.

The spring and autumn seasons both begin with equinoxes;
conversely, summer and winter both start with a solstice.
People surnamed Walters were linked to wolves and foxes.
It is impossible successfully to wipe out swarms of locusts.

The nineteeth-century virtually ended on August 4, 1914.
Virtually no one reads Whitehead's *Principia Mathematica*.
Napoleon died breathing wallpaper painted a toxic green.
A symptom, not a diagnostic condition, is the pain sciatica.

Matthew's Gospel clearly favored Jews over Gentiles.
Bomb and drug sniffing dogs promptly *sit down* to accuse.
Franklin Delano Roosevelt suffered badly from piles.
The Bias of Priene still remains in history the classic ruse.

People surnamed Russell were all originally redheads.
No one should ever try to re-word The Lord's Prayer.
Age 32—midlife!—was the average age of Deadheads.
The Po Valley in Italy, misty, is a perpetual *Brumaire*.

TRUISMS II

Jesus Christ never said a word about his earthly father.
Featherstonehaugh in England is pronounced "Fanshaw."
Still blown today on Rosh Hashana is the ancient *shofar*.
In Scotland, anyone may use your toilet—it is the law.

When working a big puzzle, always do the edges first.
Mafia never whack—"kiss"—a man in front of his family.
Isaac Newton, all of his life, was a practicing alchemist.
Bravery proves itself tried and true solely in a calamity.

Government informants are just the same as spies.
John Singer Sargent had much of a same-sex fascination.
Neither Rolls-Royce nor Lamborgini ever advertise.
A Trappist silence is maintained to foster contemplation.

A police ploy of boxing-in protesters is called "kettling."
Couscous is canonically the last course in a Moroccan meal.
U.S. National Parks prohibit hawking goods and peddling.
Baby cattle are consistently abused that people may eat veal.

Claude Monet believed black did not occur in nature,
so, his shadows were made of blues, greens, and reds.
Fistfights are a commonplace in Taiwan's legislature.
The Brits always eat bacon and peas with sweetbreads.

Sassafras, once the heart of old-time root beer,
now banned, has been replaced by birch extract.
A parachutist's supreme hazard is wind shear,
when he can be highjacked on any sudden impact.

Pietr-le-Letton (1929) was Simenon's first Maigret.
Modern versions of the Lord's Prayer are an abomination.
Serious medical depression is aligned to tattoo regret.
Much feminization of power is solved by emasculation.

It is not done to genuflect with the left knee.
Jacques Daguerre, of photography fame, was a mediocre painter.
A sacrilege is plucking a leaf from a Bo tree.
The Swiss Alps seem to loom higher when the sun grows fainter

Magda Goebbels, ever admitting her love for Hitler,
married her husband, Josef, to be close to the Führer.
Law is the inartistic non-science of the born quibbler.
The first self-portrait (1484) was done by Albrecht Dürer.

Zinfandel, being the best of American of varietals,
are by far the best wines to serve at Thanksgiving.
College pregnancies can be traced to lax parietals.
Jehovah in the Hebrew Bible is utterly unforgiving.

S. T. Coleridge called St. Paul's Romans
"the most profound book in all existence."
To the Igbo, twins are held to be ill omens.
A portrait should look into middle distance.

Without Christ, in theological terms, there is no salvation.
A distinct sexual tension can be felt in every art gallery.
Whenever a film actor asked him to provide motivation,
director Alfred Hitchcock always replied, "Your salary."

TRUISMS II

Sheep, lying down, never feel safe or at ease.
Tampon-makers can't write *vagina* on boxes.
Milton's "L'Allegro" (*not* "Il Penseroso") is a masterpiece.
G. K. Chesterton loved the use of paradoxes.

"*Thank you for taking my phone call!*"
talk-show flunkees mewl to the host,
but, of logic, this is a craven reversal,
for station hacks owe *them* the most.

In his musicals, Cole Porter refused to touch the "book."
The valedictory is poet Philip Larkin's exclusive territory.
Although expressly denying it, Dick Nixon was a "crook."
Always use warm potatoes when making *kluski slaskie*.

Christ likely carried the horizontal "rail" alone,
during his agonizing crucifixion walk to Calvary,
but not the vertical "stile" as is usually shown,
although both configured in that murderous tree.

All immature teenagers are devotees of *Mad* magazine.
Newcomers to cities tend to settle at the point of arrival.
A claw-hammer is forged much softer than a ball peen.
Plain white indicates health in any matters conjunctival.

All Yale freshman in 1910 had to wear hats.
Proximity to death made Hemingway feel most alive.
Inverted sleeping is an escape mechanism for bats.
The 9/11 assassins wielded nothing more than knives.

Most women do not know their vulval particulars.
Boar saliva has a pheromone that primes a sow in heat.
Counterbalancing carriages define all funiculars.
U.S. government subsidize vegetables less than meat.

Taiwanese cooking generally tends to skew sweet.
Acting is all about timing—and nothing more.
All rappers feel macho when singing of the "street."
Baseball pitchers cannot go nine innings anymore.

Sever the two thighs first when slicing up a turkey.
John Bunny and Flora Finch, his screen wife, despised each other.
Brahma, Vishnu, and Shiva comprise the Brahmin *trimurti*.
Forefather is common usage, but one never hears "foremother."

False promises chronicle a political candidate's ambition.
The French use only flageolet beans when serving lamb.
Nuclear fusion is much safer by far than nuclear fission.
Sarah, his wife, was actually the *half-sister* of Abraham.

Middle-seat air passengers command both arm rests.
Raymond Chandler's most dangerous characters are women.
The left side on a woman is always the bigger breast.
Torture, under any circumstances in life, is fully inhuman.

Censorship is ever the refuge of the weak and craven.
Intersections, dangerous, most threaten motorcyclists.
An "unkindness" is the group honorific for the raven.
The United Nations in 1976 termed racist all Zionists.

TRUISMS II

Never uncork champagne at any but a 45-degree angle.
There is no chapter on "friendship" in Thoreau's *Walden*.
Biblical scholarship for millennia is constant embrangle.
A "powder keg" of instability is the region of the Balkan.

Baseball's Joe DiMaggio refused all garlic in his food.
Flight attendants are not paid until the plane starts moving.
Plywood can warp easily because laminated and glued.
A good writer must have a gene for always self-reproving.

All summer squashes are similar in flavor.
Manliness is the product pulp fiction is selling.
A close trim is not a gift of an electric shaver.
Rebellions alone seem to invite the word *quelling*.

Kangaroos never do well in a human situation.
Raymond Chandler despised the novelist James Cain.
The oldest Slavic script is Glagolitic—Croatian.
At first spherical, and then elongated, is falling rain.

The color pink appears on no Rainbow Pride Flag.
Most Americans find a Third Party anti-American.
A coming train is signaled by a horizontal wigwag.
No horse is not made handsomer by a caparison.

Only a virgin can subdue a unicorn,
stare directly into blazing sun, walk
with complete immunity through sharp thorn,
and with a single glance kill a hawk.

Instantly falling in love—*parafulmine*—is madness.
Most accordions are made in the town of Castelfidardo.
Weakness is unfailingly a main constituent of sadness.
La Gioconda (Mona Lisa) was not signed by Leonardo.

No politician's handshake is personal or warm.
"Woman Above" sex posture can regulate her orgasms.
Three dimensions of shape are required of form.
An average cell contains about a hundred trillion atoms.

Bleach, surprisingly, has an expiration date.
All Scots are well-known for keeping their distance.
In Valletta, Malta, all the streets are straight.
An open display of contempt is passive resistance.

Denying God absolutely is as fully absurd
as trying to define such a Being absolutely.
Christianity was initially called "The Word."
Gertrude Stein wrote everything convolutely.

Revelations 9:4–5 says it is fine to torture heathens.
Texas sits only on the marginal outskirts of the Old South.
Jesus intentionally denominated all demons as "legions."
10,000 or more taste buds co-exist within a human mouth.

Effeminate men tend to be saps for whiteware.
Jaén, Spain, is the olive oil capital of the world.
A born New Yorker in the city is never unaware.
The sound of bagpipes, well defined, is skirled.

Salting an eggplant removes all its bitterness.
Showing only an eighth-inch shirt cuff is proper.
To the state of Maine, the Wabanaki are indigenous.
Frass is the term for the feces of a grasshopper.

No true Italian refers to tomato sauce as "gravy."
Froot Loops, multicolored, have the same flavor.
Gun salutes have different meanings in the Navy.
To Earth, Markarian 231 is the closest quasar.

The best-selling women's sweaters are blue.
Artistic talent is completely missing in Christo.
To get a horse to move away, pull a horse *toward* you.
"Cheech" is Italian slang for the name Francisco.

The letter Q appears in no United States name.
Only megalomaniacs insist on exact punctuality.
There is no art copyright on any picture frame.
Negative connotations abound with sinistrality.

Cole Porter passionately loved radio soap operas.
Dictatorships succeed by open support of the masses.
The ancient towers of Ilium (Troy) were all topless.
Refined basically for cattle is blackstrap molasses.

No person should start his religious life too early.
Joe DiMaggio thought garlic stereotyped a "dago."
The main Kentucky cigarette tobacco was burley.
There are 350 calories in a mere 100 grams of sago.

It is impossible to hold your nose and hum.
Bees in the UK are held as part of the royal family.
A line intersecting all meridians is a rhumb.
Everyone learns what he is made of in a calamity.

Dragnet's Sgt. Joe Friday (Jack Webb) hated every hippy.
Sheep are visually identified solely by tags on the ear.
It takes three months for water to travel the Mississippi
For violin strings, there is no substitute for horsehair.

Much of the gay community reveres Judy Garland.
Titus Andronicus is Shakespeare's bloodiest play.
There are no killer animals to be found in Ireland.
Of all flowers, the peony has the loveliest bouquet.

No angels (or demons) in Scripture are ever female.
Art gallery chairs, well placed, discourage lolling.
English has replaced French for all postal *air mail*.
Individuals who never say thank you are appalling.

The word "momentarily" is bastard English.
Joy perfume was named by fat, ugly Elsa Maxwell.
Between education and training, distinguish!
No clam or mollusk can survive without its shell.

Vermont is the whitest state (95.6 percent) in America.
Hemingway refused to supply blurbs to anyone's books.
The Masonic world, ritualistic, thrives on esoterica.
Each spawning river contain its own genetic Chinooks.

TRUISMS II

Under Gresham's Law as applied to biography,
colorful stories consistently drive out true ones.
Flamingos bend their legs at the ankle, not the knee.
The U.S. Congress has genius for cost overruns.

Wild game for Jews is never considered kosher.
World passports are kept dark to look more official
Red is the most commonly grown forage clover.
No compilation of human history is not prejudicial.

Milan Kundera never called his (young) native country
Czechoslovakia, for, as he said, it has "no roots in time."
Officialdom in Great Britain is solely ruled by gentry.
Rap music is a brainless slave to simpleminded rhyme.

Martin Buber's favorite psalm was Psalm 73.
No woman's hair beats Edward Weston's cabbage leaf.
Social freedom always threatens a democracy.
If a drink is not an alcoholic one, it is never an aperitif.

No love poetry exists in Wordsworth's entire oeuvre.
Broadcaster Vin Scully hated baseball's Old Timers' Games.
It was as a *fortress* that King Philip II built the Louvre.
A backyard is allowed for burial of a loved one's cremains.

Okra must not be excluded in a Brunswick stew.
Champs in boxing rings are always introduced first.
No Southern state hasn't the "definitive" barbecue.
Airplanes have never featured a gear for reverse.

A "born-again" Christian is a person who is rescued.
Harvard College has always been resolutely Unitarian.
Despondency of the human spirit is the worst hebetude.
St. Paul's Corinth was rife with debauchery and prostitution.

A V-sign facing palm inwards is an obscene gesture.
Anyone can hit a homerun to Fenway Park's right field.
Wolves in fairy tales loved disguises of fake vesture.
Any woman bringing on a hero's death is Brünnhilde.

William Faulkner never wrote for *The New Yorker*.
The nation of Ghana has endless nameless streets.
No propellant is needed for a satellite magnetorquer.
Fiber length, not thread count, matters in bed sheets.

Seventy percent of *True Crime* readers are women.
NYC's Church of the Transfiguration welcomes anybody.
Korean *sujeonggwa* is perfected by a persimmon.
China's Yellow River, or *Huang He*, is beyond muddy.

The biometric is the most secure type of safe.
A hitchhiking Black man rarely gets a ride.
The British name Ralph is pronounced *Rafe*.
Astride, you straddle; "on the back," bestride.

Lewis Carroll, 31, tried to wed, at 11, Alice Liddell.
Nabokov requested no girl appear on the jacket of *Lolita*.
A clam is a shellfish that cannot see or hear or smell.
When hunting, it is its *tail* that helps steer the cheetah.

TRUISMS II

Every virus compulsively must copy itself.
Survival is a basic substrate of all Jewish humor.
Catholics don't say cross—but *bless*—oneself.
A two-flue was the iron of a whaling harpooner.

A snail in its perambulations never gets lost.
Diaghilev never commissioned an American composer.
Flavor is inevitably sacrificed in any defrost.
Hire a dozer for excavation; for pushing, a bulldozer.

Black writers Chester Himes and Richard Wright,
James Baldwin and Ralph Ellison refused to admit
Uncle Tom's Cabin worthy, calling old Tom "white,"
but he bravely rebels and is whipped to death for it!

Every life as it spins comes full circle like a wheel.
Amos 'n Andy never mentioned race in their broadcasts.
A new convert to anything ever shows excess of zeal.
Narcissistic aging women are demons for fibroblasts.

Pug dogs are given compulsively to sneeze.
Legs must come greatly into play doing a sidestroke.
Scented candles bode ill to the superstitious Chinese.
Frank O'Hara toasted his lovers by drinking a Coke.

Repentance always implies forgiveness.
A tomato should never go *near* clam chowder.
The Puritans, to a one, reviled Christmas.
For a teaspoon of baking soda, triple baking powder.

Writer Raymond Chandler disliked Roman Catholics.
Feigning or pretending in the final analysis is lying.
Conforming is valued by the military, not mavericks.
No crawl space is not improved by dehumidifying.

As a child first is, so in essence he or she remains:
a timid infant becomes a shy adult, a curious child
continues to be inquisitive, seeking what explains,
a soft-hearted tot growing fully fledged and mild.

The British, with a need for order, love to queue.
No Rorschach blot is not halved as symmetrical.
Edison's first lightbulb filament was carbonized bamboo.
Antipodes are, by definition, always diametrical.

Pop music is a genus, whereas rock is a species.
St. John's Gospel was poet John Donne's favorite.
Mostly bacteria, not old food, comprise all feces.
Fascists, demanding conformity, badly belabor it.

Judaism only became a recognized world religion
after the Hebrew Bible was translated into Greek.
Virtually never seen is a (long nested!) baby pigeon.
No penalty exists for leading out of turn in bezique.

There is no stasis or evasion, not even in death,
which transforms to memory and remembrance,
but is human continuity, bottomless as to depth,
true recollection or merely ghostly resemblance?

Hedda Hopper's hats, Imelda Marco's shoes,
Maria Callas' scandals, Perle Mesta's teas,
Elsa Maxwell's parties, Clara Bow's screws—
those hoarders never had enough of these.

The Empire State Building has its own zip code.
After an amputated leg, Cole Porter wrote not another note.
Traveling in straight lines go the rays of a cathode.
Forty percent of Millennials now cast a non-white vote.

Norman Mailer believed round sums (for fees) "unlucky,"
found women writers unreadable, and hated *all* authority.
The most miles of running water are found in Kentucky.
Mediocrity always perfectly coincides with the majority.

Ayn Rand insisted Communists never smiled—
—she also held Robert Taylor in great disdain
who in the film *Song of Russia* got her riled
for telling a Russian, "That is wonderful grain."

Pilate's wife was the first Gentile to believe.
Actors sadly need to live their lives out loud.
Extra-large women benefit by a Dolma sleeve.
Conformity is the essential nature of a crowd.

In the state of Maine, politically divided
between the coast and its interior, flexibly,
every district, on laws mutually decided,
casts its electoral college votes separately.

The more you own, the more you are possessed.
Table-hopping was forbidden in the Stork Club.
Lord Gordon Byron was *the* poet of the anapest.
A customer keeps the *right side* of a ticket stub.

Fussy Edward VIII's favorite dessert was fruitcake.
Hallowe'en is the most popular "queer" holiday.
Virtually no one can see the habitat of a corncrake.
A "green bell pepper" taste is found in cabernet.

Everybody has Mamie Eisenhower's fudge recipe.
Divas Maria Callas and Renata Tebaldi reviled each other.
Only the Keys in Florida are completely frost-free.
English ivy (*hedera helix*) is the hardiest ground cover.

Popover batter should be cold before baking.
No Englishman, until he explains America, feels content.
Trembling at worship explains Shakers quaking.
It's illegal to photograph the metro system in Tashkent.

Jesus Christ, battened to the cross, was Truth
crucified on the mechanical boards of Logic,
for Logic, stern, discovers nothing, in sooth,
but He embodied the universal Word symbolic.

Colonial Boston, New York, and Philadelphia had
more contact with London than with one another.
2,200 degrees (F.) scorches every rocket launch pad.
If the species isn't a shorebird, it cannot be a plover.

TRUISMS II

He who makes no mistakes seldom makes anything.
Dr. Seuss stated drawing was easy, writing always hard.
A shank always goes to the *right* in as golf upswing.
The fat of choice in almost all Mexican kitchen is lard.

Never pick to eat any cep or mushroom with gills!
All terrain in the state of Florida is as flat as a manhole.
The U.S. stole from the Sioux all of the Black Hills.
Breathing, not spouting water, serves a whale's blowhole.

Tuscany and its inhabitants, from ancient Etruria,
remain different from other Italians, and distinct
—black eye, angular face, wiry, darker euphoria—
bearing in every way that specific Etruscan tinct.

Virility is connoted by men using power tools.
Faulkner called Hemingway a "coward" for his bland style.
To kick sideways is an actual ability of mules.
Mark Twain in photographs is never seen to smile.

Comare is Italian slang for mistress or "godmother."
Airplane flight crews eat different fare than they serve.
Sisters delay having periods when having a brother.
Always turn into the direction of a skid or swerve.

Cane sugar once gave Coca-Cola its great taste—
high fructose corn syrup compromised its flavor,
and its ring now sits flat on the palate, debased,
without a touch of its initial sweet tang to savor.

Solitude may find you, not free of, but full of self.
Roald Dahl said women wrote the best ghost stories.
Since everyone else is taken, one should try to be oneself.
Colonial New York was the prime stronghold of Tories.

Sinatra refused to take a single breath in the middle
of sung lyrics meant to express a complete thought,
because he found that had the effect of a taradiddle
and compromised values that he otherwise sought.

Cooking for another person always perfects the art.
Electrical systems are the weakest part of motorcycles.
His Christian name René was never used by Descartes.
Kilohertz as a term has replaced the word kilocycles.

A classic martini is never shaken, always stirred.
Green buoys (cans) have odd numbers, red even.
Elmer Crowell was the greatest carver of a bird.
Mortal sin in Mosaic law is attributed to leaven.

The New Yorker has always been hostile to puns.
Lover and beloved, tragically, speak a different dialect.
Singer Mel Tormé was a serious collector of guns.
Mohammed Atta, the 9/11 lead assassin, was an architect.

Franz Rosenzweig declared that love is sweet
only when it is directed toward a mortal object.
Misalignment is usual in human pairs of feet.
Infants are 90 percent of victims of child neglect.

TRUISMS II

John S. Sargent never cited Singer signing his work.
Jews cite the O.T. as the ownership deed to Israel.
Quite vivid is the "pull" of Van Gogh's brushwork.
Baldness in males, inherited, is mainly matrilineal.

In the Ethiopian calendar, Pontius Pilate is a saint.
Older brothers boost the odds of younger being gay.
A major paraphilia of domineering men is restraint.
Cottage cheese, like yogurt, depends on sour whey.

The center of a frontier town was the shop of a smithy.
All noir detectives in fiction are weary of the world.
Raymond Chandler dedicated no book to his wife, Cissy.
In gales, the top gallant sail on ships was the first furled.

At the Hôtel de Crillon in Paris, all guests dine
in their suites by room service; *petit dejeuner*
is eaten (*à l'anglaise*) in the breakfast room, fine
as to fettle like a coddled, pampered gourmet.

In Peter George's dramatic novel *Red Alert*,
on which the film *Dr. Strangelove* is based,
the title character is unmentioned; that insert
both Kubrick and Southern fixed post haste.

The best way to learn to write is, basically, to read.
Murderers seek to be caught as sinners want to confess.
Although dormant, living are the cells in every seed.
Recency bias is no different than political correctness.

Vichy will always be the capital of collaboration.
Print media formally capitalizes Black, not white.
Koch Industries conglomerate is a closed cooperation.
Roosters are always mutilated before a cockfight.

Rev. Jim Jones murdered his entire flock
with grape Flavor Aid laced with cyanide,
not with Kool-Aid as repeats common talk,
when 909 innocents (276 children) died.

A true republican (small r) avoids being waited on.
No Georges Simenon novel is not bleakly empirical.
A mushroom grown in horseshit is the champignon.
Cruel exaggeration is the principle of the satirical.

Russian people, inordinately, love strong-arm rule.
Women jazz singers are, predominantly, sapphonic.
Every abuser of children is worse than an animalcule.
Otto von Bismarck was hostile to every Roman Catholic.

The classic tumor cliché is it's "large as a grapefruit."
No full opera production of Maria Callas was ever filmed.
Twenty phonemic language vowels exist in Yakut.
Mercifully stun a lobster electronically before it's killed.

Three short blasts on a boat state: "I am backing up."
To Tarzan, blacks are superstitious, Arabs rapacious.
Organ music means that a soap opera is wrapping up.
Most life went extinct in the Paleogene Cretaceous.

No moronic meme beats a baseball cap worn reversed.
A budding maple tree causes a nosedive in sap for syrup.
The South Pacific island of Nauru is said to be cursed.
Scholars trace the rise of feudalism to use of the stirrup.

Cuttyhunk Island in 1692 was the first place
in the New World colonized by Englishmen.
Slang for where the action is—the "coalface."
Cavalier poets belonged to the "tribe of Ben."

An authentic Texas chili is utterly free of beans.
Palestinian commentators in U.S. media do not exist.
Conspiracy theorists are suspicious of all vaccines.
An aristocratic pursuit in Eliot's *Middlemarch* is whist.

Baseball's Joe DiMaggio disliked pasta *al dente*.
Virtually nothing can kill a yucca or wisteria plant.
No party at Harvard succeeds without cognoscenti.
The S meant nothing in the name of General Grant.

L. Frank Baum's Emerald City was originally white,
"No more green than any other city," but it achieved
its green look only because all its residents, for sight,
had to don green spectacles, thus, seeing so, believed.

Julia Child said the only unfixable meal is a *soufflé*.
Any ocean temps at 79 degrees (F) breed hurricanes.
Bad portents are linked to *Giselle* (1841), the ballet.
"Anticipate the anticipations of others." J. M. Keynes.

Mexico City was initially called Tenochtitlan.
Lobster should only be eaten with drawn butter.
The classic FBI subterfuge is the delivery van.
Pushing, not throwing, is the act of a shot-putter.

Queen Elizabeth II always carried a Launer handbag.
Starting salary for NFL water boys is $53,000 per year.
All currency for Native Americans was *wampumpeag*.
Forever working, even during sleep, is the human ear.

A perfervid Anglican is a contradiction in terms.
Pour the heaviest liqueur first into a layered drink.
Refrigerator handles literally pullulate with germs.
There is always a touch of yellow in salmon pink.

If you are not ten minutes early, you are late.
Never use a speed-pourer in an expensive cognac bottle.
Dominance hides contempt, authority hate.
Women are "immature" and "deformed," said Aristotle.

Concord, Mass., was *the* 19th bastion of abolitionism.
Any translation that is not literal is counterfeit fable.
Mental collapse is often the upshot of perfectionism.
Silver is the very best conductor for an electric cable.

Hannah Arendt remained a sharp critic of Zionism,
regretting that it chose to carve a narrow minded
nation-state, rather than seeking by ethical tropism
a detente with the Palestinians, remaining blinded.

TRUISMS II

The painter Claude Monet was visually impaired.
85% of blacks who smoke, smoke menthol cigarettes.
Plato believed women should be communally shared.
Fast-food chains put the knife to luncheonettes.

Every modern Gnostic is also basically a feminist.
St. Luke needed Theophilus to make him "certained."
That person is his own devil who is a perfectionist.
Every room Howard Hughes occupied was curtained.

Synthesists are addicted to the correlative conjunction.
In Chinese cosmology, *yein* (evil spirits) constantly hover.
All possible inputs in math are the domain of a function.
Shakespeare's father, who worked in leather, was a glover.

Ants occupy every world continent except Antarctica.
Li'l Abner's hair is always—only—parted on the visible side.
The fragrance of the maquis perfumes all of Corsica.
Eskimo's consider the warmest clothing to be the caribou hide.

Vergangenheitsbewaltigung—to try to overcome
the past—plagues every German-speaking nation.
The third row forward—#8—rules a rugby scrum.
No Jamaican or Dominican gets along with a Haitian.

It takes a mile for a train to come to a full halt.
No numbers from 0 to 999 contain the letter A.
Pure sodium constitutes up to 40 percent of salt.
Bright green by far is the superior color of hay.

Postcard writers are basically obscurantists:
just a line to say we're having a lovely time.
Confinement is the prime fear, say hypnotists.
Only what is beyond comparison is sublime.

In the U.S. Congress, insider trading is common.
Only three people may occupy a lighthouse light-room.
Highest gibbets are always reserved for a Haman.
A woman may legitimately serve as a bridegroom.

A lee shore wind was the dread of square-riggers.
Brits find it odd U.S. toilets contain so much water.
Chlorine gas was introduced at the Battle of Ypres.
The slow hand clap signals a venomous applauder.

Almost all body plastination is done in China.
American chefs ignore in cooking the herb sorrel.
Use glass bottles to hold nitroglycerin for angina.
No coat is warmer than a fur made from a goral.

Sassafras was the most expensive 17th-century item
sent back to England by the New World colonies.
There is no inherited sin or penalties for a Muslim.
Trusts are nefarious secret gambits of monopolies.

In Ephesians "God's people" became Gentiles.
Lesotho's national dish is chakalaka and pap-pap.
Traditionally knit socks, not woven, are argyles.
First used to clothe Hessian soldiers was burlap.

TRUISMS II

Poet Walt Whitman wrote a temperance novel.
Deer antlers are a major component in Chinese medicine.
Nevada is the only state allowing a legal brothel.
Drinking hot tea fights high temperatures among Bedouin.

New Zealanders tend to pronounce it "fush and chups"
while Australians give it out like "feesh and cheeps,"
which is all about vowel shifts, not a man in his cups,
regarding the fill/feel merger and odd lingual sweeps.

Shrewdness seldom goes with an open nature.
Woodrow Wilson hounded Eugene V. Debs into jail.
The legal profession is farcical for nomenclature.
Tattoos (raised dots) can be administered in braille.

The French people gave us the word "vermouth"
by trying (badly) to pronounce German *Wermwut*.
Cops are required at any American polling booth.
Optical glass production depends on silica soot.

To be rewarded with male children and wealth,
the Chinese pray to Kuan Yin, goddess of mercy.
Every good butler goes about his work by stealth.
Without bending one's knees, it is not a curtsey.

Gum disease may indicate erectile dysfunction.
Chinese burn fake "ghost money" in ancestor worship.
Regret, not pity, defines feelings of compunction.
An anomaly with Trappists is their entrepreneurship.

Of all butterflies, the monarch alone pilgrimages:
although millions of them depart Mexico in Spring,
not a single one returns in the Fall—for in stages
they die, and off to Winter fly their hardy offspring.

No product ever fits back in the package it came in.
After 300,000 deaths at the Somme, it ended a draw.
Chef Prudhomme, once fat, looked unhealthier thin.
Rape and prostitution always escalate during a war.

Ceraunophiles have a passion for violent weather.
Network television, dull, is strictly "talking heads."
The symbol of cowardice is the white feather.
Every national culture has its very own flatbreads.

Eastern Ukrainians demand to be a part of Russia.
Perception of the external world is mediated by ideas.
Ceded to Poland was 70 percent of East Prussia.
Nothing isn't ghostly to those who live by their fears.

The Lydians of Asia Minor invented money.
Boats must always pass each other port to port.
Holy Koran affirms the existence of djinni.
Profit from falling stock prices by selling short.

The Gulf Stream travels at four miles per hour.
"Jerusalem" is the last word said in Passover seders.
Bourbon, by far, goes best in a whiskey sour.
Macho men among professors are the lowest graders.

TRUISMS II

Austria Hungary's Lemberg became Lviv, Lwów,
L'vov, Ilyvó, Lavov, Leopolis (meaning "lion city"),
Lviv in 1941, then Ilov, or so Armenia did endow,
and, and then again, Ukrainian Lviv by committee.

Gay couturiers demand a model be a wraith.
Mafiosi always lace their coffee with Sambuca.
Doubt is not an enemy, but an adjunct to faith.
West Africans smoke it before eating barracuda.

Black oak burning smells like barbecue sauce.
In no existing system are gains not offset by losses.
Traditionally dry are the many wines of Alsace.
Church gargoyles are all about frowns and fauces.

Pandas digest only bamboo, as koalas eucalyptus.
NHL goalies for luck hit their sticks against a post.
The Song of Zechariais is called the *Benedictus*."
Maillard reaction to bread alters the flavor of toast.

Nobody specifically suffers from dropsy anymore.
It is your malar fat-pad grandmothers love to pinch.
Give wide berth to any town without a bookstore.
There is a thirst that only tonic water can quench.

Winds blow generally north-east and south-west.
Tarragon is the most assertive in a Sauce Fines Herbes.
All rabbits died used for a pregnancy "rabbit test."
Bosnians, a Serbian minority, feel uneasy with Serbs.

The deepest of human secrets lie inside our hands.
Gain used Pachelbel's Canon in a fabric softener commercial.
In Persian, the word Iran means "Land of Aryans."
No crop sustains livestock better than hardy mangel-wurzel.

Catholics insist remains be buried, even cremated ones.
Breaking silence is taboo in an English club room.
Tourists rarely visit Bishkek, formerly Pishpek and Frunze.
No one knows the origin of the name Khartoum.

It is far better to travel hopefully than ever to arrive.
1960s colored food photos make everyone nauseous.
Euthanasia took the life of England's King George V.
Corn—like earthworms, tapeworms—is monoecious.

Otters hold hands in water when they are sleeping.
Life is mainly a kaleidoscope of fragmented sequences.
Most cereal grains come from "love-lies-bleeding."
Mensa claims that Finland produces the most geniuses.

U.S. foreign aid amounts to a measly 0.1 percent
of the GDP of the United States, compared to three percent
at the time of the Marshall Plan, an altruism sent
abroad, back when a noble, altruistic America nobly spent.

If your face should turn out to be ugly, learn to sing.
Ten percent of human taste buds are inside the cheek.
Shanghai does not understand the dialect of Beijing.
A close bond sanctioned pederasty to an ancient Greek.

TRUISMS II

Nepotism, rather than talent, rules Hollywood.
Consciousness balloons over the murder of a child.
Strong cordage comes from bark of ribbonwood.
Abbott and Costello, splitting up, never reconciled.

T. S. Eliot never consummated his first marriage.
An unctuous undertaker always refers to the "decedent."
The *nepenthe* mentioned in Homer was borage.
An anaphoric pronoun consistently has an antecedent.

Executed murderers are favorite cadavers to dissect.
Victorians sent secret messages by colored carnations.
Speakers of Japanese, syllable-heavy, rarely inflect.
Poland, of all world nations, has the least immigrations.

No excess of Russians is not quickly forgiven
for the mere existence of Leo Tolstoy's Natasha,
for beauty is redemptive and faults are shriven
by way of a given nation's noble hagiographa.

Everyone employs hushed language discussing death.
Chopin, who had stage fright, often played in the dark.
Rafael Trujillo used the word "*perejil*" as a shibboleth
to kill all enemy Haitians who trilled the *R* like a lark.

The most popular Swiss language is *Schwyzertüütsch*.
San Franciscans all abhor the slang term "Frisco,"
the way fussifiers tend to argue for broach or brooch
and precisely how rock-and-rollers feel about disco.

Russia bore the full brunt of Adolf Hitler's war:
over 80 percent of all Allied casualties were Soviet.
Love is a joy, whereas duty is a burden or chore.
Both a *ficelle* and a *baton* are children of a baguette.

Barbers, masters of the phatic, thrive on small talk.
A pacifist, Dietrich Bonhoeffer *plotted to kill Hitler.*
Charles Dickens' obsession was taking a long walk.
Rogues in England were associated with a fiddler.

No song of Cole Porter is not erotically suggestive.
Tabloids construct the reality they claim to report.
Bone broth, with amino acids, is healthily digestive.
The CIA and FBI show little interagency support.

London has never cared about the delicatessen.
No lawyers in *The Pickwick Papers* are redeemable.
Paul Gaugin favored the yellow green *cresson*.
Any détente between Arab and Jew is inconceivable.

In remote Siberia, all men are in search of God.
It is considered ill-mannered to cram a platter with sushi.
Five shooters usually comprise a firing squad.
Jesus had more trouble with a Pharisee than a Sadducee.

Infantilized Roman Catholic priests, loyal to mother
—so preferring boys—are demented child abusers.
Surveillance radar is badly thwarted by cloud cover.
Sixty missiles are carried by guided missile cruisers.

TRUISMS II

Embalming fluid (to show health) contains red coloring.
Shops prioritize telephone calls over walk-in customers.
Bloodshot eyes on a corpse indicate death by smothering.
Ruth Ginzburg was the richest of Supreme Court Justices.

All Marx Brothers had a second-grade education,
which is the primary reason that they are so inane.
The only factually valid one is a literal translation.
America's first sunrises are always seen in Maine.

Edward Teller, a monomaniac for the hydrogen bomb,
was jealous of, and deeply hated Robert Oppenheimer.
Quell meant once to kill, to torment or torture *qualm*.
Hijacking friendships is the vice of a social climber.

Globalization not only favors rich countries over poor,
but, criminally, private wealth over the public good.
Fearing intimacy, oddly, causes the paraphilia frotteur.
Mossad devised for captives the brutal torture hood.

Johnny Appleseed was a serious Swedenborgian.
Orchestra conductors, weirdly, invite mythmaking.
God, dealing faces, accords fortune or misfortune.
An old name for making lace was "snowflaking."

Scratch a Russian and find a savage Scythian,
angrily insisting on his right to be uncivilized,
iconoclastic, rude, barbarous, extreme, simian,
lacking restraint or moderation, even despised.

Impotence is a diriment impediment to marriage.
Hitler's fixation on wolves bordered on mental illness.
The standard greeting between Swedes is "*Hej*."
Thought, an aspect of dharma, should lead to stillness.

Atomic deuterium is readily available in seawater.
The best novel on journalism is E. Waugh's *Scoop*.
Sexist: an alumnus (male) is *son* of his alma mater.
The coconut is technically a (one-seeded) drupe.

The Second Amendment encourages insurrectionists.
It is illegal to collect rainwater in Colorado and Utah.
St. Paul was jailed in Ephesus for not respecting Artemis.
Villains in campfire horror stories always have a claw.

Pecan growing consumes vast amounts of water.
Ritual demands a Chinese bride wear some gold.
Any good wife has been first a loving daughter.
Old ships always kept apple barrels in the hold.

As an adult, Elvis Presley never once wore blue jeans.
Witness God merely in the venation of an insect wing.
In Nicaragua, newlyweds are presented a bowl of beans.
Proverbs 25:2: "It is the glory of God to conceal a thing."

In the song "Girl," the Beatles refrain is "tit-tit-tit."
It is difficult to get a fire started when using maple.
The gentlest horse snaffle is the "eggbutt" curb-bit.
Thirty paper sheets can be held by a standard staple.

Fallibilism is the quintessential atheist's gambit.
The Pegasus of the general masses is the common mule.
A secret corner is the favored Congressional ambit.
The common behavior of twins proves a human bascule.

Mexico is the only place where tequila can be made.
W.H. Auden once proposed marriage to Hannah Arendt.
English fiction weighs highly the libido of a milkmaid.
Socrates made no statement forming of a commandment.

We name winds, not by the quarter they're going to,
but rather by the quarter from which they're coming.
Overfamiliarity is a *faux pas* during one's interview,
and, frankly, displaying low energy is unbecoming.

Legionary ants are known to kill chickens.
The Proud Boys have re-equipped the Ku Klux Klan.
When the heart quickens, blood thickens.
No one harbors more secrets than a hotel doorman.

A spider, with eight legs, is not an insect.
Rolling film credits give movie-goers vertigo.
Men in Shanghai are notoriously henpecked.
Menacing was the road from Jerusalem and Jericho.

No animal is as savage as the saltwater crocodile.
Impotence in the face of marriage is an impediment.
Designer Karl Lagerfeld was a fanatical bibliophile.
The Crimea first registered Black Death as a pestilent.

Every country should ban the selling of *foie gras*,
which kills birds with the agony of hepatic lipidosis
and is not only also an offense against the moral law
but can cause a fatal disease in humans: amyloidosis.

"Fearful oaths" in boys' fiction means vile cursing.
On the gridiron, Wake Forest never beats Clemson.
Beware that creature whose truth needs rehearsing.
A politician's primary passion is his or her pension.

Hardboiled noir detectives resent female blandishments.
"New car smell" has notes of vinyl, elevators, decomposition.
Far worse than death in ancient Greece were banishments.
Scripture says nothing - has no advice—on sexual positions.

King Henry VIII had an affair with Elizabeth Boleyn,
according to contemporary scholars, and sired a child
by the name of Anne, and, committing incestuous sin,
married his very own daughter, making both defiled.

A "bug" penetrating a wall is illegal breaking and entering.
Tolstoy's believed a true Christian should renounce the flesh.
The education of a sheep dog is anchored on concentering.
To the knackery, not the slaughterhouse, goes all horseflesh.

Karl Marx to his wife wrote beautiful love sonnets.
Napoleonic Code: still used in Belgium, Luxembourg, and
 Monaco.
Six times worse than a wasp's are poisons of a hornet's.
Graham Greene in Truffaut's *Day for Night* made a movie cameo.

TRUISMS II

William James's wife despised novelist Edith Wharton.
Venetians grew rich importing/exporting with the Levant.
A child's memory of cruel abuse will never be forgotten.
Although in Brittany, it goes by the English name, Ushant.

No photograph has the depth of a painted portrait.
The proper adjective is Dantescan, not Dante-esque.
Profane describes every strategy in going corporate.
No sculpture-encrusted façade isn't churrigueresque.

Tuna should never be served heated—or *even warm*!
Deuteronomy 20:10–18 urges Israelites to slaughter.
Robins, territorial, solitary by nature, never swarm.
No true father finds any suitor worthy of his daughter.

The kitschy word "gals" is a classic 1940's noun.
Exorcists must know the *name* of the possessing demon.
Most painted colors in the Lascaux Caves are brown.
Still eaten in Ireland is the red seaweed, carrageenan.

Without power, there is no security, said Machiavelli.
Lyricists are considered subordinates to musical composers.
Squibnocket cultivars made the best beach plum jelly.
Avaricious heirs often lack ambition waiting for estovers.

Tolstoy refused to identify *War and Peace* as a novel.
Protestants regard Catholic saints as a form of polytheism.
Israelis also appropriated from the Palestinians falafel.
Wednesday of all weekdays leads most in absenteeism.

A human's field of vision embraces less than half
a circle horizontally, and even still less vertically,
with one's direct vista like a standard photograph
and the peripheral or indirect view seen furtively.

Dr. Jekyll in Stevenson's tale of his becoming Hyde
was—and should be—officially pronounced *"jeekyll."*
Durkheim found Catholic law a curb against suicide.
Dormouse in the *Alice* tales lives in a well of treacle.

Frank Lloyd Wright was convinced of his belief
that large cities were unfit for human habitation.
The nature of satisfaction is that it is only relief.
Grain patterns all interlock at a tree bifurcation.

A gentleman should know how to fract a chicken,
roll out pastry, chop a fennel bulb, steam a clam,
flute a mushroom, dredge a fish, any sauce thicken,
coddle an egg, lattice a pie, expertly slash a ham.

Detective Sam Spade never found a home on television.
Third World to U.S.—"Fund us not to go Communist."
St. Paul attacked the primitive practice of circumcision.
Women alone, and not men, may see a urogynecologist.

St. Bonaventure is the patron saint of bowel disorders.
Assumptions, alone, do people go "laboring under."
Fear of *general* depletion is the phobia of hoarders.
James Joyce, the genius writer, was petrified of thunder.

Sounds enter a person's being where words do not go.
Grapefruit juices neutralize the good effect of statins.
Staten Island is NYC's whitest (and right wing) borough.
Not allowing skin to breathe is a negative of satins.

There was Anna Wintour, the *Vogue* compère,
and Anni Winter, Hitler's Munich housemaid,
along with Anno Winter, an ice-covered year,
and Anne Winters, actress in the movie trade.

Cape Cod mornings in all seasons are bedewed.
Nuclear war plans in *Dr. Strangelove* are accurate.
Chastity and modesty is the connotation of a snood.
Japanese food presentations are always immaculate.

Exodus provides a frame for the life of Christ.
New York City mayors all fail in presidential runs.
Guile is ever uninvolved with the verb *entice*.
A male heart is hardened at the sound of drums.

Babe Ruth did not retire as a New York Yankee.
90, the oldest of Psalms, Moses wrote in 1450 B.C.
Never found in the United States is authentic Brie.
More light is given to the Southern side of a tree.

Kenyans now win all international marathons.
The word *insect*—each is segmented—means "notched."
For centuries, spoken, never written, was Afrikaans.
Contact repulses voyeurs—their joy is what is watched.

Touch is the wellspring of the four sister senses.
The climate of western Europe is modified by the Gulf Stream.
Women's voices change when experiencing menses.
An aircraft propeller delivers a reverse—backward—airstream.

Florida, Illinois, North Dakota are the flattest states.
None hated Indians more than General Phil Sheridan.
No revision of position is allowed in formal debates.
Any arbitrary longitude line may serve as a meridian.

No *téléclitoridienne* can be guaranteed an orgasm.
Pyrex was originally invented as a lantern glass for trains.
The beating heart of all Jamaican patois is sarcasm.
About ten pounds is the size and weight of human cremains.

Since 1992, South Africa has 11 official languages.
Only a lawyer would ask Christ, "Who is my neighbor?"
Punishment is legal motive for exemplary damages.
Expiating his sins was the primal drive of a Crusader.

It is in eighth grade kids are considered meanest.
Wearing yellow (cowardice) is a rodeo taboo.
A common Luddite antagonism is any machinist.
One's immune system is improved by a tattoo.

Coconuts provide the main income of the Seychellois.
The Choctaw believed in head-flattening for male infants.
Marx's "*bürgerliche Gesellschaft*" means all bourgeois.
Of the existence of UFOs, there is not a single instance.

TRUISMS II

Law prescribes at least fifty yards between privies.
Jesus quotes from Deuteronomy more than 80 times.
The very last word is a climax in Joyce's *Ulysses*.
Processed foods (and cooking) kills all enzymes.

Nothing is uglier than a standard bicycle helmet.
Hurricanes somehow fix on destroying trailer parks.
Waterfall bangs as a hairstyle function as a pelmet.
No living beasts have thicker skin than whale sharks.

Apple trees blossoming are, quite factually, a bouquet.
Insurance covers hurricane wind damage; never flood.
White clothes (shoes included) are required in croquet.
Many hair moisturizers are fabricated by volcanic mud.

The English longbow won the Battle of Crécy.
The first plant defying a Spring frost is chickweed.
Music hall comedians in Britain are always racy.
The hairline of a hirsute male is swiftest to recede.

Flowers not only have a face but carry an expression.
Owners of beach houses lost in gales: read Matthew 7:24–27.
A woman's pregnancy can bring on manic depression
The general number points on a maple leaf is eleven.

The British people are subjects, not citizens.
No grin does not have something of the grim.
Stinging nettles are the strongest natural histamines.
The most common surname in Korea is Kim.

St. Jerome, a holy Church Father, studied Hebrew
in the hot desert in order to keep his mind off sex.
There are more than seventy-five species of Zebu!
Only an Etruscan could become a Roman haruspex.

The U.S. funds illegal settlers on the West Bank.
"Absolutely" has, weirdly, become a synonym for yes.
A good wine match for any food is Sauvignon Blanc.
Predicting a hurricane path or track is always a guess.

Music critic Theodor W. Adorno, envious,
who loathed Schoenberg and Stravinsky,
also rejected Beethoven's *Missa Solemnis*
as "incomprehensible," *sempre meno forte*.

A true Christian must comfort the afflicted
but yet manage to afflict the comfortable.
Life invariably allows one to be unrestricted
before one can then become truly miserable.

Predictive text on a computer bullies a reader.
Avocado farms don't accroach but *emit* carbon.
Wet forests breed the Northern White Cedar.
Nothing kills sheep more quickly than charbon.

Doubt purifies, rather than repudiates, belief.
Soya bean crops consume huge amounts of water.
The "face" on Mars is an extraterritorial massif.
No place on earth than Aziziya, Libya is hotter.

Jesus never rebuked anyone who worshipped him.
No tree's featured in British place names than the ash.
Mystery writers seem driven to use a pseudonym.
The mode and method of New Yorkers is being brash.

The Holy Grail could alone be seen by Sir Galahad
—his purity allowed him to pull the sword from the stone—
who, chaste and free of vice, nobly once declared,
"I never felt the kiss of love, / Nor maiden's hand in mine."

Alfred Kinsey was vigorously, not publicly, bi-sexual.
Defecating brings a heart rate down eight beats a minute.
A latitudinarian in the classroom is always ineffectual.
Of all birds, English poets most celebrate the linnet.

President Millard Fillmore never had a vice president.
All numbers on checks are always listed upper right.
Five spaces (half-inch) is the standard paragraph indent.
All jar and canning lids should be only finger tight.

Porcupines have sex: the male enters from the rear,
as the female lifts her tail over her back as a shield.
Weather on the Faroe Islands is virtually never clear.
All tropical fruits (unlike most) need to be peeled.

"Qwerty" type layout minimizes adjacent keystrokes.
Tomatoes and cucumbers should not be eaten together.
Only a single seed is contained in the acorn of oaks.
The shape of each bird is based on its contour feather.

Many believe that Sennacherib's lavish *jardin*
in the ancient city of Nineveh, now Kouyunjik
in northern Iraq, was the actual Hanging Garden
of Babylon, described by Berossus of Marduk.

Christianity does not encourage circumcision.
Cream of Wheat seeks to copy—simulate—grits.
Most of Shakespeare's lyrics depends on elision.
Marrying very late is common among the Swiss.

Thunderstorms preceding a cold front are violent.
Denmark possesses the oldest flag in the world.
Scorn's most perfect utterance is remaining silent.
No rhizome with adventitious roots isn't gnarled.

R.W. Emerson dismissed travel as a "fool's paradise."
An ancient Egyptian stylus was a trimmed river reed.
Mortar for China's Great Wall employed sticky rice.
None of the primary colors are fully found in tweed.

The testimony of Jesus is the spirit of prophecy.
Gilgamesh is now considered by some as a gay epic.
No machine exists that is able to harvest broccoli.
Only a true moron connects astrology to the genetic.

The F maritime signal flag indicates "disabled."
Every video game has its own peculiar argot.
Film actors all get more work when "labeled."
Unless starving it first, never eat wild escargot.

TRUISMS II

No nation does not have a recipe for fried bread.
A Chinese chef's first test is mastering Peking Duck.
No human being's hair has ever been naturally red.
Every large rock concert constitutes a living ruck.

Writer V. Naipaul described his homeland, Trinidad,
"a little island which has done almost nothing for me."
The most paranoid city on earth is remote Ashkabad.
A saline, seashell wine flavor characterizes Chablis.

No poem of John Donne's was printed in his life.
In England, no gathering doesn't form a queue.
America is rabid with invasive purple loosestrife.
A bear claw necklace most honored a brave Sioux.

Lidian Emerson, often ill, was a laudanum addict.
Nuna in Aramaic means "fish," a Christian symbol.
Silence was a strict monastic rule of St. Benedict.
Dimples, to stop needles, are strategic to a thimble.

All victims, fundamentally, are dangerous.
Surströmming (it stinks!) is relished in Sweden.
Mussolini—a myth—never improved train service.
"Naked" is the standard epithet for heathen.

The U.S. Congress is basically run by children.
Insight is granted to a select and disinterested eye.
The hypoallergenic adhibits to anything silken.
A hair cut on Wednesday is bad taboo for a Thai.

NATO largely provoked the Russia/Ukraine War.
Circumcision is neither necessary nor beneficial.
Dance halls are all fitted with a semi-sprung floor.
Hastiness is the primal template of the superficial.

Jesus Christ is never seen as a boy in his teens.
Never sit on a boat's lee side when sailing in the wind.
Water has less fat, but oil better flavors sardines
Consanguineous marriage was cause of the Hapsburg chin.

"Thunder and lightning," "Ozzie and Harriet," "Post
and beam," "Ike and Mike," and "hammer and saw"
are never spoken in reverse order, as if a sclerosed
part of our dumb brain meted out some phonic law.

To signify outs, baseball umps, holding their elbows
and a fist with a jerk, is close to pretentious idiocy.
Fauvists sought out the strongest colors to juxtapose.
Ocean waves transport not matter, but rather energy.

The strongest world currency is the Kuwaiti dinar.
The Iranian rial is the world's least valued currency.
No living animal has a stronger bite than a jaguar.
Mormon dogma flourishes with Biblical inerrancy.

A granary should always have a north-facing window.
Frank Lloyd Wright held scorn for basements and attics.
Women, not men, statistically prevail in playing bingo
A rolling ship can be corrected by the use of gyrostatics.

Bud Selig, a commissioner during the steroid era,
has an actual plaque in the Baseball Hall of Fame!
No one knows the exact population of the Berber.
Wed women in Malaysia keep their maiden name.

Incumbent U.S. presidents in midterm elections
almost always lose the House of Representatives.
Hanged men undergo *rigor erectus*—erections.
Raised voices are town meeting augmentatives.

John Wayne, right wing, sat out WWII, a slacker.
Wise furniture movers get mates to walk backwards.
Finger-feel is a crucial adjunct to every safecracker.
Flutiness distinguishes melodic song in blackbirds.

The best plumbing in the world is found in Japan.
Mary Surratt knew nothing of plans to kill Lincoln.
The first monarch of all England was Aethelstan.
Emotional excitement of any kind induces blinking.

More than a full 80 percent of the world's ocean
is unmapped, unobserved, and fully unexplored.
Stepping over any food is appalling to a Laotian.
Only green and buff is an official checkerboard.

Crossing the Jordan is the Scriptural signate of death.
NFL's artificial turf is a major cause of concussions.
Marriage is conceived an outlaw activity in *Macbeth*.
Interruptions are the major vice in panel discussions.

Herriman's Krazy Kat is neither male nor female.
What a true prophet speaks, that will come to pass.
Writing is required for the crime to be "blackmail."
Wittgenstein would go silent, *thinking* in his class.

It is, correctly, Smoky Bear, not Smoky *the* Bear.
The Samaritan was Christ's template for kindness.
Provocative describes a female wearing knitwear.
No vaccine currently exists against river blindness.

A sitting U.S. president has never visited Bolivia.
Deuteronomy was Moses' Farewell Address to the Hebrews.
Academy Award audiences fairly reek with *invidia*.
Ten Voss—$300 per 20 oz.—is costliest of all shampoos.

"Secular Buddhists," frauds, have turned meditation
into a cure for anxiety, barren of anything spiritual—
a way to improve business performance, a vacation
from prayer, a tool to cope with daily life. Satirical!

The ears that refuse to listen to good advice,
accompany the head when it is chopped off.
Opposite sides always add up to seven in dice.
Virtually every malady begins with a cough.

It is against official rules to play polo left-handed.
Sheer will can serve men like Seven league Boots.
Flossing, tying shoes, can't be done single-handed,
nor can cutting large vegetables or rounded fruits.

TRUISMS II

Hospitality to a Muslim is a very sacred trust.
An actor's deep-seated needs has a gay subtext.
A rouladen of meat should always be trussed.
Birth control pills can dampen a mood for sex.

In 2010, teaching of cursive script was omitted
from Common Core standards for K–12 education,
and, as a consequence, its sad victims are not fitted
to write. Lazy teachers chose an easier truncation.

Ho Chi Minh worked as a saucier for Auguste Escoffier.
Wearing high heels can adversely affect a woman's orgasm.
The highest position of all station cooks is the saucier.
New crops, plants, and cultivars depend upon germplasm.

Wasting food is among the worst of blasphemies.
Major restaurants serve roughly 300 meals a night.
Personal taste in looks is the strangest of alchemies.
A matador, officially, wears (sissified!) pink tights.

Salad bars are an open petri dish for bacteria.
Blindness is considered advantageous in a muezzin.
America planned to ship all slaves to Liberia.
Colors in a painting are all enhanced by gum resin.

Cycles of light affect a woman's fertility.
Offer workmen nothing until their jobs are done.
Equities as assets show the most volatility.
French playing cards mark an Ace (no A) with a one.

No word in the Eskimo-Aleut language exists for "waste."
Gender conferences are always irrationally argumentative.
To caramelize it for flavor, you have to "cook" tomato paste.
Epileptics, dry-eye victims, and redheads photosensitive.

A non-binary gender person could describe itself
as having no gender; many genders; a masculine
gender; one that is female; or on any other shelf
that's *neither* fully male nor female, a living Zen.

Charles Lamb compared all instrumental music
to a poem that is made up entirely of punctuation.
Mettle is the projected trait of a Russian *muzhik*.
Deviated septum victims live close to suffocation.

Half of all Southerners opposed the Confederacy--
90,000 (from Tenn. and Va.) fought for the Union.
White separatism is the same as white supremacy.
Roman Catholic and Orthodox have intercommunion.

Caricaturist David Levine thrilled doing big noses.
Bach's B Minor Mass was not performed in his lifetime.
Edible are all the buds, petals, and hips of all roses.
Breaking down food is the singular purpose of chyme.

Somalis are always dining with "Duke Humphrey."
The Bard's biographers assign him their own quirks.
Wheat is unable be grown in any tropical country.
There are no longer known any surviving gasworks.

TRUISMS II

The second movement of Beethoven's *C minor, Op. 111*
musicians consider the greatest piano sonata ever written.
Half of U.S. abortion recipients live below poverty level.
L. Ron Hubbard was banned from entering Great Britain.

A flaming chalice is what Unitarians use for a cross.
Elton John never wrote a single word that he sings.
Areas in the Pacific Ocean are islands full of dross.
Interruption is the one voice of all telephone rings.

Bitterness, in virtually every instance, defiles.
David Bowie never had different colored eyes.
Neurotics always demand on seats on the aisles.
Automakers, at testing sites, are paranoid of spies.

These are official colors, together wed:
North Korea's flag is red, blue, and white.
yet France's flag is blue, white, and red.
and a U.S. flag is red, white, blue in sight.

Doubt is central to the "theology" of a Unitarian.
Scratching a buttock itch is one of life's great pleasures.
The British press loves scandal more than American.
Board feet for soft wood can be complicated measures.

No art compared to music is as remote from life.
The Senegalese are addicted to the French baguette.
Any detailed kitchen work calls for a paring knife.
Placement is the key in properly wearing a barrette.

Contempt for society fuels a satirist's passion.
St. Paul says to wash your wife with the water of the Word.
Borrowers of self are the purchasers of fashion.
Nothing faster shreds a snake than Africa's secretary bird.

Late risers forego the best part of the day.
1970's British rock groups all loved blurring genders.
Than Regency fops, no one was more fey.
Texas has the largest list of registered sex offenders.

Bob Dylan (who lived nearby) never sang at Woodstock.
The most valued medium in ancient sculpture was bronze.
English walnut is the expert choice for making a gunstock.
The Dutch language (vocabulary) predominates in Afrikaans.

Natives in the Congo put mayonnaise on everything.
Desert Island Discs validates one's fame in Britain.
The hexagon structure helps stabilize a benzene ring.
Prophet Joseph Smith dictated what a scribe had written.

British Horlicks was, first, an infant and invalid food.
Korean letter shapes mimic the pronouncing tongue.
Cooking times should be increased at high altitude.
All poetic meter approximating speech is "sprung."

Shirley Temple reached her peak in 1937, at age 9.
The cycles of nature prove reincarnation a solid fact.
Thoreau's cabin at Walden was strictly made of pine.
Film actors are almost always advised to underact.

TRUISMS II

Everyone who says *Hollow*een, not Hallowe'en,
is pig-ignorant of its etymology and source in faith.
George Washington's favorite color was green.
Slang for an ounce (3.5 grams) of pot: an "eighth."

Every last U.S. mass school shooter had been bullied.
The English people do not identify with being European.
Tongue and teeth greatly matter deciphering a lip-read.
Christ felt at ease with a Galilean more than a Judaean.

Citizens of North Korea pay no income taxes.
St. Teresa of Avila was transverberated by a spear of gold.
The Gnostic word of mystic meaning is "Abraxas."
The gifts of Christian ministry in Ephesians 4:11 are five-fold.

Tennessee fans fetishize their checkerboard endzone.
Da Vinci, scientist, is said to have never bedded a woman.
The Armistice saved wholesale slaughter in the Argonne.
Hooding a helpless prisoner is the definition of inhuman.

The Book of Enoch had been rejected by the Jews
because it contained prophecies pertaining to Christ.
Celebrity makes a grave mistake giving interviews.
A gouger's ploy is making things arbitrarily priced.

George Herbert's poem "Love" saintly Simone Weil
declared to be "the most beautiful poem in the world."
Earth's axial tilt and sun are the parents of a sundial.
Queen Elizabeth II most valued her three-strand pearls.

While attention is the very substance of all prayer
we must empty ourselves in order to receive God.
No wood is harder than New Zealand black maire.
Every Arab rug (for God) is intentionally flawed.

When Marie Stopes wrote her sex manual *Married Love*,
she was a virgin—a later marriage went unconsummated.
A noted female paraphilia fixes on a men's leather glove.
Modern armories are, inexplicably, still oddly castellated.

Whatever separates, paradoxically, also connects,
just as any absence to be interpreted as a presence.
Curved lines are a fetishistic need of Chinese architects.
The secret part of a mansion's garden is a "pleasance."

The penis has the shape of a boomerang during intercourse,
Hebrew tribes stole the idea of Genesis from ancient Egypt.
In three-dimensions, every left-handed helix is sinistrose.
Every male turning twenty is most nations' first conscript.

Adolf Hitler never once visited a single bomb site.
An upright ear on a pig indicates an unquiet disposition.
The Japanese language has six different words for white.
To conceive a girl, have sex in the missionary position.

Jesus never instructed by way of command.
No homerun ball was ever hit out of old Yankee Stadium.
A tan is impossible on the palm of your hand.
Britain's national architectural style is primarily Palladian.

"Pain is the root of knowledge," declared Simone Weil,
"Religion as a source of consolation an obstacle to true faith."
Never having evolved in nature is a single instance of a wheel.
No manual operation of man does not call for a kind of lathe.

A happy child in Dickens is as rare as an adequate mother.
Kisiskatchewanisipi is the Cree name for Saskatchewan.
Killers in English "whodunnits" are often the stepbrother.
An abbot in a Trappist monastery has the honorific Dom.

Every pomegranate is said to contain *exactly* 613 seeds.
The CIA state-sanctioned assassinations are called "wet jobs."
Strangely, able to grow without moisture are natural weeds.
Heads, like hearts, announce their condition by way of throbs.

Primatologists all prove to be women who are neurotic.
Vigorous chewing, promoting bone growth, aids gum health.
Blindness is a condition of most species of fish aphotic.
Jesus attached no end of alarming caveats to earthly wealth.

Gays are mainly manufactured by their mother.
Snow works far better than rain to stem droughts.
Christ's hardest command: to love one another.
Steaming greatly lowers cholesterol in Brussels sprouts.

Televangelists generate opulent untaxed revenue.
Chef Paul Bocuse thought food "presentation" unimportant.
Chippewa craftsmen invented the birch-bark canoe.
Harmony usually grows out of the recognizably discordant.

Odysseus' *eloquence* wins him dead Achilles' armor,
causing boasting (and jealous) Ajax to commit suicide.
Slick politicians all avoid any question from farmer.
Against all Palestinians Israel enforce full apartheid.

Dorcas, no longer, was once a popular female name.
Canned music in shopping mall atriums is unbearable.
Cool temps are required for any computer mainframe.
Muscular dystrophy to this day remains incurable.

The common cold mutates too frequently for a vaccine.
Circus performers carry an elephant's hair for good luck.
Chow mein is fried noodles; tossed noodles, *lo mein*.
Washing methods are highly intricate for a garbage truck.

As a subject, urology stole impotence from psychology.
Regarding penile curvature, most of them lean to the left.
Philosophy prevents inconsistency by the use of tautology.
Surveillance in any and all instances is a form of theft.

Erik Satie identified as a "phonometrician," *not* a composer.
Surveys show women find men's cologne unattractive.
The purpose of a monastic cloister is specifically exclosure.
Protein decay cause of all things bacterially putrefactive.

Dr. Philippe Woog, the inventor of electric toothbrush,
inevitably set to work on the female Eroscillator 2 Plus.
That pre-sunrise song in October is a blue rock thrush.
No seat belts—strangely enough—exist in a school bus.

TRUISMS II

Mosquitoes are particularly attracted to smelly feet.
Comic books were the main reading of Sinatra's Rat Pack.
The soft shell of a young crab is as edible as crab meat.
All cognac is brandy, however, not all brandy is cognac.

Badgering God for help—Luke 18:1–8—is legitimate.
Two-thirds of Utah is owned by the U.S. government.
Both Matisse and Picasso were masters of the linocut.
In the human face there is no repetition of lineament.

An autobiography can be read in every human face.
Over 70 years, Queen Elizabeth II never visited Israel.
Bad luck—ever a feeble excuse—never lost a race.
55.6 percent sugar is Kellogg's *Honey Smacks* cereal.

To chamber a wine, strictly avoid a room that is warm.
The grace of returning letters to their senders is lost.
Toxic when uncooked, Taro cooked is an edible corm.
A massive storehouse of carbon is Earth's permafrost.

Carving meat across the grain makes it more tender.
A football game cannot end on a defensive penalty.
Puberty cognitions exacerbate dysphoria in gender.
Only a fool thinks biography doesn't unlock poetry.

Kool-Aid is the official soft drink of Nebraska.
No crime in writing is worse than obfuscation.
Poison ivy and poison oak do not exist in Alaska.
Following fashion of any sort is an affectation.

Blancmange is the grandmother of puddings and ice-cream.
Marianne Moore ran all her poems past her mother's censorship.
A Northern Italian almost never becomes a mafia *caporegime*.
Israel has assured all shortages be maintained in the Gaza Strip.

A canter is faster than a trot but slower than the gallop.
Slavish adherence to rap music is a gauge of a new illiteracy.
Small enough to row, yet also able to sail, is a shallop.
Koreans drink maple sap, unprocessed, straight from the tree.

Never walk in a field where cows are with their calves;
also, a *yellow* object can panic a cow, its high contrast
clear to them for, with their dichromatic vision, halves
of blue and yellow can create a sudden, scary telecast.

Four writers, *only*, can be said to be happily married:
J. Donne, Fielding, Hawthorne, and Robert Browning.
Style is circumspect and always refuses to be hurried.
A dead body at first sinks, then floats, after drowning.

Pope Leo XIII in 1888 condemned the modern use of electricity.
The Forsyte Saga is incontrovertibly unreadable.
Ayn Rand called Kant "the most evil man in mankind's history."
Perceiving an end to space is literally inconceivable.

St. Augustine's *Confessions* are made directly to God.
Poet John Milton declared censorship a murder.
Forever argued: a horse should go barefoot or shod.
"Birdwatching" is a word hated by every birder.

TRUISMS II

Pull a horse toward you in order to get it to move away.
Anything built in Jerusalem must use Jerusalem stone.
Nicolae Ceaușescu, a mad bear hunter, shot dozens a day.
An apex in projective geometry is at infinity on a cone.

Kosher salt does not require rabbinical supervision—
it is merely a coarser salt that better adheres to meat.
Britain's Royals disregard the need for circumcision.
Extremely old folks still refer to a recipe as a receipt.

Hyacinth leaves, steamed, are used in soups and stews.
In Shakespeare's *Troilus and Cressida*, Achilles is a coward.
Houses with hearths, also gas-heated, have two flues.
Wealth, no matter the fool, makes a person empowered.

Serbs live to deny the Muslim character of Bosnia.
Edison created the electric chair, to validate AC current.
Sleeping pills are proven ineffective for insomnia.
Pointing with a finger is not done by a proper servant.

Maple syrup is the secret ingredient of a master cleanse.
Jerusalem Syndrome: visitors think they've become prophets.
France never thought the Nazis could cross the Ardennes.
Most designers are convinced dresses are ruined by pockets.

Concealing a hand in one's coat in a formal portrait
was meant to signify formal, gentlemanly restraint,
a gesture that Greek orator Aeschines did interpret
as the way to speak in public, bold, proper, quaint.

Stephen King's novels all subsist on borrowed argot.
Adam's *left*-finger taps God's in the Sistine chapel.
The Chicago River flows *backward, out* of Chicago.
No one beast in a pack sounds alike among the jackal.

Harvard named Jeffrey Epstein a "visiting fellow"
after the paedophile gave $200,000 to the college.
The snack for immigrants at Ellis Island was Jell-O.
Elephants must carry *no back weight* in haulage.

Leo Tolstoy believed that no great men exist.
A sponge or starter—*biga*—enhances bread's flavor.
No ideology excludes the fatuity of a raised fist.
Any tasteless food is, literally, impossible to savor.

God *forgets* a person's sins—Hebrews 10:17.
Too much testosterone—yes!—*lowers* male fertility.
A blue cover shows highest sales in a magazine.
One third of the planet's soil has degraded arability.

Hitler's favorite movie was *Lives of the Bengal Lancers*.
One can't know both position and velocity of a particle.
South Pacific, uniquely, had no choreographer, no dances.
Each word a, an, and the is formally an adjectival article.

Jell-O contains 90 percent sugar, but then without it
the dessert would have neither flavor nor any smell.
Absent an app, a technophile will suddenly sprout it,
Living in the sand upside down is every clam shell.

TRUISMS II

Supermarkets mist produce only to make it *look* fresher.
One LGBTP community—note P—adds "pedosexuals."
A diamond can never be formed without high pressure.
N'aille pas au bois de la vie, qui a peur des feuilles.

Those who say "*eye-rack*" for Iraq are ignoramuses.
Dr. Spock discouraged left-handedness in children.
It is, formally, officially, a *bloat of hippopotamuses.*
Turkey's Göbekli Tepe Temple is the oldest building.

For Palestinians, being rude to old people is criminal.
Simone Weil saw the *Iliad* the model for waging war.
The same technique as hypnosis motors the subliminal.
Sleeping on one's back greatly exacerbates a snore.

Strangely, both Broadway musicals, *The King and I*
and *Fanny* incongruously ended with death scenes.
In Elizabethan slang, to have an orgasm is "to die."
Commonly served with tea in Ireland are fifteens.

There is no anti-venom for the Sind Krait snake.
In 1899, J.B. Rhodes, a black inventor, created the bidet.
Vigils, spanning day to night, inspired the wake.
Good writing in any embodiment is the enemy of cliché.

Red China has occupied Tibet since 1959.
like Israel the West Bank and Gaza Strip,
along with Jerusalem, as if a branch line,
while Turkey occupies Cyprus, hip to hip.

Armenia occupies much of Azerbaijan,
Morocco, the majority of western Sahara.
Russia occupies Crimea, some of Ukraine,
along with all of Transnistria in Moldova.

Alfred Hitchcock claimed Jesuits taught him true fear.
Unforgiveness forever floats on the waters of Marah.
A phallic intention informs every prehistoric *menhir*.
Crocodile dung served in ancient Egyptian mascara.

St. Mark is cited [Mk. 14:12–14] in his own Gospel
as that man who carries a jug of water on his head—
it is also claimed that, half naked, he was the apostle
who, as the Lord was arrested (Mk. 14:50–52), fled.

Adolf Hitler, the Führer, never wore a wristwatch.
A gentleman is one who uses a butter knife dining alone.
General Zhukov's Nazi attacks were based on hopscotch;
The femur, hardest to break, is a human's hardest bone.

We're condemned for life to bear the names we carry.
Architecture—mandate's involved—is always political.
Less plants are found in a given forest than a prairie.
No Levite descended from Aaron is factually Levitical.

Uncharitable tongues make the liveliest company.
Jews put stones on graves to keep the soul earth bound.
The Russian church denied Tolstoy a funeral liturgy.
A mall's play zones are a pedophile's proving ground.

TRUISMS II

Greeks made Memory the mother of all the Muses.
Virtually every nation eats a form of Mulukhiyah.
Converts are not accepted to the faith of Druzes.
The symbol of good taste in Japan is the fuchsia.

No warm, happy or successful relationship exists
between mother and son in the novels of Dickens.
Minor surgery can safely remove the walls of cysts.
Color vision is less acute in humans than chickens.

Most Scots prefer a viscous porridge—very salty.
Journalism, not art, is basically an ephemeral craft.
Jaggard's Shakespeare folio (1619) is deeply faulty.
Congressional allocations are entirely built on graft.

Bedwetters in sleeping deeply seek to avoid reality.
"Straight" self-describes 87% of all cross-dressers.
Headwinds fighting trade winds rule the Tasman Sea.
In Yiddish, an *esser* eats, unlike gobbling *fressers*.

Early investors in Ponzi schemes always win big,
and when the scheme collapses all latecomers lose.
Permian Basin offers the best success for an oil rig.
Rain on a roof provides a perfect nursery berceuse.

V. S. Naipaul held contempt for people overweight.
Scripture never states the wood used for Jesus' cross.
Sleep is induced by an old cradle rocking's crepitate.
Alzheimer's can be prevented by use of dental floss.

Jews go unmentioned in Whitman's *Leaves of Grass*,
which includes every other racial and ethnic group.
The entire musical *Oklahoma!* was filmed in Kansas.
"Shock troop" is a calque of the German *Stoßtrupp*.

Other people's sexual lives all remain mysterious.
"Bad grammar" is bad grammar—it should be *poor grammar*.
Jealousy, to one's own health, is mainly deleterious.
Shiny shirts in Congo are thought to be the height of glamor.

The names Abner, Apollo, Lucian, Anwar, Thea,
Oran, Ker, Jomei, Epifanio, Chand, Noor, Seight,
Phoebe, Meira, Kiran, Oralee, Lux, Chiara, Adah,
Leora, Zia, Bodhi, Ivar, Mahina—all mean *light*.

Adolescence is a continuous bewilderment of cognition.
It is fashionable in the art world to despise Renoir.
Lyrics invariably precede music in musical composition.
The crust of planet Earth constitutes mainly feldspar.

"Bon Appetit!" is, unstylishly, a waiter's remark.
Cardinal Newman faced a libel charge, was found guilty.
Jaywalking is virtually mortal sin in Denmark.
Singer Leonard Cohen ever wore a "stingy brim" Trilby.

A child's view of God is often based on his father.
Mahler was more truly himself when evoking doubt or despair.
Windows are the great-grandchildren of an embrasure.
A woman's figure is always enhanced by her wearing knitwear.

TRUISMS II

1 Thessalonians is the earliest extant Christian text.
The Fountainhead (1943) is a capitalist manifesto.
Statistics report Japanese comparatively undersexed.
No milk surpasses for health that of a water buffalo.

Laissez-faire capitalism, to Ayn Rand, is unknown
as an ideal and, foolishly, has *never been practiced.*
Use a straight femur for the best beef marrowbone.
A vowed Nazirite was the ascetic John the Baptist.

"Trial and error," when spoken, are never reversed.
Indian and Pakistani aphorisms are always vaporous.
Andrew Carnegie considered owning wealth a curse.
Parricide is the subconscious drive of the traitorous.

The sharp teeth of dogma give the bite of a dictum.
L. S. Lowry claimed he could not paint a tree.
Child abusers count on the shame felt by his victim.
Chinese never add milk, sugar, or lemon to tea.

Feces of each animal in a crash of rhinos smells different.
Norman Mailer believed condoms diminished manliness.
Russia, fearing freedom, needs a dictator who's belligerent.
Every world species of butterfly and moth are adactylus.

There is no such object as an empty space.
No mime does not perform wearing clown white.
Few Black novelists do not write about race.
A "moderator" nuclear reactors use is graphite.

"Eating lobster is only an excuse for eating butter,"
declared fat Rush Limbaugh on February 15, 2005.
Cow's milk is 97-degrees straight from the udder.
Bees chew wax soft from a gland to make a hive.

Pantalettes, in fashion, put an end to hoopskirts.
Children all *expect* the monstrous in fairy tales.
Theatrical roles endow a given face to introverts.
Fraction pricing first began at Bloomingdale's.

Never use resinous woods when cooking on a plank:
alder, cedar, maple, oak, hickory, and apple are best.
Gristle and membrane adhibits to a meat's foreshank
and must be tenderly slow cooked in liquid to ingest.

A Bhutanese woman's hat (*belo*) represents a stupa,
and, as worn, her head suggests a Buddhist temple.
Resurrection is involved in the emergence of a pupa.
Beans are higher in phytates than the healthier lentil.

U.S. state citizens identify as Americans first, while
EU countries insistence on their nationhood prevails.
Specific "degrees" inform the language of hairstyle.
Rapes are notoriously committed on walking trails.

Empty bottles left on a table in Russia is not done.
1860's coca wine Vin Mariani fathered Coca Cola.
Neither a prime nor composite is the number one.
Eating tainted meat transmits the virus of Ebola.

TRUISMS II

The Book of Revelations centers on the number 12:
apostles, gates, foundations, angels, tribes of Israel.
No shaped bowl does not take the form of a pelve.
Nothing mocks life like a funeral made convivial.

Jesus never once described the condition of heaven.
Children far exceed adults at coping with suffering.
Yeasted bread stales, moisture remains with leaven.
Absorbing nutrients can be aided by soil buffering.

Ants are not attracted to artificial sweeteners.
The tongue is the only body muscle attached from one end.
The west is considered boobopolis to easterners.
Republic of the Congo holds the richest hoard of pitchblende.

Ezra Pound praised Hitler as a modern Joan of Arc.
Bhutan has never been conquered, never colonized.
Nesting on the *ground* is the habit of the *skylark*.
Unimaginative people can't be easily hypnotized.

No translator—interpreter—is not an impersonator.
The Dalai Lama of Tibet considers himself a Marxist.
Guilt is ever the connotation of the word *collaborator*.
An artist's oil paint can be given texture by chalk dust.

No one has written the *Animal Farm* of capitalism.
Using a comma after the number in addresses is witless.
Heating up a magnet will utterly kill its magnetism.
"Golden Sombrero" is baseball slang for going hitless.

Putting faith in any British weather forecast is folly.
Child bedwetters tend to rise early to hide their shame.
Mali is a Welsh girl's name, often heard as "Molly,"
Curiously, alcohol—methanol—exists in aspartame.

Extended eye-contact in Great Britain skeeves them.
Charles Dickens helps us see all extremists as grotesque.
No pain receptors exist in a brain or human brain stem.
A standing position of a stork is a perpetual arabesque.

Ignorance, beyond a certain point, is a public menace.
Never stand on an escalator's left-hand side in Britain.
No racket may exceed 29 inches in professional tennis.
No provision is flexible in a constitution that is written.

Separated chopsticks in China indicate a broken relationship.
Wodehouse found no humor in pushy parents, only relatives.
Jews hold worship of any living person as a false messiahship.
General Patton made never a single statement without expletives.

Lettuce is a member of the sunflower family.
Dived and dove: both accepted past-tense of dive.
No rectification can ever redress a calumny.
It is considered vulgar for a gentleman to strive.

Most gays on the whole love Broadway Cast albums.
To know an author, read his letters, not the books.
Dentists fill cavities with silver-mercury amalgams.
Early teenagers are the main market for jokebooks.

To write multiple adjectives in proper drape,
list them, depending on their function: size.
opinion, age, color, origin, material, shape,
value, temp, and amount—not by surmise!

England and Portugal have the longest dual alliance:
it has lasted unbroken since 1386 and stands today.
Originality is invariably a variation of defiance.
Accepting one is lost is the beginning of finding one's way.

On TV's *Gilligan's Island*, it was never revealed
if Gilligan was that character's first or last name.
A major blind in our Civil War was a cornfield.
Marry sweet, fruity flavors when serving game.

Until 2007, black slavery was legal in Mauritania.
The character of Claudius in *Hamlet* is never named.
Sexual criminality has been linked to pyromania.
Fear of feeling inadequate makes a person shamed.

It actually snows metal on the planet Venus.
Texas repeatedly goes permit-less for owning guns.
Every jolly drunken satyr may be called Silenus.
The Far East predominates in wanting only sons.

A catwalk model must strut, not smile, pout,
bounce, cross her legs, follow a single line,
find a "rest face," show an attitude, not flout
keep core tight, and gracefully pivot in fine.

Recognition denied is condemnation to invisibility.
No gift for a twin is as endearing as her sister.
Georges Franju claimed every film is a documentary.
Old Master for their ink drawings loved bister.

Confronting a bear: "If it is brown, lay down.
If it's black, fight back. If it's white, goodnight."
You must interpret a bear's demeanor, its frown.
Polar bears, forget it. They hunt humans on sight.

Hair is part of a player's uniform in the NFL,
so, it's legal to grab in the process of a tackle.
Created for Rebel Angels, not man, was Hell.
Synagogues are modeled on the Tabernacle.

The holy trinity of Korean food are the *jangs*—
ganjang (soy sauce); *doenjang* (soybean paste);
and *gochujang* (chili paste), fermented tangs,
alternately salty, spicy, and all umami based.

A bear will immediately attack anyone fleeing.
Latvia is a nation where women outnumber men.
Roog, the Serer God, is a hermaphroditic being.
Sitting is the proper meditating position in Zen.

Adult cats only meow at humans, not other cats.
Ptolemaic astronomers believed the sun a planet.
Every Scottish piping band includes wearing spats.
A Greek housewarming gift is the pomegranate.

TRUISMS II

Only a Native American may own an eagle feather.
Dr. Johnson declared Milton's "Lycidas" a bad poem.
There is a suede finish in the inside of ooze leather.
Different wines comprise various sizes in a Jeroboam.

Elvis Presley's hair was originally reddish blond.
Cromwell slew Irish children, stating "Nits will be lice."
Risk can also have greater potential in a junk bond.
Draining holes and angled comprise a proper fish slice.

An amateur of genius is evidence of God.
Henry Miller called America an "air-conditioned vacuum."
Voting in Russia pivots constantly on fraud.
Warp thread must be stronger than weft on a weaving loom.

Chestnut trees are always the first in autumn to shed.
Jesus waited *two full days* to resurrect dead Lazarus.
Both birth and death prescribe the ramparts of dread.
Prayer, begging intercession, is an aspect of avarice.

Bi-weekly has actually two different definitions—
twice a week, as well as once every two weeks.
There is, technically, no *meaning*, in prepositions.
Trustworthiness is associated with chubby cheeks.

Bulimics have an aversion to incorporating health.
Rhythms: the longest English word sans normal vowels.
Cold War technology fully concentrates on stealth.
It is the red cells and our bile that embrowns the bowels.

Speculation, in any form, is almost always a low dodge.
Kansas was mainly settled by folks from New England.
Afghani food is widely (if unkindly) dismissed as stodge.
Suitable terrain significantly aids and abets a brigand.

The Great Pyramid of Giza has eight *sides*, not four.
Edward Gorey never used the alias Edward O. Grey.
Figurative objects are never employed in Islamic décor.
Scene stealing by actors is accomplished by byplay.

Lord Kitchener despised Lord Curzon, and vice versa.
Awkwardness is epitomized by American men hugging.
Scrutinize closely a resume whenever hiring a bursar.
No Russia hotel is not wire-networked with a bugging.

Interesting, for blandness, is the coward's adjective.
Boniface VIII, for Dante, was the most corrupt Pope.
High fructose corn syrup is food's most evil additive.
A bright diamond is, oddly, black carbon's allotrope.

Barnes and Noble stores never locate in a bad area.
If stuck in a riptide, always swim parallel to shore.
All yogurt is referred to as "sour milk" in Bulgaria.
Only a *single pane* of glass defines a French door.

The sole letter missing from the Periodic Table is J.
Cormac McCarthy hated semi-colons and quotation marks.
Saint Augustine believed singing the best way to pray.
Scorpion and Felix was a novel written by Karl Marx.

TRUISMS II

When new electricity replaced wood fires at home,
minerals once found in vegetables from wood ash
fertilizer in gardens vitaminizing the healthy loam
vanished caused spate of new diseases in a flash.

Theocracies, invariably, are all police states.
The MGM lion (logo) is not roaring, but yawning.
Dining at any Korean table is all about plates.
Diamond merchants notoriously sell by fawning.

Luvabitchers regard all non-Jews as racially inferior.
Gluten-free fanatics have demonized virtually all food.
Pharisaical piety was manifest solely on the exterior.
By way of black iron oxide is a normal handgun blued.

Lettuce is a member of the sunflower family.
The trebuchet revolutionized medieval warfare.
Post-disaster Federal help is always a calamity.
Whole generations in America stay on welfare.

When every contestant wins a prize, no one does.
Mobsters and their family lives are wholly segregated.
Most plane or helicopter pilots are nicknamed "Buzz."
Sodium, potassium, and water must never be agitated.

A revolt against formula is the key to originality.
Lara Logan compared Anthony Fauci to Josef Mengele.
The Republican mind finds discomfort in illiberality.
A white wine must accompany *spaghetti alle vongole*.

Iceland does not have any public railway system.
Georges Rouault is *the* painter of Original Sin.
In knowing you know nothing begins all wisdom.
The Civil War was partly due to the cotton gin.

Christ's name in Dante's *Inferno* is never spoken.
Second-rate people never become revolutionaries.
Bone marrow turns red blood cells to hemoglobin.
It is folly to name minors as direct beneficiaries.

No street in old Boston in commensurately straight.
Democritus ascribed the world to chance, not to God.
Admiration by way of envy is ever a subtext of hate.
No description of any fish accurately defines scrod.

Deaf Thomas Edison had to *bite on* his piano to hear.
Guests of a common host needn't wait to be introduced.
A "football player" is referenced in the play *King Lear*.
Quality is always diminished in the mass-produced.

Virtually all of the plastic ever created still exists.
Flaubert refused to let *Madame Bovary* be illustrated.
Encyclopedic novelists have a fascination with lists.
Cancer is eliminated in almost every animal castrated.

Attacking an enemy's plans is war's first goal.
It takes Uranus 84 years to orbit the Sun one time.
Most carbon dioxide emissions come from coal.
No transgression can be called a victimless crime.

TRUISMS II

For his poetry volume *Pomes Penyeach*, James Joyce
wanted the cover to be precisely a kind of pale green,
specifically, the color of a fresh Calville apple, choice,
a peculiarly delicate shade with an understated sheen.

Skate where a puck's going to be, not where it is.
"White chocolate" contains not a bit of chocolate.
Regulating human heartbeat is the "Bundle of His."
Alcoholic dependence is, by nature, immoderate.

Fashion weeks always follow a certain order:
New York, London, Milan, and ends in Paris.
Russia suspect Africa starts at the Ukraine border.
Privilege is the fail-safe function of an heiress.

China has developed an anti-ship ballistic missile,
which can contain hegemonic American sea power.
Hostility in South America is conveyed by whistle.
There are no examples in antiquity of a bell tower.

No Glock handgun comes with a manual safety.
Mohels in America, unlike physicians, are not regulated.
Revisions ever follow decisions when made hasty.
Jockeys (with kit and saddle!) must always be weighted.

Virtually anybody can attain kosher certification.
Abe Lincoln could recite "The Last Leaf" poem by heart.
The back (unimpeded) is best for medical auscultation.
Multiple pieces of data completely confuse a pie chart.

Hoarders harbor an eternal contempt for wasters.
There is no McDonald's restaurant in Tirana, Albania.
College degrees are a must for salaried food tasters.
To experience shame is often one's *goal* in kleptomania.

Major nutrients are lost in carrots by peeling.
When tyranny becomes law, resistance becomes duty.
A woman is always moved when a man is kneeling.
Socrates equated "short-lived tyranny" with beauty.

"The shape of creation is a furrow fear, a pasture
of pain, a field of fists," declared Mother Jones.
Einstein claimed you grow shorter as you go faster,
Bankers find money destroyed with repaid loans.

Diamonds fulfill no role and are utterly useless,
intrinsically. Their one and only value, subjective,
comes down to desirability contrived by ruthless
marketing hustle by the world's Jewish collective.

Common dog food is nothing but packing-plant scraps.
There are 40,000 world-wide Elvis Presley impersonators.
No hood flares in the shield-nosed cobra, the aspidelaps.
Prostate cancer is found low in compulsive masturbators.

Sunrise and sunset are the busiest times for deer.
Millions up North in 1860 supported the Southern cause.
No woman—reasonlessly—can become a gondolier.
Atheist Chris Hitchens compared God with Santa Claus.

TRUISMS II

A female mohel—they're allowed—is a *mohelot*.
"Problems" no longer exist—now, they're "challenges."
No one knows to this day the location of Camelot.
Stress, doctors insist, promotes cancerous metastases.

Jews cannot eat the meat of any strangled animal.
Stuntmen never eat beforehand, lest surgery be required.
It is human prions that transmit disease to a cannibal.
Every vision of heaven in literature remains uninspired.

Seven is the key Biblical number for completion.
Bookkeeper: only word with three consecutive doubled letters.
Kidneys are the major organ in human excretion.
Email delivered the crowning blow to the art of *belles-lettres*.

Pilots touch the nose of their flight plane for good luck.
The stock market is spooked by unknown variables.
"Fauntleroy" is the true middle name of Donald Duck.
Ninety percent of arson is done by male criminals.

The British put (and eat) fish fingers in a sandwich.
Therapy in all instances is to get you to accept reality.
The Ulster dialect is by far the worst in any language.
Only Chardonnay grapes may be used in a Chablis.

Kenyans now win all world-wide marathons.
FBI called informant a "confidential human resource."
Nothing graces Advent like the "O" Antiphons.
Walking while eating in France is considered coarse.

Before you can win a game, you first cannot lose.
What distinguishes a James Bond villain is *scale*.
Elena Ferrante never gave (and refuses) interviews.
The third brother alone prevails in every folk tale.

All elections are about choosing the tallest dwarf.
Vaughan Williams "Tallis Fantasia" is entirely strings.
No U.S. Congressional lobbyist isn't a lagomorph.
Nowhere in Scripture do we see angels with wings.

There are no antidotes to kill the poison, ricin.
Painite, a gemstone, is the rarest mineral on earth.
Cut against the grain in any raw meat slicing.
Squatting is the proper way women should give birth.

North Koreans kill by organophosphorus poisons.
Lengthy reverberation-time destroys good acoustics.
Renaissance men held the heart the source of voices.
Chinese find harmony/power in five bamboo sticks.

Islamic scholars universally regard a dog's saliva as impure.
but cats, who may enter mosques, are favored for their cleanness.
Most valued for their mutton are the horned sheep of Exmoor.
Of all meats, more than bison, moose meat is by far the leanest.

Jake Barnes' voice in Papa's *The Sun Also Rises*
gave birth to all of the 1930s hard-boiled writers,
where a tough tabloid flatness of talk franchises
the adoptive role of weary detectives as fighters.

Wash but don't *peel* carrots, which carry nutrients.
Left hand use in Indonesia—for anything—is vile.
Castiglione found a princely virtue to be insouciance.
Rwanda's Nyungwe rainforest is the source of the Nile.

There's no period in *Dr No*, though it looks maimed.
Moby-Dick should never be written without a hyphen.
Absalom, Absalom!—punctuation in title exclaimed!
Finnegans Wake insists no comma put the knife in.

"The car not starting" is *the* horror film cliché.
No one cannot purchase tickets to enter fashion shows.
All-white clothing is (dopily) required in croquet.
Cowboys refer to conservatives as "Square-Toes."

Lester Young would never let anyone touch his sax.
Jehoshaphat (Joel III. 2) is the valley of the Last Judgment.
Irrevocable life insurance trusts wipe out an estate tax.
Practicing Mormons find both coffee and tea repugnant.

There are exactly 119 grooves on a U.S. quarter.
Lincoln's older stepbrother, John D. Johnston. embarrassed him.
In all comic teams of two, one is always shorter.
Tortoises, peacocks, gorillas, and hippos are all unable to swim.

A turtle must never be held by the head or its flippers.
Stating *how* a person died is avoided in all obituaries.
Virtually fought in deep mud was the Battle of Ypres.
In the city of San Francisco, there are no cemeteries.

The famous Rolls-Royce logo, the "Spirit of Ecstasy"
can be retracted into the radiator by pushing a button.
Apathy with a shrug almost always points to Destiny.
Misguided worship becomes the impiety of a glutton.

Jesus never performed a miracle for unbelievers.
"Loiner" is a demonym describing the citizens of Leeds.
Watching TV is the major slough for underachievers.
A matter of perception distinguishes flowers from weeds.

Louise Brooks, who considered film acting as ballet,
declared that movement was the foundation of acting.
Two players and a pared pack (32 cards) play piquet.
Lack of drawing skill seeks a refuge by abstracting.

Worry, by definition, is always a demon self.
Any confession guarantees the highest tabloid appeal.
Oil and gas burgeon on the continental shelf.
Jealousy is the one human emotion never to anneal.

Mirrors in movies indicate a character turning inward.
One of Sodom's sins was "fullness of bread." Ezekiel 16:49.
The heaviest rain on a mountain is blowing windward.
The Rebel Angels, writes John Milton, fell for days—nine.

The power to tax a citizen is the power to exploit.
Abe Lincoln chose not to attend his father's funeral.
The largest American city bankruptcy was Detroit.
There are only seven symbols as a Roman numeral.

TRUISMS II

Only art—art alone—can redeem the rages of time.
Zionist Bernard Lewis had G.W. Bush attack Iraq.
The nadir in all show business is a performing mime.
No prismatic color has depth without the color black.

Early docility in children suggest diet deficiencies;
quite healthy children are active rowdy, boisterous.
Obscurity is the actual demonic *goal* of officialese.
Aoulef, Algeria—0.48" rainfall—is moistureless.

No piece of paper can be folded an eighth time.
Forager Euell Gibbons, who munched acorns, hated veal.
Cement plaster cracks, not so with hydrated lime.
The closer to the axis, the less energy needs a flywheel.

None can fully explain how deep friendships begin.
The Postman Always Rings Twice was banned in Boston.
Jews formally bury a baby's circumcised foreskin.
It's impossible in winter to climb (28,251 ft) Godwin Austin.

Raymond Chandler thought all agents, crass hucksters,
saying, "Where the money is, there the jackals gather."
Little more than time-beaters are orchestra conductors.
The connotation of excess is implied by the word *slather*.

Sexual excitement is linked with murder in film *noir*.
Japanese Wagyu beef sells at $300 dollars per pound.
Couloirs are chutes; but not all chutes can be a couloir.
It takes as long as twenty seconds for a child to drown.

There are no ugly (so, unmarriageable) billionaires.
One word in English has five vowels in a row: *queueing*.
True avarice belittles buying preferred stock shares.
Splitting 10s in blackjack is as novice gambler's undoing.

Tigers have striped skin and not merely striped fur.
The human nose can remember 50,000 different scents.
At both his birth and death, Jesus was offered myrrh.
Beauty staples sold to women all have bogus contents.

Rain almost preternaturally falls on wet people.
An inhabitant of Botswana is a Motswana.
No part is not edible on any given Adam's Needle.
A hundred versions exist of the *Ramayana*.

Trust no apology that is also riddled with excuses.
British royalty (a) "never tire" and (b) "all love hospitals."
Peace in Black slang—two fingers up—is "deuces."
Political placard holders are, to a one, all lickspittles.

The color blue is never mentioned in Homer's epics,
nor is it referred to in Hebrew writing; the ancients
had no word for it, nor Japanese or Chinese poetics,
including all the Icelandic Sagas—no acquaintance.

Quote an author to his face, and he's your friend forever.
Rivers are the main thematic imagery of *Finnegans Wake*.
Whencesoever? Whithersoever? Choose whichsoever!
Of Quaker headgear, one never sees a pale wideawake.

TRUISMS II

Broadcast seeding is ineffectual with large seeds.
Trying too hard to the British is held to be a vice.
Protestants call saying the Rosary "telling beads."
Auto dealers never state a car's invariable price.

Airplane pilots never eat the same pre-flight meal.
Joseph Conrad is sorely missing a sense of humor.
Able to swim—undulate—*backwards* is the eel.
Being spread is the main endowment of a rumor.

Edward Gibbon regarded Christianity as deplorable
and yearned for the proud gentilities of classicism.
Delay is seen as unconscionable at a female urinal.
Theodore Roosevelt equated treason with pacifism.

A person is revealed by the brunt of his mockeries.
Cowboys had a built-in loathing of sheep farmers.
A refuge for the inartistic creationless are potteries.
Populism finds a propellant in hatred of foreigners.

All Charles Dickens' heroines were "airheads,"
George Eliot's too complicated, too reflective.
Raymond Chandlers' are in and out of beds,
while Edgar Poe's are morbid and defective.

Most toilet paper that is sold in France is pink.
Matthew Arnold dismissed Mark Twain as a philistine.
It is the nature of supplement ads to hoodwink.
In Islam, the list of angels guarding hell is nineteen.

Saying "I promise" performs the act of promising.
Digestion takes place in a ruminant's abomasum.
Rating women comes down to crude anatomizing.
Equality of sacrifice demands equal tax on income.

An Irishman never says yes, but rather "It is so,"
"Aye," "All right," "By all means," "Agreed,"
"Certainly," "In the affirmative," "Righty ho,"
"Very well," "OK, roger, my friend," "Indeed."

The elbow is the strongest point on the human body.
"Doors to manual:" airplane order prior to a landing.
Tattoos, considered vulgar, are reviled by any Saudi.
Space actually stretches—but it is not expanding.

Few TV shows maintain traction past a fifth season.
Queen Elizabeth II had her shoes broken in for her.
Spirit and matter are indistinguishable to a Milesian.
The inner bark (ground) can be eaten of a balsam fir.

"We are now temporarily halting withdrawals"
is the equivalent of a savings bank's suicide note.
Honorary degrees carry not a jot of serious laurels.
Asphyxiophiliacs—gaspers—fixate on the throat.

The rare azure on the Ukrainian flag is a blue,
(Pantone 2935) in the parlance of color canon,
unlike the far gentler Pantone (293), royal hue
on the Dutch flag or Norway's (Pantone 281).

TRUISMS II

Spare output is the mark of a gentleman writer.
The spoken Maltese language sounds like clucking.
Smoke, not fire, is the main killer of a firefighter.
Deductibles in insurance is a form of blood-sucking.

Tabloids delight stoking rivalries between women.
Jacques Pepin pays no more than $12 for his wine.
Tigers in Korean fables greatly fear the persimmon.
Israelis all use ⊥ to avoid the (Christian!) plus sign.

The child of an old man's an orphan, his wife, a widow.
St. Paul stated, "Anyone unwilling to work should not eat."
The last, apocalyptic battle will take place at Megiddo.
Fully two-thirds of the world's carbon is found in peat.

An individual has to dig, before he is able to delve.
Nutmeg—with myristicin—becomes a hallucinogen.
Jesus equates synagogues with prisons (Luke 21:12)
Reproduction is low with a (small) Rock Cornish hen.

Overly talkative wives render their husbands silent,
but silent husbands force their wives to be talkative.
No ultimatum does not bear an order to be defiant.
Perfume is never worn other than to be provocative.

Galaxies move away from one another with and by
velocities that grow in proportion to their distances.
A pot is officially required to house growing Bonsai.
Class reunions are a taboo for Jehovah's Witnesses.

No language was more pluricentric than ancient Greek.
Any audience or assembly is *required* to be judgmental.
"Italian seasoning" basically means oregano and fennel.
The torque in all the natural world is strictly accidental.

The British Crown owns a McDonald's franchise.
Priciest wines come from sloped south-facing vineyards.
Meat is moister, more tender in a chicken caponized.
Not a speck of real chalk is used in cue chalk in billiards.

Mongolians of old washed themselves with urine.
Czechs resent being thought of as *Eastern* Europe.
Julia Child hated and avoided the word margarine.
It was Iroquois people who discovered maple syrup.

Food photographers hate to shoot brown edibles.
The Seven Years War (1756+) was the first world war.
Paradox is the active force in all Jesus's parables.
In every ocean on Earth, another floor sits under a floor.

St. Augustine had an illegitimate son by a concubine.
U.S. treaties with Indians were means of subjugation.
Antoni Gaudi, who loved curves, hated a straight line.
Mystery in women has been lost in their emancipation.

For all his talent, Frank Sinatra could not sing "scat."
The United States never rebukes or criticizes Israel.
Cowboys are touchy about anyone touching their hat.
The personification of all evil in the Bible is Belial.

TRUISMS II

Cultural awards today consider first the demographic
and the art itself a distant second—merit be damned.
Asked "Are you sisters?" greatly irritates a sapphic.
Stress hormones greatly abate when holding hands.

Edward Steichen refused to photograph anyone "not thinking."
A shrimp cocktail is lame when missing horseradish.
The Sundance Kid could hit a target only when he was moving
No one individual may officially celebrate Kaddish.

No one can pay attention to a dinner while conversing.
Finnegans Wake to be comprehensible must be heard.
Never expect a Supreme Court opinion ever reversing.
123456 remains the world's most common password.

Risotto should only be cooked with arborio rice.
To award land west of the Jordan, Moses used raffles.
Altitude is required for growth in edelweiss.
Marco Polo never wrote, but rather dictated his travels.

A moron in power means voters are well-represented.
No horns match for beauty the "grey ghost," the kudu.
Komucha, the drink—black tea fungus—is fermented.
The Zangbeto, haystacks-like, are guardians of voodoo.

Detective Nero Wolfe's favorite food was shad roe.
Crossword compilers insist that they are *composers*.
The favorite body target of gout is a person's big toe.
The right to gather firewood is protected by estovers.

A full half the hemisphere makes up the Orient.
Mexico, in 16 presences, never won a World Cup.
A peripheral job is American Vice-President.
Only 400 souls love on the islands of Sverdrup.

Sleeping on one's back is considered best for health.
Twelve is the last number to be written as a word.
To "state," the US Constitution prefers *commonwealth*.
Slouching pants is sexual invitation to a jaybird.

Newton gave mathematical form to Galileo's insights;
James Maxwell's equations did the same for Faraday.
Amendment Three is most ignored in the Bill of Rights.
Hallowe'en mavens in the U.S. ignore All Saints Day.

Wine talk rapidly (and invariably) becomes rudely exclusive;
civility in sharing wine is to put one's critical faculties on hold,
for its many pedantries, terms, tend to be interpreted as abusive
and instead of providing any warmth, they turn the hearer cold.

Inconsistent premises can make any argument valid.
Pastries are actually cited in the plays of Aristophanes.
Every character in Edgar Allan Poe is sickly or pallid.
Richard Nixon loved gobbling ketchup with cottage cheese.

Term deposits are a guileful way to prevent a bank run.
The fuller the fridge, the more energy efficient.
Buddha, seeking enlightenment, deserted his wife and son.
Trust, regarding faith, is a necessary coefficient.

TRUISMS II

Unguided by faith, reason abets mis-knowledge.
The Three Stooges were on Adolf Hitler's death list.
Faithless electors can subvert the Electoral College.
Mutual fault-finding is a commonplace in bid whist.

Only a fool tests any African river with both feet.
Alder is the preferred wood for plank-cooked chicken.
Any and all pasta should be made of durum wheat.
The Hawker Hurricane plane won the Battle of Britain.

The first Levi jeans were all made from hemp.
A benefit of old age is it does not last very long.
Stuttering can make a man militarily exempt.
Azerbaijan and Armenia have never gotten along.

Composer Erik Satie went nowhere not carrying an umbrella.
New Yorker cartoons are *meant* to be snobbishly meaningless.
Meditation goes from the outside to inside in every mandala.
Nigerian-based internet solicitations are bent on deceiving us.

Allen Tate and wife, Caroline Gordon, whom he married
and divorced twice, always took meals in separate rooms.
British troops in Colonial Boston were constantly harried.
For healthy cookies, butter should be replaced by prunes.

A physical letter belongs to the person who receives it,
but its content is the property of whoever it is wrote it,
and, while faith is owned by a believer who believes it,
no quoted quote is retained by the quoter who quotes it.

Bryher thought books should be big and fat to be sat on.
To marry quickly, as the French say, is *perdre le nord*.
U.S. citizens referring to America never include Latin.
Taiwan's the sire country of the computer motherboard.

Christmas-haters are mostly single and anti-family.
Lincoln died attending a *comic* play on *Good Friday*.
A person's defined at root by response to a calamity.
There is no actual butter in or on a Butterball turkey.

From age 18 to marriage Queen Victoria was in love
with handsome tutor Lord Melbourne, 40 years older.
Crying "Mrs. Melbourne!" giving the rumor a shove,
while uncivil, many admirers believed it consoled her.

Greta Garbo wanted to play Dorian Gray for MGM.
Nothing's more garish than a villain wrestler, a "heel."
James Joyce used black pencils, never a fountain pen.
Cut whole from trees, rounded, made the first wheel.

No human model could pose for Saint-Gaudens' *Diana*,
who, firing an arrow, stood solely on the toe of her foot.
Unable to be stored, Hebrews daily had to eat the manna.
A self-centered personality describes an average Rajput.

Gravity, neither a push, nor a pull, is a *downward* force.
Thanksgiving always spawns new tricks on cooking turkey.
Pagan mythology perfectly fed the culture of the Norse.
Three-year-old horses alone can run in the Kentucky Derby.

TRUISMS II

Hollywood and being gay is never a happy match.
Ego is an analgesic that dulls the pain of stupidity.
All U.S. submarines are fitted with an escape hatch.
Puberty emerges early in countries of high humidity.

Knocking thrice is a military code for "last man out."
Gopher wood, used for Noah's Ark, remains unidentified.
Red faces in 18th-century portraits indicate the gout.
Cigarette smoke fuses benzene, carbon and formaldehyde.

There are no poisonous snakes in New Zealand.
Coast-to-Coast radio, hucksters, hawk bogus products.
Hunters most crave for trophy the horns of an eland.
Located at the *west end* of a cathedral is the narthex.

Karl May, Hitler's favorite author, was a pacifist.
Sunday means nothing to Seventh Day Adventists.
Harm and hurt stand in opposition to a masochist.
The suicide rate is very high among the dentists.

As they were relatives, it was reportedly said
that the poet John Donne's mother possessed
the executed St. Thomas More's severed head
and, by it, a bold political defiance expressed.

Martin Luther King, a serial womanizer, declared
(quote) "Fucking is a form of anxiety reduction."
The psyche of abused children is never repaired.
Weight and cellulite are *not lost* by liposuction.

Social Security in the U.S. is constantly running a deficit.
Salt & pepper shakers should always be passed together.
ATMs dispense gold in Abu Dhabi, the richest emirate.
The scarcity of it being white gives luck to such heather.

1930's slang loved "Swell!" "Dizzy!" "Nerts!" "It's a peach!"
"saw buck," "flivver," "shake a leg," and "You shred it, wheat!"
An obligation can be sidestepped by way of "anticipatory breach."
Leo Tolstoy, who abhorred killing of animals, never ate meat.

No airplane—it needs air—is ever hermetically sealed.
The *Woodstock* Festival took place in *Bethel*, New York.
A microcosm of civilization is figured on Achilles' shield.
Two prongs, for a true resonation, requires a tuning fork.

All fetuses start off with female characteristics.
The Bahamas is a favorite haunt of James Bond villains.
All advertising sales are strategies of linguistics.
Salt, less so in broth, is the central ingredient in bouillons.

"4:20" is a popular coded slang for marijuana.
The cheetah is the only cat that can't retract its claws.
Oddly, English is the official language in Guyana.
After Act 1 of *Parsifal*, one abstains from applause.

The altar is always at the *liturgical east* in a church.
Sri Lanka has the highest suicide rate of any country.
Navies during war of neutral ships have "right of search."
Social responsibility is ever obliged of landed gentry.

TRUISMS II

Composer Erik Satie subsisted on a diet of white food.
Marcion, fiercely anti-Jewish, hated the Old Testament.
No great movies were made until close-ups were used.
In selling, conviction is, of persuasion, ninety percent.

Lenny Bruce: "Guys give girls *The Prophet* to get laid."
In Dante's geography, the bottom of Hell is center of Earth.
No girl looks unattractive in a French or Dutch braid.
As soon as bought, diamonds lose much of value and worth.

Religion for Abe Lincoln constituted a bland deism.
American men—immature—love wearing baseball caps.
The absolutist mind has affinities for Manichaeism.
Damage can result from the shock waves of thunderclaps.

Cats spend as much as 68% of their lives asleep.
Flower bouquets left at tragedy sights are never *opened*.
West Indian cooking depends on the cassareep.
A pedigree search is vain without denoting the proband.

The American evangelical zealot is a *sexual* person:
Joseph Smith; Jimmy Swaggart; Henry Ward Beecher;
Jim Jones; David Koresh; Aimee Semple MacPherson;
Jim Bakker; M. L. King; Elijah Muhammad, a lecher.

The future—by very definition—is not time.
A translator's mission is personally to disappear.
Dawn is ever the best time to harvest thyme.
King George III banned any staging of *King Lear*.

Springfield is the standard, go-to, cliché television town:
cf. *The Guiding Light, Father Knows Best. The Simpsons.*
An adjective—cf. *the homeless*—can be used as a noun.
Garbage dumps happily accommodate poisonous jimsons.

Congressmen have an "AIPAC guy" sending them checks
and in return, *quid pro quo*, tell each one exactly how to vote.
No Anabaptist barn ever displays the Pa. Dutch sign of a hex.
Discontinued from lack of use is the rare $10,000 dollar note.

All autobiographies are but narratives of ascent.
David Koresh's mother was 14 when he was born.
Stepping on rugs with shoes is taboo in Tashkent.
High fructose syrup usurps one third of U.S. corn.

Protestants view purgatory as a Catholic fraud.
Africa's most catholic country is Mozambique.
The Jain faith does not believe in a creator God.
A quarantined ship to harbor needs a *pratique*.

Most freshwater anglers consider carp a trash fish.
The unstable becomes the unusable becomes the expendable.
All N.Y. politicians pose, for votes, eating a knish.
Never feed a workman if you want him to be dependable.

Bosnia is not landlocked: it has the Neum Corridor.
For pioneers, hygiene was impossible in cold weather.
Georges Bizet for Carmen invented the word *toreador*.
Crocodile skin is the world's most expensive leather.

TRUISMS II

Confederate diarist Mary Chestnut hated the song "Dixie."
Ash trees are all being decimated by the emerald ash borer.
The Roma people are offended by the racist term "gypsy."
No travel writer should claim to identify as an explorer.

Lionel Messi was the first athlete to point to the sky.
"Kadrun" mocks Islamic fundamentalists as a desert lizard.
Literacy rate is almost 100% in the country of Brunei.
At least three hours of bad snow officially defines a blizzard.

Children draw turkeys from hand-outlines on paper.
Elias Canetti declared happiness the life goal of illiterates.
Ho Chi Minh when a younger man worked as baker.
Chile of all the nations on the planet is most cupriferous.

No Uruguay/Argentina football match isn't violent.
No products ever fit back easily into their original box.
For contemplative reasons a Trappist monk is silent.
Distinguish" dreads are Jamaican, African are locks.

A clam has no head, no brain, neither ears nor nose,
no biting mouth parts, no arms or legs, cannot smell,
see, or hear, and although the bivalve shell can close,
when it opens it cannot shriek, sing, squawk, or yell.

Belfasters pronounce Belvoir Park *"Beaver Park,"*
and New Zealanders love to eat *"fush and chups,"*
while Bostonians, instead of dark, all say *"dahk"*
and in Liverpool the word *cups* is heard as *"coops."*

Refrigerating baked goods only makes them staler.
Of 20,000 Khmer Rouge prisoners, 7 alone survived.
His writing is required to prosecute a blackmailer.
In a house without any books, everyone is deprived.

Official Jewry crucified Jesus mainly for blasphemy,
a claim of Messiah being a crime of the highest order.
The moon's speed increases when it is at its perigree.
Kashmir area is the world's most militarized border.

Camo is by far the favorite redneck color.
Protestantism does not accept the book of Daniel.
All 32 Soweto Townships suffer squalor.
St. John's Gospel, alone, alludes to Nathaniel.

All western philosophy is a footnote to Plato.
The Michigan/Ohio State football rivalry is hatred.
Israel has always been excluded from NATO.
Emerson said the human mind alone was sacred.

In a 50-50 senate, every senator becomes President.
Nothing good ever happens at an office Christmas party.
Teenage addiction often begins huffing rubber cement.
Norway is highest among nations to economic autarky.

Marriage is all about solving problems together
which they'd not have had if they'd stayed single.
Dowagers prefer a glove be made of ooze leather.
Britain's shores are mainly lined of sea shingle.

Orthodox Jews aren't allowed to bathe during *shiva*.
The Waco Branch Davidians avoided red meat as unclean.
Nothing more than simple indifference irritates a diva.
Voting, marriage, drinking, smoking: allowed at eighteen.

Once a toilet seat is purchased, it cannot be returned.
Who pronounces pasta with a short *a* loves revisions.
So lame is the Supreme Court that it has overturned
more than two hundred of its own parlous decisions.

Labels on cranberry sauce cans are upside down,
positioned so for customers for easiest extraction.
Beethoven is every pic and portrait wears a frown.
Ebola victims all suffer bouts of body liquefaction.

Rogue waves, unpredictable, typically twice the size
of surrounding waves, come from different directions.
Virtually all children in the USA live on French fries.
Blacks vote 90% Democrat in United States elections.

No women were sent to the 1606 Jamestown Colony.
"Flappers" ended with the stock market crash of 1929.
The Covid-19 pandemic spread by social inequality.
Swedish *tallstrunt* tea is steeped with needles of pine.

Maine is the only state whose name is just one syllable.
David Koresh demanded burial with the Israeli flag.
Shyster lawyers for expenses make even farting billable.
The safety of a mine's roof is only as good as its sprag.

Problems no longer exist—they're now "challenges."
Danes always refer to their writer as "*H. C.* Anderson."
A construction industry account book never balances.
Hair is of primary importance to television anchorman.

Jack is the prevalent boy's name in nursery rhymes.
Writer Elsa Morante believed that animals are angels.
"Not always" is the noteworthy negative of *sometimes*.
Human hands are universally the Third World mangles.

A bonsai's beauty lies in its struggle to stay alive.
"Absolutely" has replaced yes in American jargon.
Propolis provides perfect insulation for a beehive.
Every Hollywood marriage is a Faustian bargain.

"A whole nother" is a classic idiot American locution.
Trotsky's assassin won the Lenin Prize from Nikita Khrushchev.
Bottom trawling gear has been ruinous to the Aleutians.
Wild game gourmands rate highest breast of a mourning dove.

Albert Schweitzer in his biography of Jesus stated
it was pure insanity that made Him claim divinity.
Every boast of a butter substitute is badly overrated.
Jehovah's Witnesses abhor the dogma of the Trinity.

The New Yorker, in a transparent sham, pretends
to discern meaning in the meaningless cartoons
it prints by way of the arrogant message it sends:
its editors are all clever but its readers buffoons.

TRUISMS II

God cannot create a stone that He cannot lift.
Diluted nitric acid corrodes steel, concentrated nitric acid does not.
No human buss exhilarates like the kiss of spoondrift.
Imagination is considered a vice in the character of an astronaut.

10 is the most storied squad number in soccer.
All cuckoo clocks feature iron pine-cone weights.
A sense of belonging defines a high school locker.
The Pacific Plates are subducted under Mariana Plates.

No agents—literary, real estate, etc.—are not pimps.
Neuilly-sur-Seine is the most right-wing town in France.
Eating the whole head is delicious in cooked shrimps.
A circle is required for Native American ghost dance.

Finger holes remain all the same size in scissors.
"New & Improved" on packaging usually means less.
Federally protected are all Gila Monster lizards.
British royals, avoiding disrobing, favor the coatdress.

Bumper crops bring farmers *smaller* total incomes.
In Numbers, Noah curses the land of Canaan (Israel).
"Pannist" is formal title for a player of steel drums
Success is a block party but failure a private funeral.

Maybe is—always—a euphemism for "no."
Kids draw a woman's legs as thin sticks straight down.
The more gluten, the more elastic the dough.
Venerable Bostonian women only travelled in brown.

The CIA has always hated the J. P. Kennedy family.
Shakespeare's Falstaff was a son of Chaucer's Wife of Bath.
A compulsive self-abuser's handshake is made clammily.
Darwin, Edison, and Faraday, and all had trouble with math.

The average car dealership markup is $3,753.
Parvenus prefer to say *algorithms* instead of *rules*.
The greatest of working pumps is a natural tree.
Average is the high standard in all public schools.

"Lumbersexuals" love a beard, plaid shirts, the outdoorsy look
The credulous descry paranormalcy in any photo halation.
To have interviewed Mother Jones, one only said he needed work.
Each and every Bulgarian may rightly be called a Thracian.

Sociopaths tend to harm not themselves but others.
Al Capone's business card: "Used Furniture Dealer."
Neurotics have a tendency to overuse slipcovers.
No evangelist doesn't strive secretly to be a healer.

A goalkeeper in every penalty kick must consider
whether the kicker is left- or right-footed; the joint
of the foot about to kick; and, crucially, the didder,
when his lowered head at the ball aims full point.

Chefs love to be photographed carefully salting a dish.
Billy Sunday attacked sexual sin to groups of men only.
No extreme waters—sharp hot or cold—kill a catfish.
Solitude, which vivifies, knows nothing of being lonely.

Low incomes make the poor *more* conservative.
Artist Rosa Bonheur believed animals had souls.
Sodium Benzoate is the favored food preservative.
A seducer never forces but flatteringly cajoles.

Angry women professors love to teach Adrienne Rich.
Organ meats provide Inupiats and Yupiks with vitamin C.
Tapestry is enhanced by the embroidered chain stitch.
The working classes, not the gentry, go in for "high tea."

Nothing quite reeks like a middle schooler's locker.
Funeralists prefer "brittle mineral frame" to *skeleton*.
Determining added time muddles European soccer.
Connected fitness thrills all mavens of a peloton.

Lillian Russell had a singular passion for mushrooms.
Even Carrie Nation's silences were considered bickering.
French hydrangea (Bigleaf) neither blossom nor blooms.
Eyes are observing scenes in dream-based eye flickering.

Jesus Christ supposedly received 39 lashes—
the Roman *flagrum*—as did St. Paul (2 Cor. 11:24);
the concept of giving not more than 39 slashes
is Jewish in origin, not Roman, savaging no more.

A triple agent offers himself to the opposing side
as a double agent who has "turned" but continues
pretending to serve his original masters as a guide
while actually passing on to them falsified news.

Great Britain was, of all, the most imperial power.
Employers generally prefer their butlers to be single.
Some dieticians hate sugar even less than white flour.
A Nordic version of the pretzel is a Danish *kringle.*

A casket is always carried feet-end first, not the head,
a symbolic step, said to remind us of a person walking.
The Spanish monarchy has always been horribly inbred.
To be rejected, weirdly, is the main motive for stalking.

The world's richest person makes ca. $2,569 a second.
U.S. Govt. mediators are free to lie to hostage-takers.
Hand-fans in the 18th-century were a way to beckon.
Root beer was created a temperance drink by Quakers.

No standard list price governs college tuitions.
A hurricane can only start to form over the sea.
Government is inevitably the cause if inflation.
Ahura Mazda is the Supreme Being of the Parsee.

One-third were immigrants who fought in our Civil War.
All historians have a lady dogsbody to do all their work.
In American hotels the street-level floor is the *first* floor.
whereas abroad that is ground level by an English quirk.

Cheese is listed first among the world's most stolen foods.
American college girls have a "thing" for Seurat posters.
No narrative accompanies any of Jesus Christ's beatitudes.
Miming ships, coasters were first called "bottle coasters."

J. L. Goddard knocked Hollywood films for "too much acting."
A D'Artagnan frozen turkey of 16 lb. costs a full $225 dollars.
Instead of correctly saying *effecting*, dolts now say "impacting."
Few queer the meaning of poems more than invidious scholars.

Jewish scholars found the book Ezekiel anti-Mosaic.
New England town meetings are seedbeds of hectoring.
Garlic is, oddly, considered the universal apotropaic.
Ralph W. Emerson explored his thoughts *by* lecturing.

Cranberries are a rarely found in Italian cuisine.
Publishers have a ghoulish interest in incest memoirs.
A red seaweed used in many foods is carrageen.
#5 Gurkha Black Dragons are the most expensive cigars.

Sports rivalries are based strictly on geography.
Germany and Poland's relations are never warm.
Art has almost nothing to do with photography.
Heat creates its own wind system in a firestorm.

Microwave carousels reverse at every new start.
Johnny Carson's least liked guest was Bob Hope.
Nothing oversimplifies production like a flowchart.
Eczema patients should avoid using green soap.

Howard Hughes went through 12 boxes of Kleenex a day.
No true diary—*diarum*—shows knowledge of the future.
A God-fearing altar boy to a pervert priest is perfect prey.
Polypropylene allows the strongest non-absorbable suture.

Danakil warriors must not only kill but castrate victims.
John Donne in his Second Prebend sermon exalts America.
Rivalry is always triggered by perceived mutualisms.
Cervical cancer is indicative by a woman's metrorrhagia.

St. John promised a blessing to anyone (Rev. 1:3)
who would listen to the Book of Revelation being read.
Christ on the cross equals a "partridge in a pear tree."
Roman generals, receiving triumph, were painted red.

The umbrella came from Italy originally as a sunshade.
In Shakespeare, music is the antonym to turbulent weather.
Portugal was the most active in the transatlantic slave trade.
Something's morally, indefinably, wrong in patent leather.

The dot over a lowercase *i* and *j* is called a *tittle*.
The entirety of Asia is larger than the mass of the moon.
A Komodo dragon's toxic bacteria is in its spittle.
Oprah Winfrey wins fans by bland opinions, all jejune.

When he died in 1932, Flo Ziegfeld was penniless.
The leveling aspect of democracy breeds mediocrity.
A Buddhist seeks to perceive by way of emptiness.
Congenital diabetics are notorious for being crotchety.

Mental spalling is the refractory result of bad judgment.
In *Shepherd of Hermas*, we have but one chance at repentance.
A lunatic fringe accompanies every reform movement.
All pedigree hunters have exalted views of their descendants.

TRUISMS II

Nothing is more cryptic or ambiguous than the human smile.
The Earl of Kent's last speech in *King Lear* is a suicide note.
No prose skeeves more than *Playboy*'s rhetorical house-style.
A gathering of hippopotamuses is referred to as a "bloat."

Getting to meet Hitler was a task devoid of scruple.
"A good voice never has a beautiful face." Flo Ziegfeld.
No English football team has ever won the "quadruple."
Only objects impressive or remarkable can be *beheld*.

An orchestra conductor's flat hand begs for smoothness.
Coriolanus was likely never played in Shakespeare's lifetime.
Good manners by way of subtlety are often a mask of rudeness.
Space's four dimensions are length, breadth, height, and time.

Chef Julia Child had no great liking for pasta.
A collector must have a wife who considers her hobby him.
Trade wars always promote equal disaster.
An auto-hyponym covers both a hypernym and its hyponym.

A British valet is often a friend-slash-manservant.
It is only the blossom end of tomatoes that "cat-face."
A Jew may not be Orthodox and still be observant.
A cripple in his nightly dreams always wins the race.

Exporting democracy abroad is the height of folly.
Locals in the Congo eat everything with mayonnaise.
Toxic to people and pets are the red berries of holly.
For Christmas now in the U.S. one must say "holidays."

A pole vaulter's sport always ends in failure.
In *Mein Kampf* only married girls become a German citizen.
Touching a collar was good luck to a whaler.
Crispy brown food like barbecue is said to be a carcinogen.

Ordinary people's lives, sadly, are never chronicled.
Ecclesiasticus 41:19 urges elbows be kept off the table.
German officers gave an evil twist to the monocled.
A sleighbell—on a harness—is technically a cascabel.

The sea and sky conjoin in J. M. W. Turner's art.
The Maldives, flattest country in the world, is slowly sinking.
Couples with children almost never order à la carte.
Gunslingers in films feel it's virile to shoot without blinking.

The fruit of the kiwi can legitimately be eaten unpeeled.
Hardboiled fiction is all about who gets suckered.
DiMaggio never forgave Mantle replacing him in center field.
Shaker minds, rooms, and dogma are all uncluttered.

No one doesn't die, but someone declares, "Thank God."
The Romantic poets cherished metaphysical peculiarities.
Spring is always cold and autumn warm on Cape Cod.
Voting in Chicago is always fraught with irregularities.

Medieval theology believed Earth grew ever colder
as it left temperate Eden further and further behind.
The first United States President was a slave holder.
The historical interests of Iraq and Iran never align.

TRUISMS II

Samuel Taylor Coleridge described St. Paul's book
of Romans as "the most profound book in existence."
Prime spot in a colonial tavern was the inglenook.
Victorious from the start is the policy of nonresistance.

Diamond Jim Brady began his life selling handsaws.
Army usually loses to Navy in their football rivalry.
No planes can safely fly past the region of aeropause.
Pigs find it physically impossible to look up into the sky.

Herod the Great was not a Jew, but an Idumaean,
an Edomite—his ethnic background was Arabic.
Seki can both insult and be affectionate in Korean.
Sunni and Shia Muslims consider each a heretic.

Johann Sebastian Bach was better at composing music
than any one person has ever been at creating anything,
except for William Shakespeare who, verbally acoustic,
soared as high to match God's other angelic offspring.

Virtually no one can determine an offside in soccer.
Mark Twain said, of all places, Mauritius was paradise.
Two incidents are legally required to accuse a stalker.
The asking price always surrenders to the selling price.

A newly tattooed person may not legally donate blood.
Hitler, whose mother died on Dec. 21, hated Christmas.
Judas suicided on *Cercis siliquastruma* tree: a redbud.
No retribution is ever fully complete as forgiveness.

Wordsworth's poetry is entirely bereft of humor.
Hemingway insisted John Dos Passos was a Negro.
There are no obvious symptoms of a brain tumor.
The main—and longest—river in Spain is the Ebro.

Servers hate wasting time making cappuccino.
Psalm 2 predicts Herod and Pilate would become friends.
A soprano has less vocal range than a sopranino.
After Gettysburg, the Confederacy was on its beam ends.

No Gospel angel appears without first saying, "Fear not."
Only the King of Hearts playing card has no moustache.
Chinese wines, drunk while still warm, are served hot.
A lexicographical omission is specified by a swung dash.

Maine is the closest state to the continent of Africa.
Old U.S. wooden lecture halls were all acoustically live.
Breaking wind is the anthem of the family brassica.
Twist-cutting biscuit dough crimps it and impedes its rise.

Forty-five men wrote the Bible, of 66 different books,
odd styles of storytelling, differing points of views,
not a single women author, but some say by its looks
one Priscilla wrote the mysterious book of Hebrews.

Thug Sam "Momo" Giancana's eyes always got wet
hearing "You're Nobody 'till Somebody Loves You."
No 'Twenties dowager's hat failed to sport an aigrette.
No prose at all appears in Shakespeare's *Richard II*.

TRUISMS II

Leonardo Da Vinci never once painted a crucifixion.
Seitan in Chinese cooking is its main meat alternative.
Open-minded types are frequently lacking conviction.
Abraham Lincoln took blue mass pills as a purgative.

Prison mashed potatoes are reportedly to be the best.
Psalms 16:10 gives a preview of Christ's Resurrection.
Amazon archers found a hindrance in the right breast.
Every Persian carpet includes a deliberate imperfection.

Respect is presumed by authors who use three names.
Counter-clockwise is common direction in skating rink.
Christ's first apostle to shed his blood was St. James.
No good carpenter flushes a screw he can countersink.

Red Sox fans thoroughly enjoy double outcomes:
their team wins and/or the hated N.Y. Yankees lose.
A princeps pollicis artery gives a pulse to thumbs.
Cruise ships have residents who permanently cruise.

Religious Christmas carols are stifled on American radio.
Creativity is the reach to get beyond the feeling of loneliness.
Veal, larded and glazed, is traditional meat in a fricandeau.
None dare weigh the burden in life exacted by homeliness.

No kiss of greeting is given on the lips in Tangier.
Vanilla vines are all pollinated artificially by hand,
and strangely its flowers open only one day a year.
Volcanic eruptions alone create a rare green sand.

The Catholic Bible has seven books in sum,
never included in any Protestant Bible; to wit:
Sirach, First Maccabees, Judith, Wisdom,
plus, additions to Daniel and Esther, and Tobit.

With an individual's Saturn Return, one enters adulthood.
Alaska is the westernmost, easternmost, northernmost state.
Every brutal husband contaminates his son's fatherhood.
There is always a small assertion of rapacity in a bookplate.

Grocers habit of hiding bruised specimens in a box
of fresh fruit was a sneaky act called "stove-piping."
Star Trek's first gay character was the wry Phlox,
also, a flaming flower the pink of which is striking.

Pettiness, jealousy, and rivalry with chefs is universal.
Jessica is an original name in *The Merchant of Venice.*
Medals, trophy, prizes are totemic of perpetual rehearsal.
Wealth and privilege promote being a brat in tennis.

The British Royal House was originally Hanover house,
then was changed to Saxe-Coburg-Gotha, then Windsor.
Typography was a particular fascination of the Bauhaus.
Cold weather is highly painful to a Doberman Pinscher.

Ditheists and binitarians share the same theology.
Beethoven insisted on 60 coffee beans for each cup.
Mormons, who baptize by proxy, scour genealogy.
A pitcher often tips his pitch during a full wind-up.

TRUISMS II

Sinatra's "Rat Pack" referred to themselves as "The Summit."
75% of infectious diseases are born of lower species contagion.
Every catastrophic event causes the stock market to plummet.
A "query" is a question, an "inquiry" an official interrogation.

Gnostics break with the Jewish origins of Christianity.
Wearing anything white is anathema for a bridesmaid.
Every genius begins with an odium for conventionality.
Shingles on any unvented attic will very soon degrade.

Reindeer appear golden in summer, but blue in winter.
True Russian potato pancakes must contain bacon.
A sliver of anything cutaneous is officially a splinter.
Dreadlocks signify defiance of whites to a Jamaican.

No car ever made was worse than the 1971 "Ford Pinto,"
except for the three-wheeled UK "Reliant Robin" 1974,
or perhaps the disastrous pig-shaped dud the 1980 Yugo
and 1978 AMC Pacer, half cartoon beagle, half eyesore.

Woodthrush always migrate to Honduras and Nicaragua.
Constipation is unknown in Delhi: squatters are the rule.
The world's vanilla comes predominantly from Madagascar.
European terrorists typically appear wearing a cagoule.

No individual's credit is ever as good as his money.
Bach's "B Minor Mass" is, in itself, a cathedral of sound.
There are 110 pounds of potatoes in a standard gunny.
Duchamp's "Fountain" is the totem of art that's "found."

No social group exists without a corrupting hegemony,
an infection which sits at the root of all gathering.
A proviso among furniture polishes is they be lemony.
Consumers are manipulated by emotional tampering.

Writer Jack Boyle was serving time in San Quentin
for robbery when creating his sleuth, Boston Blackie.
Harder, denser than bone is calcareous tooth dentin.
Any shoe lying upside down badly spooks an Iraqi.

The worst mistake to do with one is pay a blackmailer.
King Lear and Edmund exchange not a word in the play.
*Un*pasteurized *raw* milk goes into cheese Emmentaler.
St. Augustine declared that singing was a way to pray.

The Executioner's Song won the Pulitzer Prize for fiction,
yet the book is non-fiction, recording documented facts.
The regal disapproval of Henry Daniell was icy perfection.
Luke is both participant and journalist in the book of Acts.

TV game shows are the destination of faded actresses.
American radio makes no use of literature, books, stories.
There is never a possibility of fully cleaning mattresses.
Their flat bottom shapes facilitate the stacking of dories.

Politicians publicly embrace religion only for votes.
Gnosticism is a total corruption of the Holy Gospels.
Groats are the healthiest oatmeal of those made of oats.
Galileans alone (but Judas, a Judean) were Christ's Apostles.

TRUISMS II

Canadian French is 17th-century French: the purest.
Mid-life women commonly change their sexual preference.
Aggregation is both the need and vice of a tourist.
Only the truest explorer reprobates a frame of reference.

Cherries (pits have cyanide) are toxic to cats and dogs,
and grapes and raisins can give them kidney damage.
Reading Isaiah, chapter 53, is banned in most synagogues.
The boon of Signing Bonuses is a Wall St. apanage.

There is a certain thirst only tonic water can quench.
A MLB player's prime goes from age 28 to age 32.
Medieval England spoke entirely Norman French.
Fat must be always equal to flour in a perfect roux.

All fashion victims, pathetically, live to follow suit.
A *left* arm gives most accurate reading for blood pressure.
"Forefathers," believed sexist, is now held in disrepute.
Petrochemicals and aerosol pollutants make up "air freshener."

California is the breeding ground of bogus religions.
The oceans of the world alone regulate global climate.
The play *Hamlet* is strictly about making decisions.
Jesus was declared innocent three times by Pontius Pilate.

No common sailboat captain isn't a mini-Mussolini.
No person would ever life his life over the same way.
A grumpy euphemism for "damn" in Russian is blini.
Only the lonely and poor work in New Year's Day.

Claymore mines are illegal for homeowners to own.
Correction, for a narcissist, is always taken as reproof.
No pain surpasses that of passing a kidney stone.
Ninjas in films are always shown abseiling from a roof.

Jesus raised his close friend Lazarus from the dead,
but left his own cousin John, alive, to be beheaded.
No company is duller than the contentedly ill-read.
The perfect sail is triple-stitched and heavy-threaded.

Intersections are a motorcyclist's worst nightmare.
Hell's Angels identify not with Johnny but with Chino.
Air Force One can be constantly re-fueled in the air.
Pollen and/or dust is actually necessary to form snow.

Bees in orchards can never puncture sound fruit.
No German necessity was needed for the Holocaust.
Anxiety can cause a child to be selectively mute.
Cows petrified poet (and ex-farmer) Robert Frost.

Americans all pronounce the word mental as "menal."
No one has ever managed to breed eels in captivity.
A U.S. weight of 100 pounds is referred to as a cental.
Aucklanders pronounce *i*'s for *e*'s—i. e., *yistidity*.

U.S. official air space extends up to 100,000 feet high.
Most American motorcycles don't have center stands.
To catch trout, always use the Blue-Winged Olive fly.
The index finger is needed the least in human hands.

TRUISMS II

Essex pigs are always black, Jefferson County white.
Tolstoy could create women, Dostoevsky could not.
Whales, eating, snuff out tons of lives at a single bite.
Marilyn Monroe despised the film *Some Like It Hot*.

Every ship carries two white lights, mounted
at different heights on separate vertical axes;
the lower is always forward, as encountered,
of the higher one—admonitory prophylaxes.

"Talk about..." the lame interviewer's feeble exhortation.
No actual muscles are located in your fingers and thumbs.
At sea, to eat raw fish without water speeds dehydration.
African sexuality is bound up with the sound of drums.

Quantity has a quality all of its own.
Mesopotamian architecture made the first archway.
Clothes are sewn, but seeds are sown.
The cathode-ray tube is the television tube of today.

Sherlock Holmes spoke of love only with a sneer.
V.S. Naipaul to British anti-immigrant voters:
"We wouldn't be here, if you hadn't been there."
Smoked, salted, but never gutted are bloaters.

No one ever chances to see a baby seagull.
Each Masonic rite has its own handshake.
Teeth are not considered bones of the skull.
One extra egg won't let a brownie cake.

Who last touches the hockey puck is credited the goal.
Victor Hugo considered himself heir to Shakespeare.
When winning in football, always run, never pass the ball.
A human's balance depends fully on the human ear.

Warmth to a pig is the equivalent of food.
Sonia Orwell's one true love was Maurice Merleau-Ponty.
There is an actual *smell* of decadence in Hollywood.
Sailors on the main all refer to a sea chant as a sea *shanty*.

Thinking is actually not possible without memory.
The more vacant the mind, the louder the laugh.
Winds in the Doldrums blow *up*, not horizontally.
No one has ever actually seen a swimming giraffe.

Wind in the Horse Latitudes are perpetually becalmed.
Let no fat soprano sing fragile Madame Butterfly.
A pregnant girl ever leaves a church-run home unharmed.
Zen Buddhism is the actual aesthetic of all bonsai.

Peace is impossible without equal justice.
No beginner in curling should use a quacked stone.
The *Pax Romana* is solely attributable to Augustus.
Every primitive tribe has its own membranophone.

In 2050, London's temps will match Barcelona.
Cancelled student debts force citizens to pay them.
Being late is the privilege of every opera diva.
Mucus is less related to a disease than phlegm.

TRUISMS II

Yahweh, oddly, gave Moses *two* tablets.
Twelve disciples, too, seems an arbitrary number.
David picked up *five* stones—by habit?
Only *three* Magi came; would more encumber?

Angels portrayed in art are never shown as dark.
The left foot should always precede the right in curling.
Some say cypress, others gopher wood for Noah's Ark.
Kicking water at an opponent is legitimate in birling.

Freighters always steam in a straight line.
Stendhal observed that bad taste often leads to crimes.
U.S. diplomats visit Israel first, then Palestine.
Sonya Tolstoy copied out *War and Peace* eight times.

W is a letter the French language does not use.
Most pedophiles turn out to be family uncles.
The world population now has 16 million Jews.
Karl Marx's wrath was born of his carbuncles.

Orthodox Islam in Iran is predominantly Shia.
Caramels in gift samplers are much preferred to creams.
Only 10 male hair styles are allowed in North Korea.
Sensory adaptive clothing is issued without seams.

Celebrities always appear to be short in real life.
Eels have no ovaries, no testicles, no eggs, no milt.
No husband with one son has an attentive wife.
Father-hatred for Freud explained our sense of guilt.

A tad of sugar fights acidity in tomato sauce.
In surfing, water is no longer water, but a rock.
For Jews, a symbol of *oppression* is the cross.
Owls, crows, and eagles all frighten a hawk.

When following the money, one always discovers the truth.
An overly aggressive wine can blot out the texture of food.
300 species of bacteria can be found in the plaque of a tooth.
Coming on time to any wedding in India is considered rude.

Germans knock on the table when approving a decision.
Only 146 doctors are fellowship-trained in obesity medicine.
To placate the gods was the primate-like goal of circumcision.
The phonograph was the favorite invention of Thomas Edison.

Wine connoisseurs rarely drink wine without food,
but whenever they do so, the wine is invariably white.
To prevent corrosion resistance are firearms blued,
which conveys solidity and added beauty to its sight.

Only Lacaune sheep milk can make Roquefort cheese.
Females alone can be Romani *drabardi*—fortune tellers.
A clotting blood disorder is called "Christmas disease."
Architect Frank Lloyd Wright despised attics and cellars.

File-cut patterns on kitchenware always help a grip.
Adolf Hitler called German crowds his "only bride."
Cognitive deficits are frequent attending a cleft lip.
No renewable energy source can beat the ocean tide.

TRUISMS II

Seven bushels of corn can make 100 pounds of pork.
Tolstoy believed children should not fondled or kissed.
For biodiversity, rainforests alone beat forests of cork.
Eggs are to laying hens, what thin layers are to schist.

A star is a hydrogen bomb held together by gravity.
King Saul was the tallest man in the Middle East.
Nothing for Victorian children wasn't a lesson on morality.
Once ordained, a Catholic priest is never not a priest.

Never ever pay the first health bill you've received.
Hard are those people whose mother never loved them.
Tears that are shed purge, and so stress is relieved.
Naught in nature for power beats the umbilicus of a stem.

St. Paul in Philippians wrote about *joy* while in jail.
No food is as disgusting as elvers cooked alive.
A code, not a language, is the tactility of braille.
Amaryllis is the great-grandmother of the chive.

There is no overt religion in *The Pickwick Papers*.
Electrolytes prevent scouring (diarrhea) in a pig.
Architect Frank Lloyd Wright abhorred skyscrapers.
The word Friday comes from Norse goddess Frigg.

Satan's interests, strangely, are solely spiritual.
No serious bike rider is not an insane competitor.
The basic structure of the universe is spherical.
American dollars are the currency in Ecuador.

Macau leads the whole world in gambling casinos.
Old Cape Cod women love and collect fabric scraps.
Hispanic people—fully separate—are not Latinos.
Only women can milk reindeer among the Lapps.

William Beveridge hated his own phrase, "welfare state."
Japan's passport is the most welcomed in the world.
Eels—*Anguilla Anguilla*—have never been seen to mate.
Quizzicality is ever portrayed with a brow that's furled.

No Gentiles appear in Saul Bellow's novel *Herzog*.
Rwanda and the Congo hate and provoke each other.
Well-known to be lactose intolerant is the hedgehog.
Coleridge said the holiest thing alive was a mother.

Chemistry as a field is ultimately electrical.
Anna Karenin is correct: she was not a ballerina.
A Maine lobster's claws are asymmetrical.
Education is both compulsory and free in N'Djamena.

Any missing limbs on a salamander are fully reparable.
Motorcyclists, with loud straight pipes, have virility problems.
Preachers who dialogue with congregations are unbearable.
Entasis, a light curve, enhances the shafts of Greek columns.

Dale Carnegie, obsequious, stressed using flattery
and advised never tell another person he is wrong.
Foreplay's point, like a heating pad, is calefactory.
Comic Bert Lahr's signature was "*gnong, gnong!*"

Brazilians, who speak Portuguese, are not Hispanic.
Mein Kampf, translated and abridged, is milder on Jews.
It's the phallic fact of a rabbit's foot that's talismanic.
There are consistently seven holes in all horseshoes.

Americans dopily say *verbage, folage* and *menstration.*
Herbert W. Clutter, slain in *In Cold Blood,* hated Catholics.
Hollywood gossip columnists called divorce "renovation."
Crows and all corvids are fascinated with shiny metallics.

The heavy pollens of milkweed cripple bees' feet.
Adolf Hitler never formally renounced his Catholic faith.
A dreamer wants better bread than can be made of wheat.
Sex outside of marriage in Indonesia is punished by death.

All great writing is lost in every last translation.
Lewis Carroll died presumably without sexual experience.
No spots appear the same way on any Dalmatian.
The foundation of all advertising is grounded in prurience.

Jesus as Redeemer meant nothing to R. W. Emerson,
who regarded death on Golgotha as a great defeat.
The best source for taking zinc is consuming venison.
One of military's great strategies has been retreat.

Most pop, country, and rock songs are in 4/4 time.
Schizophrenics and depressives crave a lot of sugar.
Metrical patterns in poetry are a form of rhyme.
Nothing tenderizers meat better than a pressure-cooker.

The English never escape their rigid class system.
Charles Dickens (cf. Mrs. Clennam) disliked his mother.
The Holy Spirit in the Bible corresponds with wisdom.
Doubt, an interrelated force, is Faith's twin brother.

Patton explicitly instructed shoot prisoners in cold blood.
Whatever you have and enjoy, a truck driver brought you.
An exploding shell spreads shrapnel on an angle upward.
No wood is more elastic, turns, or carves better than yew.

Hot pipes in a house freeze before cold pipes do.
Shearwaters actually *fly* underwater, with sculling wings.
In Italy, there is never any strictness in a queue.
An Estonian to express a sign of freedom publicly sings.

Ribcage, palms of the hand, and soles of the feet
respond with the most pain when being tattooed.
Technology in its every iteration soon is obsolete.
Sheep herders and cattle ranchers forever feud.

A human action that's conceivable need never happen.
Pederasty was a form of chivalry to the ancient Greeks.
Anchorites compulsively shun clothes of silk and satin.
Poulterers should be jailed for snipping chickens' beaks.

R. F. Kennedy always despised Adlai Stevenson.
Typewriters as an invention first gave women work.
Obsolete now is the euphemism "extreme unction."
Water inevitably gathers to fill a mountain cirque.

TRUISMS II

Oppenheimer never explained why for code
at Los Alamos he called the nuclear test "Trinity."
In planets, orbiting stars are likely bestowed
a million advanced civilizations in our galaxy.

Jesus in the Bible is called the "Son of Man" 92 times.
Monosexualism developed with monotheism.
Rap music, which depends on, badly disfigures rhymes.
True wit engages on polite irony, or asterism.

R. L. Stevenson's mid-name was first spelled Lewis.
Voles are completely and uniquely monogamous.
Of all loves a person loves, the earliest love is truest.
Rivalry is unavoidable in anything dichotomous.

Tomatoes grow poorly in Denmark and are rarely served.
The faster you shoot a sextant, the better your aim.
Lincoln's Second Inaugural speech was merely 700 words.
A writer must work in a book as a child in a game.

Saffron, orange threads, come from a purple flower
taken from the stamens of the flower, not the petals.
The powerless have always been abused by power.
After a fire, oddly, no plant grows faster than nettles.

Cumbria in England is the rainiest of all its counties.
Lester Young let no one ever touch his saxophone.
"Rosebuds" was the first (hated!) name for Brownies.
Energy dissipates as heat whenever work is done.

Americans idiotically begin every response by saying, "Well . . ."
Cobblestone on colonial streets ruined drivers' kidneys
Hannah Arendt in *Eichmann in Jerusalem* scorned laws of Israel.
Cold and warm currents meeting raise monstrous seas.

Gibraltarians want to have nothing to do with Spain.
Giant clams (*Tridacna gigas*) are unable to close tightly.
A lone sailor must never fall sleep in a shipping lane.
A hack poet's work, obscure, is proffered reconditely.

The *alula* cabbage plant is found only in Hawaii.
To Boston's "Cornhill, "street" was never appended.
Never hang from low palm fronds of a coconut tree.
No working Constitution is ever finally amended.

José Greco, the great Spanish dancer, was Italian.
Being free from temptation means *distancing* it.
The hollowest of needs tis to crave a medallion.
Proof in all of its iterations means instancing it.

Paraguay borrowed its national flag from France.
The Maori were at one time savage cannibals.
In San Jose, gun owners must hold gun insurance.
The policy of L. L Bean stores allows in animals.

Flattery is by any definition insincere.
Sharks have no vertical vision, cannot see above them.
In 1634, the Mass. Bay Colony banned long hair.
One must pass guarded checkpoints to get to Bethlehem.

TRUISMS II

Political discussion is *banned* among Masonic groups.
Sam Colt, gunmaker, flatly refused to bd called Samuel.
Training wings are *never* worn by pilots and paratroops.
Mushrooms are edible fungi, unlike a toxic toadstool.

Coca-Cola is a world-wide symbol of imperialism.
L'Eglise Saint Roch is the French church for artists.
Atheism, in the last or final analysis, is materialism.
Only the four fingers on each hand used by harpists.

You cannot flush paper down a toilet in Iran.
Roughly, one in three adults have criminal records.
A government-issued ID is required to pawn.
Even pro guitarists have trouble with barre chords.

The utter brevity of life makes all of us amateurs.
The horizon always retreats as you move toward it.
Juggling money is the sole talent of arbitrageurs.
Rather than make decisions, sick hoarders hoard it.

The first flag of Belarus was strictly plain white.
Sturgeon are disappearing from North American rivers.
A saltwater crocodile has the most savage bite.
Plains Native Americans loved eating raw bison livers.

Fifty percent of Israelis refuse to live next to an Arab.
The Republic of Kiribati is pronounced "Kiribass."
Resurrection was symbolized for Egyptians by a scarab.
Schizophrenics are often compared to a Rubin vase.

Jesus Christ never once visited the city of Tiberias,
although it was the capital of the Galilean district.
No part of the human body is fully free of bacteria.
All husbands in China are notoriously nitpicked.

Flying fish tastes like sardines, but much better.
The number 39 in Afghanistan, cursed, is a badge of shame.
No female names are listed as a Biblical begetter.
Experience is all of our blunders given another name.

"Critically endangered" is officialese before extinction.
Dallol, in Ethiopia, is the most desolate place on earth.
For carvers of totem poles, no one beats the Tsimshian.
Distance drivers must spend 8 hours in a sleeper berth.

All Ancient Egyptians looked down on shepherds.
Jackie O banned Grace Kelly from JFK's funeral.
Unable to roar—they "chuff—are snow leopards.
There is infinite knowledge hidden in a numeral.

As you work, work itself is teaching you to work.
It is the contour feathers that determine a bird's shape.
Our Mutual Friend is literary ground zero of murk.
A strong musk smell graces the fox or Concord grape.

U.S. Congress people invest in companies they regulate.
Alfalfa and clovers are the best nitrogen-fixing cover crops.
An east wind will very often a coming storm adumbrate.
Flourishing in North America was the 3-horned triceratops.

The two far right vertical stars of the Big Dipper
—"pointers"—are directed toward the Pole Star,
which is the tip of the handle of the Little Dipper
or the long tail of Ursa Minor or the "little bear."

Rapacity destroys what it is successful in acquiring.
"Mistakes were made": the Ted Kennedy euphemism.
Rats mainly cause the fires blamed on "faulty wiring."
In the 1920s a shining ideal was linked to bolshevism.

A three-dot tattoo, commonly seen in jails,
found mainly on hands or around the eyes,
a boastful statement "*mi vida loca*" details
"my crazy life," printed there to emphasize.

All around-the-world sailors who travel so all alone
suffer grievous periods of loneliness and depression.
Development gets favored taxes in an enterprise zone.
Geometric growth is discrete; continuous, geometric progression.

FBI and CIA, rivals, never cooperated pre-9/11.
East winds are rare in the vicinity of 40th parallels.
A double Mersenne prime is the number seven.
Beethoven, between major work, wrote bagatelles.

A sheep's stomach is 5 times as great as that of a pig.
Only a child of a Jewish mother defines a Talmudic Jew.
A worker is 7 times more likely to die on an oil rig.
Alligators, snakes, and owls swallow food but don't chew.

French geniuses always ate at Procopius, now *Le Procope*.
Antonio Meucci invented the telephone before A. G. Bell.
Seventh Day Adventists believe Anti-Christ will be a Pope.
A machete is the most useful tool when living on an atoll.

Haram al-Sharif in Jerusalem—the Temple Mount,
as the Jews call it, is a time bomb waiting to explode.
A *komtesse* is the unmarried daughter of a count.
Agawam, Mass. (01001) was given the first ZIP code.

Shakespeare from fair Albion never once traveled.
Design is almost always at loggerheads with comfort.
Paranoics, better to hear, keep driveways graveled.
Still extant is a 4,200-year-old Sumerian clay tablet.

Sen. J. F. Kennedy. voted against statehood for Hawaii.
The larch tree, its bark immune from fire, despises water.
Nothing was more useless than a WWI soldier's puttee.
Parents see a *husband's family* own their Chinese daughter.

The definitive Mafia Meal: sausage and peppers
with a heaping main plate of spaghetti marinara,
a side dish of broccoli rabe, fingers of cheddars,
and cup of hot coffee laced with white Sambuca.

Male helplessness is a pose, almost always a ruse.
The first rule of finance: never use your own money.
In German card games, the highest value is the deuce.
Weather on the Faroe Islands is virtually never sunny.

TRUISMS II

Breadfruit was never welcomed in the Caribbean—
natives there much preferred their traditional plantain.
Stigma is at the heart of everything plebeian.
Henry James was an Edwardian master, not Victorian.

Moses, writing Genesis, simply fabricated stories,
All fiction writing involves much impersonation.
No one meaning attaches to any Masonic allegories:
each member can accept his own interpretation.

It is officially illegal to hunt or kill penguins.
Cirrus clouds indicate the proximity of unsettled weather.
Jamming was the *bête noire* of all Sten guns.
A bird's skeleton can weigh much less than its feathers.

Fresh water, lighter than saltwater floats on top:
underground stillness keeps the two from mixing.
"Tonic" to a Bostonian is the word for soda pop.
Gas stations in concert are masters of price-fixing.

Apricots were widely despised World War II soldiers.
The Catholic Church forbids members from being Masons.
A human body's most mobile joints are the shoulders.
A "white marriage" involves no use of sexual relations.

A person today dies from hunger every 4 seconds.
"Scientist" was a word coined only in the 1830s.
Inishmaan is the shy sibling of all the Aran Islands.
Gobbling is only done by mating male turkeys.

A pig is simply a mill for turning corn into pork.
Christ valued leftovers: "Gather up the remnants so that nothing in lost."
Christian demonology has debased the pitchfork.
King Arthur revealed quests to his knights at the round table on Pentecost.

"God save the Queen" is many a nation's melody: Germany's "*Heil Dir im Siegerkranz*;" "*Rufst du, Mein Vaterland*" for Switzers; "My Country, 'Tis of Thee" in the U. S. and Lichtenstein's "*Oben am Jungen Rhein.*"

None of the 50 United States ban barefoot driving.
A halo around the moon promises a change in weather.
The socially insecure are never quite arriving.
The libidinous mind has a distinct paraphilia for leather.

Mafiosi shoot an informer under the chin six times.
Acceptance of tragedy is the foundation of Slav life.
The softer the mallet, the lower the tone of chimes.
Waterways are being throttled by purple loosestrife.

One never sees a blind person bumping into a pedestrian.
World mountaineers all carry Quiggin's Kendal Mint Cake.
The only Olympic sport joining both sexes is equestrian.
Steaming involving seaweed constitutes a real clambake.

Peacock feathers are a taboo among theater people.
Cape Agulhas, with mammoth waves, is fierce as Cape Horn.
Centrifugal cannot be said as *force*, only centripetal.
Parents urged *flesh* be changed to *peach* as a Crayola crayon.

TRUISMS II

New England in literature is always stark and grim.
Every storm and squall were fit subject for the Romantics.
Wife-carrying—*eukonkanto*—is sport for a Finn.
Girls Nights Out always prove an exercise in corybantics.

Leopold Bloom in Ulysses is not Talmudically Jewish:
his mother and grandmother were in fact Irish Catholics.
Never, ever applied to a man is the adjective "shrewish."
Muslim countries, including India, never use chopsticks.

In England, dining at close quarters in a restaurant
it is held as *unthinkable* to speak to another diner.
Castiglione said, a prince must, above all, be nonchalant.
Ancient Egyptian beauty depended greatly on eyeliner.

A woman invented fire escapes, bullet-proof vests,
windshield wipers, life rafts, items meant for safety,
like feeding tubes, specifically where welfare rests,
car heaters, home-security systems, matters weighty.

The shout "*prout*" makes a donkey pick up its paces.
Pope Leo XIII called Freemasonry the "Kingdom of Satan.
The death hand in cards is two eights and two aces.
Denmark leads the world in the consumption of bacon.

"Pie eaters" was at one time code for immigrants.
Pseudonyms on any and every level are frankly pranks.
A liar's most useful tool is trust of the innocents.
Female tanks have machine guns, cannons male tanks.

Henry James was very ill when writing *The Turn of the Screw*.
French farmers concocted *coq au vin* to eat useless roosters.
The only plant that survived the Hiroshima blast was bamboo.
Delirium, fury, noise, and agitation characterize all boosters.

A fresh egg always sinks in a bowl of water.
Feminism, seeking liberty from men, promotes estrangement.
Censorship is always implied in an *imprimatur*.
Something sub rosa is ever implied in the word *arrangement*.

One inch of rainfall equals ten inches of snow.
The Edomites in Scripture were known for their wisdom.
All reporters were banned from 9/11's ground zero.
Inequality is the proven ambition for a capitalistic system.

The noble name of Jabal Tariq was anglicized
("Tariq's Mount") to name the Rock of Gibraltar.
Two miracles are needed for a dead soul to be canonized.
Belgium is reputed nation for perfecting a psalter.

All mammals are unable to breathe under water.
The Sydney Opera House mimics sails, shells, *and* birdwings.
"Race" records were distributed by the railroad porter.
The UK House of Commons is off-limits to queens and kings.

Religion in Burundi is mainly Roman Catholic.
Anne Desclos, *Story of O*'s bisexual author, preferred women.
Every macho man fancies himself a maverick.
There are less phenolics in an apple than in a persimmon.

Charles Dickens last novel *Edwin Drood* was his best,
although he died before he finished writing the book.
The discolored comb of a chicken indicates fowl pest.
After maturation, a male fish becomes a female snook.

"America First," a fascist code of President Trump,
was first uttered by Woodrow Wilson, a Democrat.
Wily strategists look to invest during a stock slump.
Nickels were the most common coins for an automat.

Alimony cannot be discharged by a bankruptcy.
Jesus of Nazareth and Hitler were born in an inn.
Not one character in *Amos 'n Andy* had a family.
American Freemasonry does not accept women.

No wide reader does not become a polymath.
China and the Congo have virtually the same flag
Strongest winds ride the right of a hurricane's path.
Social events for women necessitate a clutch bag.

Glenn Miller didn't originate the song "Tuxedo Junction;"
that man was black bandleader named Erskine Hawkins.
A fear of poverty lies behind conspicuous consumption.
There are virtually no Shia Muslims among Moroccans.

Lawyers never want intelligent people to be on juries.
Half of Americans live within 50 miles of their birthplace.
Candid truth, not self-cozening, constitutes true diaries.
Deceit and hypocrisy make for an asymmetrical face.

Arran Victory is the Rolls Royce of potatoes.
Sherlock Holmes loathed every form of society.
Ripening with heat, *not* sunlight grow tomatoes.
A spiritual person never reveals his or her piety.

Every Hebrew letter has also a number.
The word for *father* is numerical 3.
and word for *mother* has a 4 penumbra.
and *child*, 43, combining both, agree.

The Depression really did not end until World War II.
"Gone to Australia" is Mafia-speak for a dead corpse.
Polls reveal the favored color of toothbrushes is blue.
Hickory wood, which easily cracks, very often warps.

"Mother's Ruin" by users is the preferred nickname for gin.
French explorers of the 17th-century were Native Americans.
"Nigger" is used 215 times in *Adventures of Huckleberry Finn*.
Mount Gerizim is the holiest place on earth for Samaritans.

Venus, unlike every other planet in our solar system,
spins not from west to east but from east to west.
"Incels," involuntary celibates, are men who hate women.
Every detective or mystery novel involves a quest.

Hunter Thompson knew the book of Apocalypse by heart.
Animals attend church in Mexico on St. Anthony's Day.
Style in British pubs is having expertise in throwing a dart.
Gala is now the most widely grown apple in the U.S.A.

TRUISMS II

Nobel Laureate Doris Lessing seriously considered
her loony Canopus novels her most important work.
Guilt is an emotion that is primarily self-embittered.
Tension has always existed between Greek and Turk.

"Philistine" used as an insult is both racist and bigoted.
The English mystery plays were acted out by workmen.
No boor in life surpasses anyone who is uninhibited.
To see best at night at sea, *cut all lights* in deck and cabin.

Hurricanes, unknown down in the South Atlantic, occur
everywhere else above latitude north 10º north and south.
The U.S. owes much of its discovery to the French *voyageur*.
Much in the way of taste depends on saliva in your mouth.

Belief in a Supreme Being in American Masonic lodges
is in fact required, be it Christian, Islamic, or anything else.
Dodging trolleys gave the name to the Brooklyn Dodgers.
Russian sable is the most expensive of all animal pelts.

Hung juries typically bring a win for the defense.
Africa is 28% wilderness, North America 38%.
Etiquette is always first and foremost sheer pretense.
A Hebrew tabernacle was at first a portable tent.

Emeralds, brittle, tend to chip and are rarely flawless.
The proper surname of British royalty is Saxe Coburg and Gotha.
Laughter is the one part of human nature that is lawless.
"He Makes Rivers" is the Ojibway meaning for the name *Hiawatha*.

Originals are required to meet the "best evidence rule."
Materialism is the lamest yardstick for standard of living.
By staying calm, you'll be thrown back *out* of whirlpool.
Forgetting is truly the only form of forgiving.

Gangsters eliminate the boss, never a mere cog,
to avoid major retaliation. By attacking organized crime,
Bobby Kennedy assassinated Jack. To kill a dog,
don't cut off the tail; cut off the head, then it's free time.

In Poland, 200,000 Jews were killed *after* 1945.
Fairy tales are, in fact, erotic novels for children.
Edgar Allan Poe's worst fear was being buried alive.
He who heeds all advice builds a crooked building.

Coca-Cola when first served was originally green.
No landing invasion force succeeds without air support.
Hard water on hair badly depletes the sheen.
A reply is calm, but scorn and accusation define a retort.

Finns feel much closer to Swedes than to Estonians.
Monte's Restaurant in Brooklyn was a mob hangout.
War was the ultimate dream of the Lacedemonians.
No atheist was allowed to be an American Boy Scout.

The most popular protein in the world is goat.
Jews reject the claim Abraham was a Muslim.
A common male paraphilia is the female throat.
Slurping noodles in China is a common custom.

TRUISMS II

Mohammed, to pray, turned first to Jerusalem, *not* Mecca.
Aging Queen Elizabeth I banned mirrors from court.
The Beatles were rejected as lame by the company Decca.
Ground nuts and breadcrumbs replace flour in a torte.

Speed may help a ship while running in gales.
Caskets have 6 to 8 sides; coffins are rectangular.
Cawl or lobscouse is the national food of Wales.
All falling snowflakes are essentially hexangular.

Stammerers, when children, often end up in a fight.
With Italians, slang for Frank (Francesco) is "Cheech."
An expert in still air can easily maneuver his kite.
A woman's callipygian beautify resembles a peach.

A false-hearted smile actually constitutes a frown.
Marilyn Monroe: "None of my men are handsome, none."
Curiously enough, the word noun is also a noun.
A great-great nephew of Thomas More was John Donne.

California chardonnays never go well with meals,
as they are generally too aggressive, too alcoholic.
Pottery, not carts, initiated the first use of wheels.
The Beecher family was virulently anti-Catholic.

A .32, cops call a woman's gun because it has no kick.
Jerry Vale's "Spanish Eyes" is *La Cosa Nostra*'s pet song.
A good dry-cured prosciutto should never be cut thick.
President Bill Clinton was seduced by an intern's thong.

For a knockout, punch where the jaw meets the ear.
Power comes from the short, hard snap of the wrist.
There is no power in your arms, so let that be clear.
The pop comes from the forearm down to your fist.

No groups—ghettoized—mingled at Truman Capote's B &W Ball.
Children's books are aimed for grandmas who buy them for kids.
A circular arrangement is always the shape of an African *kraal*.
Boston, unlike New York and Chicago, grew exclusive if any grids

Ribollita, a Tuscan soup, demands *cavolo nero*—black cabbage.
Sassafras, considered a carcinogen, is now illegal to be sold.
The adjective "old" is consistently the hat for the noun adage.
Vitamin C does not a thing to keep at bay the common cold.

Little Black Sambo, not African, is a Hindu Tamil Boy.
Freud thought people were ashamed of their dreams.
Japanese *Gaijin* and Arabic *Ajam* are equal to Yiddish *goy*.
Francis Bacon in his portraits actually painted screams.

There is no letter Z in the Maori alphabet.
Whenever Jesus *sat down*, it was always to impart teaching.
Chinese girls fear to wear a white barrette.
Casinos use 100% plastic playing cards to prevent cheating.

Women in photographs tend to look younger than men.
Staging oldies-but-goodies shows is rouging a corpse.
Tarantula kebabs are standard fare in Phnom Penh.
Voicelessness—silence—is the condition of all storks.

TRUISMS II

Tarzan's catch-all movie grunt "*Ungawa*" meant nothing at all.
Visitors often leave $1.87 at O. Henry's grave in Asheville, N.C.
Fisherman rape entire sea environments when they bottom trawl.
Sacred to all Hindus and Buddhists is the peepul or *bo*—tree.

Grapefruit juice, alone, speaks to a special kind of thirst.
Women's higher hormone prolactin makes them weep more.
No hunting crocodile or alligator is ever fully submersed.
Why, not where, is the meaning of the question wherefore.

Convent-bred girls always have the best manners.
Any biography of a living human being is quixotic.
The scream of jihad can be heard in its black banners.
The fatal fact of romance is that it is aperiodic.

Evita was never an implicit endorsement of Eva Peron.
NY Times drama critics can close a show in one column.
People don't nod but shake their heads to agree in Ceylon.
Only the meat cut from the *thigh* of a hog is *jambon*.

Cambodia is the most gay-friendly country in Asia.
It is physically impossible for pigs to look up into the sky.
Madeira wine is made only from the grapes Malvasia.
Ted Williams, baseball's great hitter, never wore a necktie.

Foreigners can own property anywhere in Mexico.
Beefsteak tomato was the first Campbell's Soup flavor.
Hatred is of the emotion of fear a distinct aliquot.
Euthanasia is perfectly legal in all six states of Australia.

10 pounds of milk is needed to make one pound of cheese.
Wine, aged in terracotta urns, appears *orange* in Tbilisi.
It was the German people who originated Christmas trees.
The Noel crib was first introduced by St. Francis of Assisi.

Jesus harbored a special affection for Samaritans.
On Christmas alone can priests celebrate three masses.
Cornification is physical effect of all keratins.
Many nutritious vitamins are found in blackstrap molasses.

Meekness is not pleasing to God without wisdom.
Nor is wisdom pleasing to God without meekness.
At baptism Christian infants always wears a chrisom.
The essential quiddity of the serpentine is sleekness.

There is heavenly grace in the desire of grace.
The Jewish calendar was lunar, the Roman solar.
Cusk eels live so deep they have no eyes or face.
Only euphoric symptoms are seen in the unipolar.

Ke-tchup to the Chinese is a fish sauce.
Burglars first target the main bedroom, never an attic.
North-facing sides is the favorite of moss.
Hot, humid, pollenated air is worst for an asthmatic.

Zen Buddhism makes never a mention of God
and demands of followers no Scriptural devotion.
Altering a will or deed is "constructive fraud."
Every single U.S. state has a town called Goshen.

"Unfair to labor" signs, as opposed to "On Strike,"
mean picketers are not yet recognized as a union.
A songbird with a raptor's *savagery* is the shrike.
Quakers—"Friends"—never take Holy Communion.

In the N. Rockwell's famous *Saturday Evening Post*
warm Thanksgiving scene, no alcohol is to be seen.
Shakespeare wrongly thought Bohemia had a seacoast.
Shaping a metal material by hammering is to peen.

Max Ophuls's 1969 movie, *The Sorrow and the Pity*
was officially banned from French television until 1981.
The oldest theatrical plot pits the country versus city.
Our solar system—99% of its mass—is *only the sun*.

Tomato ketchup, as its bottles state, is redundant.
Siderial day is four minutes shorter than solar day.
Ill-disposed to debate is any political incumbent.
The sound of a seagull is best-described a *skreigh*.

"Going to school" in Cosa Nostra-speak means off to jail.
Aroma applies to young wine, *bouquet* for well matured.
"Feathered" hooves and ankles are bred in a Clydesdale.
To be a "fool for Christ" is the point of being tonsured.

Yarmulkes, headscarves, turbans, all large crosses,
and Stars of David are all banned in French schools.
Not touching land for years is a gift of albatrosses.
Salute from the *en guard* line is first of fencing rules.

The CIA tortured Guantanamo prisoners by rectal feeding.
Never look for planet Venus in the middle of the night.
Offering publishers a ms. is scorned as special pleading.
Staring at most animals is seen as an invitation to fight.

Iran, Iraq, Lebanon, Saudi Arabia,
all Pakistan, Yemen, plus Kuwait,
Afghanistan, Bangladesh, and Syria
refuse to recognize Israel as a state.

The world premiere of *Madame Butterfly* in Milan
in 1904 was a total failure, booed off of the stage.
Everything is sold in vending machines in Japan.
Knowledge is the most crucial fodder for old age.

The clover family is the world's best source of honey.
Tibetan tea is drunk salted with *dri* butter in place of milk.
As little as 8% of the world's currency is cash money.
A naturally potent diuretic agent is common corn silk.

Defense against active shooters is ignored in the news,
which, because of a sad anti-gun bias, always low rates
the need by those victims who in fighting back choose
not to be left a corpse as a way of accepting their fates.

In Chinese culture, the younger generation is served last.
Bismarck, who loved champagne, saved the empties he drank.
All leather work in India is performed by the lowest caste.
Redheads, gays, and short men are all voided at a sperm bank.

No presidential pardon can ever be rescinded.
After Cubism, the grid became a format in modern painting.
The worse a listener the more notoriously long-winded.
Slow readers in high school are sent to vocational training.

Marilyn Monroe believed the most romantic spot
in all Manhattan was the Queensborough Bridge.
There are no seagulls in Malta: they were all shot.
No member of a militia ever forgets Ruby Ridge.

Brighter than all the heavenly stars is the planet Jupiter.
By raising Lazarus, Christ broke the occult hold of the Sadducees.
Gandhi blamed Indians, not Britons, for the occupation of India.
Nyepi is a full day of complete silence that is kept by the Balinese.

Cheroots, inexpensive to roll mechanically, never taper.
Initiatic knowledge is ever the key to secret societies.
Many Victorians died from toxic arsenic in wallpaper.
Only four names exist for children among the Balinese.

Confidence is never not a procedure of slow growth.
Evangelist Billy Graham never spoke out on behalf of the poor.
Zany, if and when not updated, is the Hippocratic Oath.
It is non-consenting people or parties that most tempt a voyeur.

The Oz characters were animal, vegetable, and mineral:
—the Cowardly Lion, the Scarecrow, and the Tin Man.
Nerds adore any and all computer devices peripheral.
Middle-aged Florida women look parboiled with a tan.

In *Uncle Tom's Cabin*, Harriet Beecher Stowe
has Uncle Tom steer little Catholic Eva away
from the evils of Catholicism, known as a foe,
delivering her over to the Methodists, to stay.

Redheads—sea ducks—which all feed on wild celery
are succulent, but Audubon found the green wing teal
the tastiest by far, and then a canvasback for delicacy
to round off for perfection the consummate duck meal.

Crime writers tend to be madly committed gardeners.
Spencer Tracy routinely took top billing over Kate Hepburn.
Papal indulgences were sold by *licensed* pardoners.
The most expensive of all Bordeaux wine is the sauterne.

The Ten Commandments reframe the *Book of the Dead*:
the teachings of Moses are steeped in Egyptian wisdom.
Only since 1928 were consumers treated to sliced bread.
Burma, Liberia, and U.S. alone shun the metric system.

Avoid restaurants with menus in macaronic French.
Bodyguards, said slain Jimmy Hoffa, make you careless.
The prime ornamental pond fish is the golden tench.
All cetaceans (except for bristle whiskers) are hairless.

"Fat" wine has body but little tannin or structure.
All movie cowboys always had goofy sidekicks.
A novel that does not disturb you is not literature.
Most restaurants in Thailand no longer use chopsticks.

Yahweh in the Hebrew Bible, jealous, petty, cruel
and always angry, is nothing less than a war god.
Toxicity is the primary denotation of a toadstool.
"Inclusions" is jeweler-speak for any gem that's flawed.

Ximenes is the greatest crossword puzzle constructor.
Crime novel readers identify with crooks, not cops.
Every ADHD sufferer is a chronic interrupter.
Chloral hydrate with alcohol makes "knockout drops."

California lists highest as state of the worst tippers.
Colonialism and racist overtones flourish in *Babar*.
The Germans used 150 tons of chlorine gas at Ypres.
All stars move: a misnomer is an alleged "fixed star."

No wine description isn't delivered in purple prose.
Cassiopeia is seen directly opposite the Big Dipper.
No one ever correctly pronounces the word *clothes*.
Neither caught nor identified was Jack the Ripper.

Tenure of heredity comes naturally to English people.
Dates are never stated on LPs or Broadway Cast Albums.
In withdrawal, drug addicts will often remain foetal.
Trace amounts of asbestos can be found in all talcums.

Extra dry champagne is always sweeter than *brut*.
Beached whales are buried in sand by front-end loaders.
280 pounds, grounded, is the weight of a spacesuit.
Rot-resistant wood shingles are best made from deodars.

The tiny seeds on strawberries are the actual fruits—
the fleshy and delicious red part their "receptacle."
Neither algae nor fungi—plants—have any roots.
Negative connotations attach to the word *spectacle*.

Historian Arthur Schlesinger, Jr. cited anti-Catholicism
as "the deepest bias in the history of the American people."
Homosexuality is not necessarily linked to transvestitism.
In the training of canines, the hardest of all are beagles.

Raw water is a cultural constraint for the Chinese.
The Gospels say not a word about eastern thought.
Being rich is the primary virtue of college trustees.
Each and every person who is paid is also bought.

Every cow has four distinct stomachs: the omasum,
the reticulum—the part which produces proteins—
the rumen, and the enzyme-producing abomasum,
which, working together, metabolize eaten greens.

The Book of Enoch, never part of the Christian canon,
is often quoted by the writers of the New Testament.
The only unmarried U.S. president was James Buchanan.
Tension and urgency often call for poetic enjambment.

Young American girls, curiously, say *noé* for no.
Entrée (appetizer) as used in the USA is a misnomer.
Analogical reasoning comes natural to a crow.
American nurses refer to an unruly patient as a "gomer."

TRUISMS II

Everything in the universe strains toward intelligence.
Writers on the subject of wine are utterly bereft of humor.
The sole value for every Hollywood star is relevance.
There is not one single heritage site in all of Timor.

All gourmands when ordering Truite au Bleu all fussily insist
that it be traditionally served curled—that is, *recroquevillent*.
No revolutionary gesture is as overused as the sign of a fist.
A complete mystery is the death of the poet François Villon.

A .45 shot makes a loud noise; a .22 mainly takes a silencer.
Jesus, who captivated crowds, needed to withdraw to be alone.
Nothing has a sweet, musky evergreen scent like a Douglas fir.
Verjuice (unripe grapes) is the ancient secret of *moutarde* Dijon.

An Amazon had to kill a man in order to be married.
Lights left on all night—a pose—encourages intruders.
In Svalbard, Norway, it is illegal for corpses to be buried.
Of Welsh nobility, and not British, were the Tudors.

It is nearly 4,000 miles to the exact center of Earth.
A nun's linen guimpe made her feel chaste and protected.
A major horror in Herbert's *Dune* is of a water dearth.
Political incumbents are most always—98%—re-elected.

A Sally Lunn teacake, preferably, must be served hot.
Nichols & Stone makes the solid signature Harvard chairs
A frown in any fellow is a distinct sign he is fraught.
Ambassadors give most of their work to a *charge d'affaires*.

The Egyptian hymns to Aten anticipated the Psalms of David.
Umberto's Clam House in Manhattan is famous for mob hits.
Anything painted the color yellow is among the quickest faded.
Northerners know nothing about the Southern dish of grits.

Albert Einstein, monk Thomas Merton, and
Vladimir Nabokov, although it seems bizarre,
along with the pop singer Barbara Streisand,
throughout life never learned to drive a car.

In mixed company, the English do not present persons:
any presentation is a statement as serious as a contract;
introductions to them—casualness or aplomb are sins—
are considered like sacraments, doctrinal, godly, exact.

Planets, wanderers, are proscribed from star charts.
The sole creature that missed the Ark is the unicorn.
Cows of all creatures lead the bestial world in farts,
with circa 220–440 pounds of methane, all airborne.

The chicken industry hates wasting feed on useless roosters.
Henry James in writing always separated *does n't* and *has n't*.
Making money, not art, is the sole goal of movie producers.
Large size is usually a disappointment in a Christmas present.

Forgiveness does not necessarily involve reconciliation.
Vietnamese *pho* is eaten with chopsticks and spoon simultaneously.
Painting over antique wood or boards is an abomination.
True wit offers its in response immediately and extemporaneously.

TRUISMS II

There is no onion or cheese in traditional Quiche Lorraine.
Scripture predicts the presence of many scoffers in the Last Days.
Isaac Asimov, a Sci-fi writer, flatly refused to fly in a plane.
Root vegetables of any kind always taste better when braised.

Vindaloo is not a hot spicy regional dish of Bengal
but a cooking method of the Portuguese colony Goa.
Nothing irks Biblical Israel like the Canaanite Baal.
Natives often wipe their bums with rocks in Samoa.

The word for okra in French is, curiously, *gombo*.
Traditionalists beat egg whites in copper bowls.
The closest relative to human beings is the Bonobo.
Otto Weininger believed that women had no souls.

Every major mountain has the "crux of the climb,"
that one pitch for climbers that must be overcome.
One palace has no Royal Family link: Blenheim.
Having its very own pulse is the human thumb.

Vietnamese *pho* is traditionally always slurped.
Ishmael's chowder recipe in *Moby-Dick* mentions no milk.
Every second child in a family is born usurped.
Strong fibers for insulation can be found in vegetable silk.

Tripiers, among butchers now a vanishing profession,
have the smelly task of cleaning and parcooking tripe.
Self-diminution is a consequence of every concession.
"Sewing-machine" speed is the eating action of snipe.

Childhood is the single promise that is never kept.
Waterzooi, a chicken stew, is the classic Belgian dish.
The shortest Bible verse is John 11:35—"Jesus wept."
Half of good health is turned into healing by a wish.

Most serial killers, when young, have hurt animals.
I Love Lucy humor (!?) never survived the 1950s.
The Korowai tribe of New Guinea are still cannibals.
Most men look abnormal watching a strip tease.

A felon may not vote, own a gun, serve on a jury,
obtain a driver's license, win custody in divorces,
work in a bank, health care, insurance, seek glory
in banking or real estate or join the armed forces.

Raymond Chandler's Philip Marlowe, homophobe,
dismissed gays as "pansies," "fags," and "queens."
Dashiell Hammett's Sam Spade was shot to death
by jealous Iva Archer, the last of his bloody scenes.

Although starlings, ducks, and doves fly arrow straight,
goldfinches undulate, and nighthawks lurch erratically.
No young girl's hair is not beautified by a braided plait.
Resisting roll in flight dynamics seeks a balance laterally.

Peppercorn rents are given to maintain a mere legality.
Nothing was ever funny about comedian Red Skelton.
All U. S. lobbyists thrive on Congressional venality.
Revolution is goal of revolt—resistance, of rebellion.

No "Damascus Road" experience is casually ignored.
In 1965, Che Guevara renounced any Cuban alliance.
Maine, Vermont, Alaska, Hawaii: all ban the billboard.
Science fiction is the bedridden cousin of true science.

Being alone is a means of being part of a greater whole.
Clover-fed pig manure is richer than that of pigs corn-fed.
Hitler on Churchill: "a superannuated drunk sustained by
   Jewish gold."
Most used food color, petroleum based, is FD&C 40 Red.

Many parties are thrown chiefly for the *un*invited.
Sigmund Freud thought any father-hater was a hero.
The self-love of a narcissist is always fully requited.
Mathematically considered, an even number is zero.

The poor cannot afford "concealed carry" permits,
nor old people, Indians, most women, and blacks,
those people most in need of them when intermits
are called for during all *criminal* weapon attacks.

Herman Melville wasn't taken seriously until 1921
—to show the idiocy of critics and a reading public—
although *Moby-Dick* was published back in 1851,
a literary masterpiece received as if it were mudbrick.

Scatology in poems always dazzles a teenager.
It is easier to read magazines turning pages backwards.
Money on a horse race is, not a bet, but a wager.
Falconers never bother to teach—too lazy—buzzards.

MGM refused to make a $69,000 investment—a flop,
they felt—for *half* the profits of the smash hit *Oklahoma!*
Lettuce and radishes prove to be the best catch crop.
Ceiling/floor tilers are prime targets for mesothelioma.

Rare book dealers *loathe* wearing white gloves,
which reduce sense of touch, increase the hook
of accidentally tearing a page by dulled moves,
smear a page, flake off bits, even drop a book.

T. S. Eliot dismissed his great poem *The Waste Land*
—seriously—as "just a piece of rhythmical grumbling."
It is impossible to get a tan on the palm of one's hand.
Thrown dice, to be legitimate, have to be tumbling.

Joy is the most infallible sign of the presence of God.
 "Estée Lauder" in real life was short fat Josephine Mentzer.
Bachelors are limited to special public places in Riyadh.
Finances—who has and hasn't money—is a universal censor.

Most all English Liberals and Radicals sympathized
with the rebel South during the American Civil War—
Lord Palmerston established a separate, undisguised
embassy for Texas in St. James, offering full rapport.

The Orient Express Train first ran on June 1, 1889,
and the date of its very last trip was May 17, 1977.
Carving birds is most easily worked on soft pine.
Maple leaf points on a Canadian flag are eleven.

TRUISMS II

There is never deep dive coverage of Israel's crimes.
Monasticism ever burgeons when the world is at war.
A marinade called for in meat most benefits by limes.
U.S. Marines always refer to themselves as the Corps.

George Bernard Shaw declared that Dickens' novel.
Little Dorrit was more seditious than Marx's *Kapital*.
Exorbitant parking fees are common in today's hotel.
Women surveyed most favor kisses on the clavicle.

There is no fee in Indiana to carry a concealed weapon,
but in Illinois every gun permit costs a thousand bucks.
A surgeon, to cut a hole in a bone, calls for a trepan.
Watts, in electricity, are ever the units of radiant flux.

When people have accents in their names, like Salvador Dalí
and Véra Nabokov, they *always* pettily insist on its inclusion.
No gender specific pronouns exist in the language of Bengali.
Border hostility among all nations is a foregone conclusion.

A mature tree over one year will absorb
as much as 48 pounds of carbon dioxide
from a given atmosphere's general orb,
releasing its oxygen in exchanging pride.

Muppet man Jim Henson never raised his voice.
American parents don't raise their children, culture does.
To raise one well, never give a child a choice.
The universally used defensive explanation is "Because."

Farming, paradoxically, is a prime cause of erosion.
Sycamore seeds have wings that help them float.
Lupins and violas disperse their seeds by explosion.
The most consumed meat in all the world is goat.

Not sworn by God, any and all oaths are jibber jabber.
It was John Enders, not Jonas Salk, who created the polio vaccine.
Clotted cream is had by way of thickened milk clabber.
White supremacy identifies by—code or slogan—the number 14.

King Farouk I's 200 automobiles all had to be red,
the only cars in his nation, Egypt, allowed to be so.
Americans oddly leave *furled* flowers for the dead.
European pastry chefs consider merengue a dough.

Out of sheer politeness, in conversation, an Arab
will not look at you, to him being a sign of respect.
Creator of Muslim Brotherhood was Sayyid Qutb.
There are 172 nationalities in the city of Utrecht.

Wildfires in boreal forests, a glut of carbon dioxide,
lead the entire world in record-high CO_2 emissions.
A pinky ring never made a normal male dandified.
All "legacies" win a place in Harvard admissions.

Cobweb tattoos, usually located on the elbow
or neck, symbolize any lengthy time in prison.
If done in jail, no multi-colored ink will show,
where access to any colored inks is forbidden.

TRUISMS II

"While supplies last" is nothing but a product ploy.
India's yearly population growth doubles that of China.
Being inarticulate befits the persona of a cowboy.
The Grapes of Wrath was proscribed in South Carolina.

The formula for red Campari, which involves
herbs, spices, barks, the citrus chinotto, peels,
and around which woody cascarilla revolves,
is a solemn family secret that no one reveals.

Yaks tend to suffer and die at low altitudes.
The Hebrew Bible is a bigoted polemic against Philistines.
No expiration dates exist with frozen foods.
Siblings never marry in the same year in the Philippines.

No meal ever eaten in Tibet excludes *tsampa*.
Cuba and the Vatican have never severed diplomatic relations.
The lightning capital of the world is Tampa.
Henry James wrote *The Golden Bowl* by sequential dictations.

The Jokhang temple is the holiest shrine in Tibet.
Starfish, an invertebrate, has neither brains nor blood.
To every pretty girl, every other pretty girl's a threat.
The tree on which Judas hanged himself was a red bud.

Two knocks in Trappist sign language means "enter."
Bobby Kennedy hated Jimmy Hoffa, Gore Vidal, Roy Cohn.
Scientists are all agreed that the universe has no center.
The most popular peasant name for Shakespeare was Joan.

Andean peasants (Indians) do not speak Spanish.
On the outside of a carousel, the horses all go faster.
Major organized crime is notoriously clannish.
The most responsible Boy Scout was quartermaster.

Pirate boarding parties leapt from the quarter deck
when attacking, where they found two ships touching.
Modigliani had a fetish the elongated female neck.
No seamstress does not take special pride in ruching.

Moses is mentioned only once in the Haggadah.
Subway cars are paradise for the deviant frotteur.
Coca-Cola company's supposed "secret" formula
is merely a marketing strategy, and nothing more.

QB Tom Brady will not eat tomatoes, dairy,
white sugar, flour, coffee, mushrooms—same
with eggplants, any "nightshades"—all scary,
because, raising the body's pH, they inflame.

In mystery novels, never trust anyone serving
warm milk, ladyfingers, a gift of chocolates,
porridge, anything with cream sauce, herring,
Dover sole, a cup showing any sign of droplets.

Leo Tolstoy came to abominate the art of fiction.
Victory is an ongoing process, never an event.
Southern Italy is the prime region of malediction.
In soccer, to disguise a booted ball, kick it bent.

TRUISMS II

Galileo, ignoring his professional colleagues abroad,
refused to write any of his astronomical tracts in Latin.
"Graveyard of the Atlantic"—the coast of Cape Cod.
There are two opposing faces of the silky fabric satin.

"Babe" Ruth had a mincing gait as he rounded the bases.
To dismember toxic fugu takes special Japanese knives.
Rule, authority, and sovereignty is lost in familiar faces.
Most British music hall jokes are about shrewish wives.

Any action on Mt. Rushmore in Hitchcock's film
North by Northwest—a "shrine of democracy"—
had to take place *between* the heads, not *on* them.
which was an official U.S. Dept of Interior policy.

Once a journalist, Dickens liked the immediacy
of publishing work in periodical, not volume form.
The chase is far more exciting than the discovery.
A true Scottish silver brooch features a cairngorm.

Apple juice is standard filler in cocktail fruit juices.
Confederates had red-cedar canteens, the Union tin.
Muslims repudiate all *uqqal* believers—the Druses.
Touching noses is the form of greeting for Bedouin.

The "books" of Broadway musicals," never original,
unashamedly all copy the plots of every other genre.
To counter magnetic deviation is the job of a binnacle.
In 2013, Uruguay was the first to legalize marijuana.

The polygraph, as thought, is not the "lie detector;"
the detector of the instrument is in fact the *operator*.
Perfume was created as a women's heat convector.
Floor 4 is never numbered in any Chinese elevator.

Vincent Van Gogh seriously had a "shoe period,"
painting and repainting that one item over and over.
Only 52 days of the war are covered by the *Iliad*.
Ashkenazi Jews may eat corn and rice at Passover.

Few American housewives can expertly construct
a soufflé, a Béarnaise sauce, or a good consommé.
Old time teachers preferred *deportment* to conduct.
The Pilgrims held Christmas profane, not a holiday.

American kids commonly say, "I pledge *of* allegiance."
Advertising your benevolence is to detract from it.
Only public officials can commit criminal malfeasance.
No curtain looks elegant hanging from a grommet.

Huge deposits of lithium exist in the Salton Sea.
In Italian opera, the soprano always kills the tenor.
At four o'clock in England everyone stops for tea.
No human body part is as soft as a thumb's thenar.

Crime novelists and all mystery writers love plots
involving trains: closed spaces, strangers, tunnels,
sleeping cars, corridors, loud noises like gunshots,
the atmospheric miasma from smokestack funnels.

TRUISMS II

Clamorous philanthropy is an appalling vice.
Of Dickens's fifteen major novels, ten involve prison.
Always deduct some value if you lower the price.
Jesus Christ was crucified on Passover, the 14th Nisan.

Each leg of a camel is endowed with double knees.
Six wheels (thus, no 4WD) are found on a cement truck.
Alcohol is officially banned for Australian aborigines.
Strength of character in people always appears eccentric.

R. L. Stevenson's *A Child's Garden of Verses*
—he was a sickly boy—is all about being in bed.
France leads the known world for uttering curses.
The Parsi community in India is the most inbred.

One toasts a crumpet; however, one heats a scone.
The "last mile" in Sing Sing was a walk of 15 feet.
Deposits in chronic gout—urates—are chalkstone.
Seafood with most nutritious minerals is crab meat.

American Writing Paper Corp. in Holyoke, Mass.
under tight security, manufactures all paper, rare,
sized, covered with a thin finish and quality class
for all U.S. passports, fine lines etched with care.

Palomino is a color, Appaloosa (horse) is a breed.
Sleuth Hercule Poirot always misquoted Shakespeare.
If not Hebrides handmade, it's illegal Harris Tweed.
There are expiration dates to be found on a brassiere.

Fagan in *Oliver Twist* was in all likelihood a pedophile,
and Uriah Heep in *Copperfield* a compulsive masturbator.
Adolf Hitler all of his life was a confirmed Anglophile;
Thumbs up, in fact, was the call for death to a gladiator.

A bad sting from a bullet ant can last for 36 hours.
The objective of a negligee is to *appear* as *deshabille*.
The Burj Khalifa in Dubai is the tallest of towers.
Still missing are 7 Imperial Easter Eggs by Fabergé.

Pizza is rated the most well-liked food in the world.
Vernacular architecture is about *in*expensive materials.
It helps to separate aromas in a wine when it is swirled.
Sugar is the selling ingredient of all American cereals.

Real estate agent prices very rarely represent the buyer.
Both Crystal Pepsi and New Coke were dismal failures.
The Vietnam war—unintentional—*defines* a quagmire.
Changing the name of a ship was taboo among whalers.

Every good Samaritan is perforce a bad economist.
It is the *loop breaks* in fingerprints the FBI looks for.
A main symbol of revolution is showing a raised fist.
Colored smoke signals for help in Army semaphore.

No crowd can ever make itself look beautiful.
Democrats in Arizona are rare as Hell's Angels.
All laws of economics are feeble and mutable.
Little can match a kidney stone for most painful.

TRUISMS II

Raymond Chandler's *The Little Sister* is a plotless mess.
The Puritans fined profane Christmas revelers 5 shillings.
A *baton sinister* indicates bastardy in any heraldic fesse.
The alphabet in ensemble casts alone determines billings.

Tolstoy scarcely ever spoke in public in his life.
Ivy is poisonous, so is the golden chain laburnum.
A sign of a worthy husband is the health of his wife.
Healing is actually possible in a broken sternum.

Argument is customary during a rabbinical pilpul.
Humphrey Bogart loved to say the word—lisp—"Thursby."
No official dog breed includes the term "Pit Bull."
Classic 1960s slang for the marijuana plant was "herbie."

Any cormorant must wet its tail before it can fly.
No "Book Club" edition has value to a serious collector.
Italian boys named Guido prefer to be called Guy.
Mystery stories often involve a suspicious church rector.

Jurors in a trial must examine facts, never opinions.
The best place in the world to see rainbows is in Hawaii.
Self-governing was a farce in all British "dominions."
New York subways are lame next to the metro in Almaty.

Before Dickens's *A Christmas Carol* ever appeared,
Christmas Day was never a public holiday in Britain.
Pioneer mountain men spent an entire life unsheared.
The state of Michigan is shaped exactly like a mitten.

British judicial wigs, made of bleached horsehair
have two pigtails with four tight rows of small curls.
The darker grey the wig is, presenting a sort of flair,
the more pronounced the status symbol of its purls.

A larva is found in mezcal, never a bottle of tequila.
Women must weep (on film) to win a Best Actress Oscar.
Pesticides have toxically polluted the entire river Gila.
Feeling success mere luck is the syndrome of an imposter.

Gravity's Rainbow was first titled *Mindless Pleasures*.
Virtually every note that Dinah Shore sang was off-key.
A bird's skeleton usually weighs less than its feathers
Djibouti and Somalia in almost everything never agree.

Northern Chile is dry, southern Chile is mainly all wet.
All lawyers are banned in Thomas More's *Utopia*.
A copper wire is a magnet as electricity flows through it.
The sole African country never colonized is Ethiopia.

Lesbians never appear in Dickens work, except once,
in *Little Dorrit* when Tattycoram elopes with Miss Wade.
The dream of gold prospectors is discovering a bunce.
In the game of bridge, the highest suit rank is the spade.

Readers love to see private eyes outsmart officials,
which imagines a child-father situation in reverse,
with authority being seen as pompous superficials—
a delicate child fighting a powerful father's curse.

TRUISMS II

Old pioneers referred to rhubarb as the "pie plant."
Evelyn Waugh said no Americans outgrew puberty.
Esculent is the high-and-mighty cousin of succulent.
"Interesting" is the coward's go-to word of ambiguity.

The wife of a rajah is always called a ranee.
A clenched fist: symbol of the family Rothschild.
Uganda and Rwanda and Congo never agree.
A Brit to drink a session beer will order a "mild."

New Englanders refer to a bobwhite as a quail,
where a ruffed grouse is also called a partridge,
but down South, the way that customs prevail,
a grouse is a pheasant and bobwhite a partridge.

No tourist is ever permitted to visit Fort Knox.
The U.S. Social Security system is a Ponzi scheme.
Never give Chinese gifts of watches or clocks.
Few outside New York can identify an egg cream.

It takes a sloth up to a month to digest a single leaf.
Novelist Henry James never slept with a woman.
No pain can exceed the echo of joy in present grief.
All of the C.I.A.'s torture techniques are inhuman.

Pocket lint and fabric fluff is identified as "gnurr."
The cardinal (bird) has no counterpart in Europe.
To Ralph Waldo Emerson, no wall wasn't a door.
Mounted warfare was engendered by the stirrup.

Sports talk show hosts, many of them, grow neurotic
in an underpaid business that virtually anyone can do
by having daily to discuss salaries, huge and exotic,
of multi-millionaire athletes which all of theirs outdo.

Agatha Christie, the dullest writer, had no style.
Ecuadorian pickpockets are the best in the world.
Teeth all show in the closed mouth of a crocodile
—a fact not so whenever an alligator's is furled.

In an odd death case, immediately suspect the heirs.
Goldman Sachs is the Deep Black of all chicanery.
Gambling in every form is a game of musical chairs.
Envy, in a perverse way, is fundamentally flattery.

The greater scaup duck is also called the blackhead,
broadbill, bluebill, raft duck, shuffler, flocking fowl.
Part of Roman Empire's fall was toxicity due to lead.
The "eyes" are tube-shaped and immobile in an owl.

More than 40% of Americans are blatantly obese.
Frank Sinatra preferred "The Summit: over "Rat Pack."
Obfuscation is the singular objective of legalese
The casino edge is only 1% in the game of blackjack.

Joe Sewell who struck out at bat only 114 times
in over 8000 plate appearances in MLB baseball
during a 14-year career, besting anyone's primes,
the hardest to K in history, a man above them all.

TRUISMS II

Ede & Ravenscroft, Ltd. make all barristers' wigs.
Clark Gable had a top billing clause in all MGM contracts.
The fruit most mentioned in Holy Scripture is figs.
Exposure to the sun greatly increases the risk of cataracts.

Thermostats in automobiles are always unreliable.
Chickadees spend much of their time upside down.
A child's recollections of cruelty are unrectifiable.
The Japanese have no one word for the color brown.

Trefoil sent to a gravesite means getting even.
Basil tendered as a memorial stands for hating.
Oleander, never means that anyone is grieving
but *beware*, and begonia stipulates desecrating.

Brown Pelicans are never, ever found inland.
The *homo* of homosexual means "the same," not "men."
Car lights must be kept on all day in Finland.
Turkish is a language, Turkmenistan tribes, Turkmen.

Maigret thought all crime is related to childhood.
Woodcarvers all refer to a thimble a thumbstall.
Spinsters never have the cachet of bachelorhood.
The universal game of pool is always eight-ball.

Ransom notes, for disguise, always misspell a word,
and its letters never clipped from esoteric magazines.
A person buried is different than one being interred.
There are at least 50 bones in the shells of testudines.

Carolyn Keene, creator of the *Nancy Drew* books,
in real life was Mrs. Harriet Adams of New Jersey.
A blasphemy—God's hooks (nails)—is "gadzooks."
The Old Testament, unlike the New, is short on mercy.

The French all loved Jerry Lewis, Josephine Baker,
and Louis Armstrong who said, "You frogs ape me"
No legal oath is ever sworn by a practicing Quaker
Dublin's Wellington Bridge in 1922 became the Ha-Penny.

Chambers is the best crossword puzzle dictionary.
"Whodunits" are in fact games, played to sets of rules.
Food, etc. costs 1/4th less in a military commissary.
The Taliban prohibit Afghani women from all schools.

Paul Revere, the colonial patriot, was also a dentist.
Bluebirds most prefer apple-tree holes for nesting.
No Indian or Pakistani isn't a Kashmiri irredentist.
Planting a tree is the supreme act of eco-investing.

Stabbing suicides never do so through their clothes.
Customs agents are incentivized ($) to catch scofflaws.
Southern girls refer to their boyfriends as their "beaux."
All cat's front paws are sharper than their hind claws.

All bankers receiving more than $10,000 in a deposit
immediately file/notify the U.S. Treasury Department.
Anger is the prime emotion of every Hebrew prophet.
Second floor is always hotter in a duplex apartment.

The British disdain *lumps* of sugar in tea.
Water after the first bubble must not boil.
Brew must steep for minutes, two or three
—otherwise, bitterness can sour it, to foil.

Warm milk should then be standing by,
also, a strainer, a proper ceremonial tool
with its own specific resting spot nearby
and a waste basin for any slops that cool.

The faults of a thief are the virtues of a businessman.
Whittlers draw blades *toward* themselves, never away.
The sweetest oak acorn—edible—is the chinquapin.
Long shafts and heavy heads are best playing croquet.

A wood duck can actually climb and nest in trees.
Nose crusts can be formed in the merest of seconds.
Plucking your eyebrows can force you to sneeze.
Altitude makes the blood flow double in Tibetans.

Small dirty bills are retail currency in the heroin trade.
The point of cars in mystery stories is to break down.
Colonials fought the revolution mainly by ambuscade.
Numbers are always recited backwards in a countdown.

Many Ponzi schemes are successfully pulled off!
Death by hanging severs the second cervical vertibra.
Hemophilia was in the bloodline of the Romanov.
"Worms" in mezcal—edible—are in fact moth larva.

Detective Sam Spade never carried a gun.
Assault weapons sell well in any militia magazine.
Nothing's more contagious than a sudden bank run.
Calming properties adhibit to the color soft green.

Don Diego de Deza, the Spanish Grand Inquisitor
from years 1498 to 1507, burned 2,592 heretics alive.
Anyone over age 18 can become UK Prime Minister.
Women in tennis need a two-hand, backhand drive,

Intuition is what makes a superior customs official.
Most astute safe cracking is done on out-of-date safes.
Runway fashions are the very definition of superficial.
Victorian literature proliferates with urchins and waifs.

To break a hold, stomp hard on the aggressor's instep.
Nero Wolfe, solving crimes, best did so in an armchair.
No drunken soldier can march with a Nazi goose step.
$200 a week is standard pay in America for an au pair.

A whetstone always has a rough and a smooth side,
and Arkansas slip stone is held best for sharpening.
Bliss is simply the ignorance of every teenage bride.
Not rushing the "close" is the trick of telemarketing.

Theft is subjective; as to absolutes, who doesn't steal?
Elevenses often doubles in Britain as a second breakfast.
Smugness, not subtle, when playing cards is a reveal.
There is something slavish about a choker/necklace.

The English always pronounce *scone* with "gone."
A polygraph subject must consistently sit motionless.
The true surname of editor William Shawn was Chon.
The natives of Gascony are known for boastfulness.

Luther always tore out of Bibles with rudeness
the Epistle of James, condemning it with a groan
as an "epistle of straw," as it advocates goodness
and says nothing of Justification of Faith alone.

A wren cocks its tail up, a flycatcher holds it down.
"Dark money" secretly funds the American right wing.
Insurance deductibles as a tactic is a legal shakedown.
The way that an Estonian expresses rebellion is to sing.

"Rule, Britannia!" is often written "Rule Britannia,"
omitting both the comma and the exclamation mark,
which, by altering punctuation in a simple manner,
alters the song's interpretation with an equal bark.

If Edgar Allan Poe is the father of the detective story,
Voltaire, with *Zadig* (1748), is its great-grandfather.
Cheeks are the tastiest part of any filleted John Dory.
Desert was proving ground of an early Church Father.

Brideshead Revisited is wholeheartedly misogynistic.
White-throated sparrows cry "Old Sam Peabody, Peabody."
No cult fraud in California doesn't claim to be a mystic.
R. Wagner said he never learned to play the piano properly.

Common pigeons are exactly the same as doves.
Popeye the Sailor's pipe never stays on one mouth side.
Professional hockey goalies avoid oversized gloves.
The bridal gown is centered spouse of the average bride.

Mr. Hyde hates Dr. Jekyll knowing he can be killed
by his counterpart committing suicide as Dr. Jekyll.
The original pronunciation of "Jekyll," when trilled
in Stevenson's native Scotland, rhymes with "treacle."

It took *Crime and Punishment*, a book written in 1866,
as long as twenty long years to be published in English.
Generating concern is the primal masquerade of politics.
In each rain forest depredation, species are extinguished.

Ducks that eat more fish will have a sharper bill.
North Carolina supplies most goods for a furniture store.
Taboo is eating while gazing in a mirror in Brazil.
The Japanese in their sushi prefer to avoid all albacore.

Adolf Hitler never ever held an actual job.
Depressives always keep very strange hours.
Delicious stock can be made from corn cob.
Each sunflower head is made of tiny flowers.

The left side of Lincoln's face was smaller than his right,
a particular aberration called "cranial facial microsomia."
It is illegal in the U.S. to be a spectator at a cockfight.
Abandonment in childhood explains most monophobia.

TRUISMS II

In WWI, Germany was never defeated in a land battle.
Self-pity is a crucial element in every autobiography.
Long distance riders should use an "endurance" saddle.
No political biography isn't a puffed-up hagiography.

Spanish Needles yield immense quantities of honey.
Human beings very rarely laugh when they are alone.
The sole mechanism of, and for, control is money.
It matters not a whit if dice are shot, rolled, or thrown.

A "hangman's blood," a beer cocktail is made of gin,
whisky, rum, port, brandy, stout, as well as champagne.
Showering without any curtains is common to a Finn.
No country does not have its own version of chow mein.

Being too opinionated gets a person out of jury duty.
Sucking hard candy, one swallows air and create gas.
Moscato d'Asti, sweetest of wines, is not over fruity.
Dumping garbage on any land is a "continuing trespass."

Presentation is essential to a sense of meaning.
The sleeve was couturier Cristóbal Balenciaga's obsession.
Standing in a bread line is never not demeaning
Ten months is generally the standard length for a recession.

Prophecy is an attempt to prevent what is prophesied.
The Macbeths, weirdly, actually had a good marriage.
Chinese on Qingming offer food to ancestors who died.
Diabetes uncontrolled can easily lead to a miscarriage.

A foundation of all capitalism, sheer taking advantage,
—"I've got it; you have not!"—is unapologetic usury.
A Boy Scouts' neckerchief is a perfect cravat bandage
All ideal bathroom books must have a fractal quality.

Horatio Alger, Jr. never put girls in his books.
Only three monks know the secret of green Chartreuse.
The most superior lima beans are Fordhooks.
Holding great power almost always leads to its abuse.

Violence is essential to the functioning of slavery.
Hitler suffered "meteorism"—uncontrolled farting.
Sweetness is the opposite in a dialectic with savory.
Alterations are the perpetual bane of flow-charting.

Edgar Allan Poe had a great sense of humor.
After a child dies, a marriage will often end.
Five years is a survival rate with a brain tumor.
The tightest knot (figure 8s) is a Flemish Bend.

The rope ends in a Gordian knot cannot be seen.
Bilirubin, the pigment in feces, makes it brown.
A hammer for metal work must possess a peen.
Grand juries hand up a ruling, juries hand one down.

Jews are allowed to make jokes about Jews,
and the same goes with Blacks about Blacks,
but if Muslims employ the Prophet to amuse,
they will be condemned to no end of attacks.

TRUISMS II

The word for "we" in the Russian language is *my*.
No song opens better than "Bad, Bad Leroy Brown."
A total atheist is allowed to serve as a Jewish rabbi.
Cornwallis was absent at the surrender at Yorktown.

Abraham banished his first-born son, Ishmael,
along with Hagar, so did Buddha, a son and wife,
St. Augustine's son (o. w.) lived a meager spell,
thrown away, all, as if repudiation defined a life.

Tomato sauce adheres best to *lumaconi giganti*.
Rap as "music" is totally, certified, batshit insane.
"Novel"—a term hated by novelist Cabrera Infante.
Swastikas remain an important symbol to a Jain.

The struggle for survival obliterates all thought.
It is considered taboo for skiers to announce a last run.
Czech peasants—*robota*—created our word robot.
Thomas More was the great-great uncle of John Donne.

Edward Gorey's *The Helpless Doorknob* are cards
that as a set of twenty, fully permuted, can be read
in 2,432,902,069,736,640,000 (as to figural regards)
different ways, according to the way they're spread.

Pitying a person is basically a benign form of abuse.
Adolf Loos, the architect, said "Ornament is a crime."
All the Greek gods effectuated by means of the ruse.
A major weakness in poetry is use of the eye rhyme.

A skier ahead of you always has the right of way.
In 1950s marriage models, only husbands had jobs.
History sees a difference between China and Cathay.
Meat is sweetened when grilled by adding corncobs.

Richard Hughes, author of *A High Wind in Jamaica*,
never saw, visited, or decided to travel to that island.
Two of the three strings are the same on a balalaika.
The Atacama Desert in Chile is world's driest land.

Doris Lessing's work is overwhelmingly misandrous.
The Earth forever spins on its axis from west to east.
Happiness is never linked to a storybook enchantress.
Sugar in any form is an important nutrition for yeast.

Novelist Iris Murdoch never wrote using a typewriter.
Spain remained largely neutral during World War II.
Only tortured bulls are slain by a cowardly bullfighter.
Natural habitats are never fully replicated in a zoo.

Don Quixote's Part Two, much duller than the first,
portrays a milder, wiser, less belligerent anti-hero.
Dudleytown, Connecticut is reported to be cursed.
Algebra is impossible without the existence of zero.

It is much easier to fast after first starting to fast.
British workers order a full pint, never a half-pint.
To help tack, rudder, are the sails of a mizzenmast.
Christian faith was essential to the medieval knight.

TRUISMS II

British working people almost always vote Labour,
as the snobbish Tory party seems to them surreal
Distance carries no significance in tossing the caber—
it is how the caber *lands*, straight up being the ideal.

To slow down skiing, employ the "pizza slice"—wedge.
Bret Easton Ellis never wrote a character pure of heart.
Birds must all grow feathers *and* foot-grip fully to fledge.
It is self-defeating to cheat when reading an eye chart.

Mobster Sam Giancana collected Dresden figurines,
sterling tea services, and whole sets of Meissen china.
The New Yorker wastes tons of paper for "blow-ins."
There are five different and distinct shapes of vagina.

Every old building in Manhattan carries a certain history.
Black writer James Baldwin refused to eat watermelons.
Only in an ecclesiastical sense may we have a consistery.
Fully 8% of the U.S. population are fully convicted felons.

College basketball coaches are all crazy, vain, neurotic.
In '37, Gertrude Stein voted Hitler the Nobel Peace Prize.
An old ploy in country music sales is to seem patriotic.
British veterinarians are officially not allowed to advertise.

Stage scenery for the play *Macbeth* is always ebonized.
The object of torture's torture, of persecution, persecutions.
Two miracles are required for a person to be canonized.
57 submarine volcanoes constitute the chain of Aleutians.

Chanterelle mushrooms, fruity, are quite safe,
but the Jack o' Lanterns, look-alikes, are toxic
like any white-gilled ceps with a bulbous base
and a skirt or a ring on the stem, evil if exotic.

The IRS audits merely five returns out of 1,000.
Second Wave feminism said women need meaningful work.
Arsenic has proven the most historic poison.
More endearing than offensive has the connotation of quirk.

Socrates, who alone in all Athens never touched
a child, was still executed as "Corrupter of Youth."
A black-painted house is a taboo among the Dutch.
Small shelf life exists in a bottle of opened Vermouth.

Almond crops are entirely dependent on bee pollination.
Wittgenstein thought sex—sensuality—*undermined* love.
Sparrows, finches, woodpeckers dispense with migration.
No children should ever play around the plant foxglove.

Vladimir Nabokov claimed that his Russian works
were more beautiful than any of his American ones.
Greek ancestry is common among the enemy Turks.
"Green sickness" is said to prevail in virgins and nuns.

Whales can risk drowning if they should fall asleep.
A satin fabric has two faces—shiny versus opaque.
Guyanese cuisine keeps for months with cassareep.
Steaming is the method of a cooking in a clambake.

TRUISMS II

Sammy Davis, Jr. grotesquely, self-indulgently bathed
in three colognes—Lactone, Hermes, and Au Savage.
The top drug corporate kingpins always go unscathed.
No old pioneer mountain man wasn't a bird of passage.

Buffaloes always live in single-sex herds and join
strictly during the late autumnal breeding season.
Protestant hearts tend to swell recalling the Boyne.
Walt Disney architecture delights in the bartizan.

Singer Dean Martin nightly always said his prayers.
Respect for obedience was badly tarnished by Nazism.
Congressional lobbyists do their work backstairs.
Awkward fumbling is the best definition of tribadism.

Mexico's Mazateco Indians converse just by whistling,
same with *silbo*, spoken on the Canary Island of Gomera.
No sardine in terms of sweetest taste can match a brisling.
A special toy for New England kids is the maple samara.

JFK loved Richard Condon's *The Manchurian Candidate*,
a best-selling novel with a Presidential assassination plot.
No boxer over 118 pounds can qualify as bantamweight.
Only music in quadruple time can be called a "fox trot."

The Bechdel Test for a film must have two women in it
who speak to each other, about something beside a man.
A clock's second hand is an abiding meal for the minute.
A definite brainlessness adhibits to a person with a tan.

There is a strange element of narcissism in shyness.
5000 victims were killed for the 6/20/1944 Hitler bomb plot.
The first requisite for creating a pig pen is dryness.
Blond hair is oddly described as *blue* hair (*plava*) by a Croat.

All fates, in the end, are by far much worse than death.
Mushrooms are in fact a flavor, not a food.
Putting stones, not flowers, on graves is a shibboleth.
Chastity is always announced in a snood.

Sweat droplets in cartoon comic are called "plewds."
Frank Sinatra, who hated to be alone, needed chums.
Taste is enhanced—berries, grapes—as frozen foods.
Ardor for battle is escalated by the sound of drums.

The first telephones invented required two hands.
The Rat Pack called all non-celebrities "John Q. Putz."
The health of Earth's ecology depends on wetlands.
Perfect mosquito repellent is burnt husks of coconuts.

Only *written* Chinese is universally understood by all.
The need to be ardently social is the death of the mind.
Sublimity as such can only be found in something small.
Sentinelese islanders, reclusive, are famously unkind.

No photo or drawing should let you trust a mushroom.
Japanese typewriters, so complicated, were seldom used.
Notable lack of conversation bespeaks a reluctant groom.
"Leathers" become a delight for any fruit that is bruised.

TRUISMS II

New Yorkers and pre-WWII immigrants call sauce "gravy."
Precise times given in Dragnet were farcically irrelevant.
Submariners are all strictly *volunteers* in the U.S. Navy
It is the older matriarch who in herds is the lead elephant.

Men and women in every way sit down differently.
40% of the world's methane emanates from livestock.
Racism was the fulcrum of successful minstrelsy.
A synthetic stock makes for the most durable gunstock.

Vladimir Nabokov alleged the swan an "overrated bird,
the postures of its neck grotesque, aesthetically absurd."
All equivocating minds thrive on using the weasel word.
Apartheid from S. Africa to Palestine is now transferred.

No painter can match Velázquez for technical skills.
With a Magi's gold, the Holy Family traveled to Egypt.
A mushroom is likely poisonous if white are its gills.
Sports, not education, defines United States collegiate.

The nation of Israel does not have a constitution.
British toffs use *guineas* in transactions, not pounds.
Justice, refusing mercy, is a demand for retribution.
An English lady generally travels wearing browns.

Mahler's Symphony No. 7 is too paranormal to be good.
An eye pupil expands 45% when seeing something pleasing.
African blackwood is the world's most expensive wood.
Sexual interest in prepubescents takes the form of teasing.

Pigs dig truffles, which smell like their sex hormones.
Westward Ho!—the only English town with an exclamation mark.
Social options in Montreal are limited for anglophones.
Convicted sex offenders inhabit Florida's Palace Mobile Home Park.

Obsession is the incapacity to tolerate alternatives.
The Howards of Britain are the preeminent Roman Catholics.
Hating the EPA makes a mockery of conservatives.
Psychotics are mentally deranged; unfeeling are psychopathics.

The least happy nation state surveyed is Madagascar.
Shakespeare's family background were Catholic recusants.
No reputation is more defamed in culture than a Lascar.
The 'great north migration" created the Harlem Renaissance.

No male was handsomer than French actor Alain Delon.
Polynesians shuffle-walk in water to avoid (*nohu*) stonefish.
Sir John Falstaff, of favorite foods, much preferred the capon.
Be as you wish to seem, knowing that seeming can be a wish.

V. Nabokov, having Lolita die at age seventeen,
proves that the author of the novel himself kept
—never mind using lustful Humbert as a screen—
his own decadent passion for a young nymphet.

It takes four days to reach the moon, eight months to Mars.
Eva Brain despised Hitler's German Shepherd, "Blondi."
Parkinson's Disease risk is reduced by smoking cigars.
Sex for pleasure was denounced by Mohandas Gandhi.

Evelyn Waugh's constant theme: husbands betrayed.
When you raise girls, you're raising children for strangers.
Eritreans lead in victims of the modern slave trade.
For those who fear of it, the world is replete with dangers.

Capitalism follows to a T the laws of Carl von Clausewitz.
Many dog lovers have little or no affection for the human.
Only Damson plums may provide a base fruit for slivovitz.
Gases do the main fermentation in sheep and cattle rumen.

Nuns in gatherings tend to twitter like sparrows.
Taxes in the state of Massachusetts are plain brigandage.
One foot is the perfect depth for tillage harrows.
No gender separation exists on a holy Hajj pilgrimage.

Lambskin is by far the finest material for suede.
Every large crowd comprises a mindless machine.
Mozart despised the trumpet and the sounds it made.
Coffee is a good source of niacin by way of caffeine.

There are matrilineal societies in New Guinea.
Evelyn Waugh said non-fathers are masters of ridicule.
Democracy is government ruled by committee.
A public school in Great Britain is a private school.

Howard Hughes was addicted to codeine; watching
Ice Station Zebra; eating Baskin-Robbins Banana Nut
ice cream (later, French Vanilla), also debauching
on chocolate, chicken, and canned peaches with a glut.

A bottom round of beef is the best cut for pot roast,
Pancreatic cancer is always found when it's too late.
Speediness is the very first requirement of a riposte.
Jealousy, paradoxically, juggles both love and hate.

Burma Shave signs calculated cars to be traveling
at 35 mph, gauged for an 18-second reading time.
Only over *trivial* details can a dispute be caviling.
Both an annual *and* a perennial is the herb, thyme.

Jacques Pepin abhors using foil in baking a potato.
Derry to Catholics, to Protestants is Londonderry.
Most school sport programs ban the hammer throw.
The Chinese *Mosuo*, "single mothers," never marry.

Reptile-venom-derived drugs best fight heart attacks.
The first fact of outer space is that it's entirely silent.
Native Americans, for sweetness, eat bastard toadflax.
Societies empowering women are much less violent.

Hitler who loved Bruckner's Fourth and Seventh
Symphonies hated the romantic music of Brahms,
whom Jews applauded with praise and presence
for his flowing hair, beard, and smarmy charms.

The kitchen sponge is the dirtiest item in the house.
Avoiding lawyers in life is a blessing from God.
To counteract a vessel's magnetic field, degauss.
With cool water is the standard way to cut Pernod.

TRUISMS II

All Hollywood army films depict a soldier from Brooklyn.
Singer Leonard Cohen impairs the spiritual by the profane.
A natural UV protection is had in anything worn woolen.
Method and formula of gambling casinos are pure chicane.

The Olympic Games torch was a Nazi invention.
Goldfinches have very little interest in eating insects.
Cyberspace makes outdated the Geneva Convention.
Confucius always ate ginger when writing his *Analects*.

It is fairly impossible to be a devout Unitarian.
Diary-keeping during World War II was a jailable offense.
Any believer in a person's free will is a libertarian.
Vietnamese, Burmese, Thai, and Malay have no past tense.

Admiral Nimitz and General MacArthur hated each other,
as each wanted to be Supreme Commander of the Pacific,
Mac was hapless egotist who sought everyone to smother,
while Chet was gentle fellow with nothing of the fanatic.

Jesus never made one reference to the Cross
without also mentioning His Own Resurrection.
The PLO is, ironically, excoriated by Hamas.
The left knee is not used in a Catholic genuflection.

Mafia's tactic after killing is to dispose of the car
in airport parking to avoid short-term discovery.
$18,000 is one-box cost of the Cohiba Behike cigar.
England's Henry VIII wrote a book—*against* heresy!

No musical climax excels that of the *Rienzi* overture.
Who sits or stands in a Pinter play means everything.
Misogyny lies at the root of the doctrine of coverture.
Marasmius oreades is the mushroom of the fairy ring.

Media mail takes a full month to get to Hawaii.
No person missing a mother's love will ever truly care.
A dactyl in hexameter poetry invites a spondee.
A full eight feet wide measures the Great Bed of Ware.

The 1' x 4' x 9' black monolith in Arthur Clarke's *2001*
was originally conceived as a transparent "tetrahedron."
Dirty dishes left in a sink prove householders slovens.
Jews believe Hebron is the entrance of Garden of Eden.

The primary force behind the "Bay of Pigs," the fiasco
first called "Operation Pluto," was Richard M. Nixon.
Americans never use the word *antipasti*, only antipasto.
Between Jefferson and Hamilton was constant friction.

Nadia Comaneci in Montreal's 1976 Olympics—
the first and only Perfect 10—actually wore #13.
Inappropriate behavior is common in bulimics.
Strings have now been bred out of the string bean.

Of Stephen King's 51 novels, 34 take place in Maine.
Columbia head Harry Cohn's idol was Benito Mussolini.
Feeling indebted to anyone is anathema to a Dane.
It is far better to stir (*pace* J. Bond) than shake a martini.

TRUISMS II

All James Patterson novels float on a river of clichés.
Anti-Chinese feeling is strong among the Vietnamese.
True beef marrow and *dry* red wine make a Bordelaise.
Very few spices are used in cooking among Cantonese.

When pairing beer and cheese, both should be acidic.
Amadeus Mozart was Franz Schubert's favorite composer.
Native Americans rate highest among sufferers arthritic.
Sirloin steak, flank, short loin, and shank are not kosher.

Stating that a person has a fund of common sense
is a subtle way of saying he doesn't have much else.
Lack of remorse makes unfit a true vow of penitence.
Sable (marten) is the most expensive of all fur pelts.

Timon of Athens, a fragment, was botched by a later hand.
Schadenfreudists always deal with, delight in, trivialities.
The Sun Also Rises, back in 1927, in Boston was banned.
All true egalitarians despise/avoid restaurant formalities.

No tie-holder as an accessory should dominate the tie.
Jews still debate serving 4 or 5 cups of wine at a Seder.
Shelf-life is 25 years for a product when you freeze-dry.
Unrecyclable—laminated, dyed, glossy—is wrapping paper.

The Chinese never use salt in a beef marinade.
On Lincoln's inauguration, Sen. Douglas held his hat.
Quince, not oranges, figured initially in marmalade.
There is virtually not a single meat-eater in Gujarat.

No notable figure is or was ever truly humble.
Lincoln's "Emancipation Proclamation" was originally reviled.
Thyme of all herbs is most strongly antifungal.
It is the mother who gives her surname to an illegitimate child.

Wind force is equal to the square of the velocity:
if the wind speed doubles, then force quadruples.
Chile and Argentina live with political animosity.
Wealth is only achieved by the easing of scruples.

Hyphenated identities are always fragile and unstable.
Yemenis are routinely turned down when seeking U.S. visas.
American products are required to have an origin label.
No temperature can range so low that a liquid never freezes.

From touching a toxic mushroom, no one can get sick
—it must either be tasted, cooked, or fully eaten first.
Pollock filets minced comprise the standard fish stick.
Roanoke Island, North Carolina is said to be cursed.

Heavy weather approaches Cape Horn from the west.
81% of the Southern Hemisphere is covered by ocean.
Three days is thought to be the limit of a house guest.
Touching anyone's head is a strict taboo for a Laotian.

Herb Caen coined the word "beatnik," disapprovingly.
Tipping is considered rude, even insulting, in Japan.
Nothing original has not first been met with incredulity.
Only true Malacca canes/sticks are fashioned from rattan.

TRUISMS II

The Merry Pranksters cross-country bus trip in 1964,
summer– with 14 original riders—lasted only 11 days.
It was religious hostility that created the Crimean War.
Beef marrow is the *sine qua non* of a true bordelaise.

Humor is completely absent in all wine writing.
The abo Khoisan own the world's richest diamond fields.
Virtually any variation of cod is called "whiting."
In Homer the greatest spoils of war were enemy shields.

Jesus never broke a single law of the Hebrew Bible.
La Revue du Vin de France is world's best wine magazine.
The quaternary digit of a byte is called a "nybble."
Against the death penalty was Dr. Joseph-Ignace Guillotin.

The Koran refers to wine—*nabid*—as an abomination.
Jesus never once used the O.T. phrase, "Thus saith the Lord."
Old Testament prophets spoke mainly of commination.
Fugitive slaves followed the big dipper, the "Drinking Gourd."

No living coconut tree has ever sprouted branches.
There are no operating railroads in the state of Hawaii.
Texas leads the USA in triple-digit acre ranches.
A matrilineal culture comes natural to the Cherokee.

The trunk of the coconut tree is actually a stem.
A Roman Catholic priest is *daily obliged* to read his breviary.
Jews, Christians, and Muslims all say "Amen."
A fee of "handling," as in "shipping & handling," is thievery.

Proverbs 7:13–20 is actually said by an adulteress.
Cassia oil is the secret to the Pepsi Cola formula.
An utter financial failure was the U.S. Pony Express.
Jewish women are not obliged to wear a yarmulke.

Silphium, the spice which disappeared, is now extinct.
The Trinity Test Site is open to the public but twice a year.
Giving the gist of the matter is the goal of being succinct.
Two hearing aids, just like two *ears*, are required to hear.

Designer Karl Lagerfeld said that wearing sweatpants
symbolizes defeat, a sign of losing control of your life.
A knockoff of Limburger cheese is U.S. Liederkranz.
To proper accompany drums—unlike flute—is a fife.

Most Jewish mothers are pushy as Zebedee's wife,
the bold parent of the Gospel's James and John.
To best see the *aurora borealis*, go to Yellowknife.
The secret of chess is learning to play *the pawn*.

Botanically speaking, the coconut palm is not a tree:
it has no bark, no branches, and no secondary growth.
Always constructed parallel to a shoreline is a quay.
Repeatedly modified, ever, is the Hippocratic Oath.

The I Ching is correctly pronounced "Yee Ching."
In the Gospels, one always goes *up* to Jerusalem.
Squareness is the curious contour of a boxing ring.
Th most abundant metal on Earth is aluminum.

TRUISMS II

Cow blood is commonly eaten in Kenya for breakfast.
Pule cheese is the priciest cheese in the world.
A calculated risk as a decision is guaranteed reckless.
It is much faster by far to knit stitch than to purl.

Betel nuts have been proven a carcinogen.
Martin Luther King was named Michael at birth.
A family's youngest sin is called a "benjamin."
The Atacama desert is the driest place on Earth.

Ophelia in *Hamlet* is in all likelihood pregnant,
as the Prince dismisses her as a bawd in a bed,
for she sings, facing her overlord cruelly regnant,
"Before you tumbled me, you promised me to wed."

Vagina in French is masculine "*C'est un vagin!*"
As a teenager, Martin Luther King attempted suicide.
Wild, not cultivated is the juniper used in gin.
Ocean depths mainly determine the speed of a tide.

Critic Edmund Wilson utterly loathed Robert Frost,
whom he called a "sad, third rate, dreadful old fraud."
Most Jews were not German killed in the Holocaust.
To fall hopelessly in love is worship a fallible god.

A single almond sucks up 1.1 gallons of water,
and it takes but 92 almonds to make up a cup.
No living animal has thicker fur than a sea otter.
Every part's poisonous in the simple buttercup.

True diamonds, rubies, sapphires, and emeralds
alone are officially considered precious jewels.
Rome's Crassus is held the worst of all generals.
Love is not a game that is played by any rules.

Human red blood cells have no nucleus.
A potato is a modified stem, not a root.
No soil is more fertile than around Mt. Vesuvius.
Statins are badly affected by grapefruit.

Salvador Dali was petrified of grasshoppers.
Generalities, while breezy, tend never to be wrong.
Obituaries are omitted in the deaths of all paupers.
In India, it is completely legal to smoke *bhang*.

A hurricane in the Atlantic is a typhoon in the Pacific,
but both storms are considered to be tropical cyclones.
Mosquitoes are of all earth's creatures most morbific.
Both the Bible and the Quran expressly ban loans.

When grapes are fermented, sugar fully disappears
into cellular energy, utterly consumed by the yeast.
Greek elders or seniors are by definition presbyters.
Half the population us under 25 in the Middle East.

Oranges were fully unknown in ancient Greece,
as well as in Italy, until the time of the Crusades.
Satin and silk wedding dresses both badly crease.
The most valued playing card is the Ace of Spades.

TRUISMS II

Viruses can never be killed by antibiotics.
Turkmenistan leads the world in super-emitting methane leaks.
The second cousin of linguistics is semiotics.
Jews traditionally see Messiah foreshadowed in Feast of Weeks.

Human beings cannot synthesize vitamin C.
No one can scientifically explain why tomatoes are red.
No fermented leaves may be used in green tea.
The best lubricant for all nuclear reactors is black lead.

Weather is short term, whereas climate is long term.
Nabokov loved to destabilize his fiction with tricks.
The life cycle is two to three months for human sperm.
Any owl that is lacking ear tufts is denoted a strix.

Israelis use the plus sign (⊥)—an upside down 'T'
—since its universal sign (+) resembles a holy cross.
Ezra Pound called fascism the "new Democracy."
Mustard with garum is the world's very oldest sauce.

All parts of the aconite plant (wolf's bene) are toxic.
The planet Mercury's entire structure is frozen solid.
Italian *arugula* is exactly same as English "rocket."
Use and address not a name on a pet that is collared.

Flirtation is the basic minuet of all romance.
Islam teaches Mohammed alive alone saw heaven.
St. Jean Vianney considered it a vice to dance.
A new beginning is any tattoo with the number 11.

A proper *étouffée* is never made with a roux—
a roux would make the dish a stew or a fricassee.
The ancient Greeks never had a term for blue.
The original U.S. Constitution was pro-slavery.

A traditional jambalaya must look brown.
Monday in Louisiana is red beans and rice day.
It can take up to 12 full minutes to drown.
Deep down, his girlfriend is the mother of a gay.

Walking on frosted grass can actually break it.
In Japan, never leave chopsticks flat on a table.
Play-acting is easy: you simply have to fake it,
No wealthy heiress has ever been truly stable.

Not one shot was fired in Hitler's Anschluss of Austria.
The best chopsticks, grown in Yoshino, are of cedar.
There are virtually no hills in the flat state of Florida.
Personality is commonly non-existent in a non-reader.

A biography empty of indiscretions is worthless.
The darker the color its soup, the saltier the *miso*.
The more earnest a person is, the more mirthless.
Gout always begins in the extremity of the big toe.

Tolstoy transformed "The Lord's Prayer" to perfect it!
Green tea should always accompany servings of sushi.
Tom Bowdler read little without the need to correct it.
The Pharisees ruled synagogues, temples the Sadducee.

Louisianans pronounce mayonnaise "*my-o-naze.*"
Bitcoin, the network, is capitalized, the "currency" is not.
Soil erosion results by an animal's continuing graze.
Operating websites can be easily taken down by a bot.

Russian ballet choreographers Léonide Massine
and Georges Balanchine fully despised each other.
The world's largest slum is located in Mumbai.
Holding babies left side is main choice of a mother.

Women comprise three-quarters of movie goers.
More English speakers live in Nigeria than Britain.
Governments must fully protect all "whistleblowers."
An elegant thank-you note is always handwritten.

Balanchine always watched his ballets danced
from his customary spot, downstage right wing.
No flirtatious look is direct but always glanced.
Singers want to act, and all actors want to sing.

A naked woman, surprised, covers her breasts:
why not shield the area between her legs first?
After three days, it is goodbye time for all guests.
Timbuktu, in northern Mali, is supposedly cursed.

A person who's prone lying flat, face downward,
whereas, a supine person is lying on one's back.
A hammer for pounding rivets must be rounded.
The sole fashion color that goes with all is black.

The diary does not know what's to happen next.
No human doesn't have phobias, rituals, anxieties.
Of Shakespeare's canon, there is no final text.
Conventional reverence defines standard pieties.

Three grapes only are used in making champagne:
Pinot Noir, the Pinot Meunier, and the Chardonnay,
but *blanc de blancs* only white grapes do contain,
with a smell of lemon meringue tart in its bouquet.

The primary component of beer is malt.
Jesus tended to feel uncomfortable in crowds.
Sea salt is no healthier than regular salt.
As heavy as a jet is weight of cumulus clouds.

Hoping to see the Lion of Judah, the Apostles
were all bewildered to find the Lamb of God.
All seven continents reveal dinosaur fossils.
Destruction of anyone's letter is mail fraud.

Cecil Beaton only liked people who were beautiful.
The smaller the bubbles, the finer the champagne.
The Collatz Conjecture in math remains unprovable.
The number one supplier of rare pearls is Bahrain.

Sifting flour make a major difference in cake baking.
Anti-Semitism's involved by Jews who change their names.
A bow is sufficient to avoid unwanted hand shaking
Anxious males who fear aging prefer "Jimmy" to James.

TRUISMS II

"My Pillow" is shredded polyurethane foam *only*.
The tastiest veal comes from non-weaned calves.
Solitude, people fail to understand, is never lonely.
Divorce decisions tend to follow the rule of halves.

Greta Garbo loved to wear boy's sweaters.
Ortolans are killed by being immersed in Armagnac.
Jesus forgave all the sins of grateful debtors.
Firms to fight takeovers employ the stock buyback.

Native American mothers never hit their children,
fearing by doing so they might turn into cowards.
Anyone journeying on sacred reasons is a pilgrim.
A wily mover makes his partner walk backwards.

Chicory can cleanse you, like glass of water.
There is no way to establish that an oyster is safe.
Complex is every relation of mother to daughter.
A pedophile's delight is dependence of a waif.

Any inordinate repetition ritual a sign of OCD.
The French use excess of garlic in cooking lamb.
Music is completely non-existent without melody.
Guam leads the world in the consumption of Spam.

Goose *foie gras* is finer than that made of duck livers.
A woodcock empties its bladder each time it takes off.
Western red cedar gives off most splinters and slivers.
The lob wedge in golf (58–62°) allows the most loft.

Singer Elvis Presley starred in 31 different movies
or, said much better, made the same movie 31 times.
Staining each other, always, are proximated rubies.
Hardness of a mallet's effects the sound of chimes.

Bedwetters all rise early to try to avoid shame.
Rembrandt painted as many as 80 self-portraits.
Farcical drama explains an author's pen name.
A paranoiac's mind is predominantly a fortress.

"No offense, but" always precedes an insult.
The Beatles all ended up suing each other.
Scientology is not faith, not religion, but a cult.
A fetal heart quickens at the voice if a mother.

"Livery Stable Blues," recorded by the all-white
Original Dixieland Band, is the first jazz record.
A uniform gives every pugnacious man height.
Nothing bears bacteria like a kitchen drainboard.

The Rankine scale of absolute temperature
was developed from the Fahrenheit scale,
just as the Kelvin scale, regarding pressure,
came from the Celsius, ratios without fail.

There is no mention in the Bible of baptismal submersion,
halos, the prohibition of gambling, alcohol use as aberrant,
the rapture, clerical dress, the "rapture," alternate version
praying with folded hands, cats, or Scripture being inerrant.

TRUISMS II

Slander is oral defamation, written it is libel.
Greta Garbo hated to be called "Greta."
The Pyramids are not mentioned in the Bible.
Avocados are unable to grow in India.

Mozart wrote his first symphony at age of 8
and composed his first opera at the age of 12.
Tears more than words carry sorrow's weight.
Only reaching *inside* something can you delve.

A chanter pipe on a bagpipe provides the tune;
the drone pipes a continuous, unvarying note.
There is a singing sound in the sand of a dune.
No serious endorsement is weaker than a vote.

Silver, purple, month, pint, and o*pus,*
marathon, as well as *discombobulate,*
wolf, and *pint,* selected for our focus,
are words that do not rhyme, to date.

Ballet impresario Serge Diaghilev despised all jazz.
Any survivor of childhood could become a novelist.
Colorlessness is the original state of the gem topaz.
Listening is basically the function of a psychologist.

North and South Koreans respect each other
but suffer from deep Chinese and U.S. hostility.
No historian ever uses the term "foremother."
Palmitic and stearic acids kill male fertility.

Anise in the Bible (*Anethum graveolens*) is dill.
Upper class women talk in extremely loud voices.
There is no FDA oversight regulating a diet pill.
A child is always spoiled by any offered choices.

Term for an older brother in India is *Dada*,
Fred Astaire could make any prop come alive.
Tree sap is the favorite food of the cicada.
Obstacles only make the stubborn soul thrive.

Brits refer to Americans as "*the* Americans."
Club root is the worst disease of all brassicas.
There was Jewish blood in all Samaritans.
Wars are all officially sanctioned massacres.

Shylock is not and never was a Jewish name.
It is mentioned nowhere in the Bible the sky is blue.
Petrichor is the designation for the smell of rain.
The central dome of the Taj Mahal is slightly askew.

One oyster can filter 50 gallons of water a day.
Coutts Bank staff members must be clean-shaven.
"Two-Spirits" identify as both straight and gay.
British Virgin Islands: the world's leading tax haven.

Most ballerinas have irregular menstrual cycles.
Crows just don't use tools to eat, they make them.
All followers of Jesus—*learners*—are disciples.
Clear mucus coughed is a sign of healthy phlegm.

For Trotsky the Nazi-Soviet Pact, August '39,
was "the midnight of the Twentieth Century."
Hinduism's divine number is the number nine.
No light should reach the crowns of chicory.

The center of London is on the site of Charing Cross.
An alley is a path between buildings too narrow for vehicles.
No Southern state creates the same barbecue sauce.
Both T. Jefferson and L. Tolstoy discounted Biblical miracles.

The best cricket bats are made from white willow.
In double-digging, sub-soil is always left on the bottom.
Elizabethans banned as a decadent luxury the pillow.
John Keats wrote the one perfect poem about autumn.

Ida Koverman who ran MGM was born a Brockway,
a Christian Scientist, not a Jew, earned $259 a week;
while L. B. Mayer, earning billions in take-home pay:
fired her after 22 years, and she died poor, an antique.

Insect antennae are always *paired* feelers.
Jews are required by their own law to wear gabardine.
Death is the Mafia penalty for any squealers.
The toughest granite on earth is found in Aberdeen.

Up to 1849, chess pieces could be any size and shape.
Steroid food explains a predominance of trans Filipinos.
Mutual consent doesn't reduce criminal statutory rape.
Neither windows nor clocks are to be found in casinos.

W.H.O. ranks the USA 37th world-wide in health care.
Philip Larkin considered sex a form of male bullying.
Vocalizing is considered by many required in prayer.
Proof of the U.S. Congress being bought is lobbying.

Nabokov's last four novels all focus on 12-year-old girls.
It is a phenomenon that birds do not fly over the Acropolis.
There were only, exactly, 56 of cute Shirley Temple's curls.
Japan's Greater Tokyo is the world's largest megalopolis.

Portland Stone has the property of being cleansed by rain,
white in the open but black under sills and hidden areas.
The tastiest sweetener for beverages is from sugar cane.
No variation is edible of the 388 species of calceolarias.

Vulcan is the only god who worked with his hands.
No straight lines can be found on Greece's Parthenon.
The radio spectrum has only twelve frequency bands.
Trappist chant, "responses," is based on the antiphon.

Fred Astaire's all-time favorite dancing partner
was, he declared, not Ginger but Rita Hayworth.
Saying "thanks" for a plant is taboo for a gardener.
To remove color from oils, use a bleaching earth.

China is the world's greatest publisher of Bibles.
There is no evidence Salieri was jealous of Mozart.
The Campbells and MacDonalds clans were rivals.
WWII airplanes were prime ground for "nose art."

TRUISMS II

Brits pronounce pizza "pitsa" rather than "peetsah."
Americans always rhyme the word *mental* with "fennel."
There are about 2000 spots on the average cheetah.
Scalers of a fort first sought to stifle a battlement's crenel.

A surreptitious glance at a clock is socially rude.
Valentina Schlee and Greta Garbo despised each other.
Naked is sexual, vulnerable; unadorned is nude.
No German fable has a kind and loving stepmother.

King Charles I was only five foot four inches in height.
Eating meat from strangled animals is prohibited Christians.
Consisting of seven colors (VIBGYOR) is white light.
The Triassic Period flourished with two-feet ornithischians.

Textron; Bell Helicopter; Dow Chemical; Lockheed;
McDonald Douglas, got rich from the Vietnam War,
as well as Boeing; Brown and Root, kings of greed,
which funded LBJ's campaign war chest, full bore.

Jehovah's Witnesses insist Jesus and St. Michael are the same.
Ballets are usually "made" (i.e., created) on a principal dancer.
The whole point of politics parties is deciding whom to blame.
The sun is the sole and single cause of melanoma skin cancer.

Garbo loved wearing a turtle-neck sweater, a skirt slim
(wool), flat-heeled shoes, and men's socks on her big feet.
In every clinch, she always reached out to embrace *him*
before the leading man did so to her, a European "greet."

St. Paul lived with Priscilla and Aquila for 18 months,
and no indication is given, anywhere, he was married.
Any and all maneuvers moving railroad cars are shunts.
Lobsters must be let go when carrying eggs—"berried."

Stuntmen aren't eligible for Academy Award recognition.
Riga, Latvia was once the most developed city in Sweden.
Twin children thrive in virtually all matters of apposition.
The word "creation" is never used of the Garden of Eden.

Ernest L. Thayer never received any royalties at all
or a single check from his ballad "Casey at the Bat,"
the most famous poem ever written about baseball,
and for comic verse the nation's uncontested *eclat*.

There was a symmetry to DeWolf Hopper's wives:
six little snippets, Ella, Ida, Edna, Nella, Elda. Lil.
None know the name origin for the game of "fives."
Any sung octave of high C inevitably sounds shrill.

Physical activity diminishes a state of anxiety.
Truman Capote had a yen only straight, ordinary-looking men.
The sole aspiration of every gourmand is satiety.
Gayelord Hauser said the most poisonous of foods was Italian.

W. R. Hearst, barred from France, hated it all his life.
London's Savoy Hotel once banned ladies wearing hats.
No one can approve a person who refers to "the wife."
The only mammals that don't taste sweetness are cats.

TRUISMS II

No person has a name in Cormac McCarthy's *The Road.*
Human inventions derive from the dimensions of nature.
Sticky skin is found on a frog, but only dry skin on a toad.
Self-interest informs most votes in American legislature.

There are as many as 50,000 Chinese characters
and 400 different syllables in Mandarin Chinese,
spoken with one of four possible tones for chatterers,
each with its own separate meaning, as you please.

Kissing in public is considered offensive in Thailand.
David Sarnoff, founder of RCA, judged television a failure.
In Oregon no one under 18 can be machine sun-tanned.
There are three times more sheep than people in Australia.

To return to Russia, toss a silver ruble into the Neva.
Gala ballet audiences, snobs, usually sit on their hands.
Although in lore Jesus was transfigured on Mt. Tabor,
the mount goes unmentioned in Scripture, as it stands.

Israeli settler colonialism is considered legally acceptable.
Balanchine's *Donizetti's Variations* is a ballet for small girls.
Leaving a tip behind in Japan is considered disrespectful.
Only nobles in ancient Rome were allowed to wear pearls.

Lobster is the preferred crustacean for *sauce americaine.*
Edward Gorey never used the pseudonym "O. Weardd Grey."
In rowing, being short is considered a virtue in a coxswain.
Costumes are believed too precious to be washed in ballet.

There is an odd stigma in Asia to a woman using tampons.
90 percent of the sensory experience of eating is olfaction.
Ice-climbing anywhere is impossible without crampons.
Even the best Venetian blinds show shadows and diffraction.

Questioning Herod, the Magi caused the "Massacre of the Innocents."
Many great composers died after their 9th Symphony: Beethoven,
Bruckner, Schubert, and Mahler had not lived to complete a tenth.
Gertrude Stein declared, "It is always a mistake to be plainspoken."

The essence of all philosophy is basically logic.
Witch's covens traditionally have thirteen members.
Proverbs are developed to be strictly pedagogic.
Blessed is he who when he gives never remembers.

There was never a student movement in the USSR.
Barristers are gentlemen in the UK, never a solicitor.
Expert (not average) golf is always indicated by par.
Christ was abjured by Dostoevsky's Grand Inquisitor.

There existed ten major Chinese dynasties:
Shang, Zhou, Qin, Han, Tang, Song, Yuan,
Ming, and Qing. But then for its societies
a Republic in 1912, all Imperial rule gone.

Chinese discrimination of black people goes back decades:
but there's no racism, because the nation is only 0.8% black.
The most valued card in a deck is always the Ace of Spades.
There is unquestionably something of a clique in any claque.

TRUISMS II

A goose bonds to the face it sees on hatching.
George Orwell hated his Christian birth name, Eric.
Cider vinegar is a perfect trap for fly-catching.
Cuernavaca: Spaniards couldn't say "*Cuauhuahuac.*"

Chinese eat the top of a whole fish, never flip it to eat,
which is bad luck: you never turn a boat over, do you?
General James Longstreet was always called "Old Pete."
The weakest of all color associations with food is blue.

No 80-year-old man is not completely assless.
Ballet dancers say "merde" to wish each other good luck.
Bad manners in the U.S.A. means "classless."
Cut from a cow's fifth rib, and so inexpensive, is chuck.

The poet Edgar A. Poe had a lifelong fixation
with the mournful sound of the open letter "O,"
"Nevermore," "Lenore," "sore," the reiteration
of "evermore," forever always linked with Poe.

Significance always sits in a letter's post-script.
The best champagnes are all aged for five or more years,
The vice of stubbornness thrills to contradict.
Stupidity, oddly, is most manifest in someone's ears.

Kids' "bunny-eared" shoelaces never hold up.
It is against the law to sell kidneys for transplant.
Mourners always leave flowers, queerly, rolled up.
Sibilants are avoided in elegant Gregorian chant.

The Chinese revere the character *fu* which means luck,
happiness, good fortune, and blessing. Across the nation,
its citizens post this small word everywhere with pluck
and take great pride in all of the meanings of its citation.

"Bill" was P.G. Wodehouse favorite fictional name.
Westerners call black tea what Asians refer to as red.
All tax havens, anonymous dodges, are a con game,
essentially by global multinational corporations led.

A visible iceberg is typically 10% of its total mass.
Black women always have the highest employment rate.
One tiny drop on the skin is fatal of VX nerve gas.
At 135 pounds, a professional ballerina is overweight.

Calvin Coolidge, the most negative and remote
of U.S. Presidents, was also the most accessible.
State and local taxes exempt any treasury note.
Strawberries transported are highly putrescible.

The rarest human blood type is AB negative
and by far the most common type is O positive.
Hosta plants are notoriously photo-sensitive.
Poetry rides on the waves of the connotative.

A picked apple should always be lifted upward
so as not to snap the stem. But if jerked down,
the stem would be ripped out, the apple scored,
and decay would begin right away in the crown.

TRUISMS II

Yale's Skull & Bones men always deny their membership.
Chinese seniors are always seated facing an entrance door.
The FBI for fingerprints is interested only in the fingertip.
No one with intelligence activity may join the Peace Corps.

The word *fence* was originally short for "defense."
Spinach, an annual, is never found growing wild.
In 1856, the UK stopped minting the groat (4 pence,)
A "boilermaker" is a mixture of "brown and mild."

A charcoal powder best cleans the teeth,
sweetens the breath, and, if gulped down,
helps palliate an upset stomach's sheath,
purifying water for a toothbrush's crown.

No *pas de deux* was ever made on an argument.
English has twice the number of words as Russian.
The obverse side of envy offers you a compliment.
German militarism defines the soul of a Prussian.

"23 No. 9" is the most difficult Rachmaninoff prelude.
The most venomous snake on earth is the western taipan.
Grain should never be the first ingredient in dog food.
As many as 6852 islands constitute the nation of Japan.

Playing solitaire and ironing his western shirts
were George Balanchine's two favorite hobbies.
Mid-thigh is the hit-goal for taste in mini-skirts.
Firearms are never carried by British bobbies.

Room temperature fruit is unbearable to eat.
All of Igor Stravinsky's music has a cruel edge.
Beet greens are more nutritious than the beet.
The loft is precarious in golf on a lob wedge.

Vivien Leigh filming *GWTW* despised Clark Gable.
The Red Pyramid is older than the Pyramid at Giza.
Siberian convicts can shorten jail time hunting sable.
No melting pot exceeds that of the area of Silesia.

Bread, even the best, is never good for ducklings.
The King Ranch in Texas is larger than Rhode Island.
Hollywood is ground zero for random couplings.
Speyside is not considered part of Scottish highland.

"Stinking Bishop," made in Scotland and the UK,
is considered to be the world's stinkiest cheese.
Calling cards of old were always left on a silver tray.
Norwegians have no expression to say "please."

Actor Erich von Stroheim, who added the "von,"
was a fake, in real life son of a Jewish hatmaker.
Infections are easily transmitted wearing a thong.
No one works under more deadlines than a baker.

Rafflesia arnoldii flower can weigh up to 15 pounds.
Women have always been GWTW's core audience.
Tradition has women traveling best wearing browns.
Full satisfaction is very rarely achieved in prurience.

Whaling men saw Melville less a writer than ship-jumper,
believed *Moby-Dick* caricatured their occupation and them,
had a vague, suspicious notion that he was a man humper
and scorned the idea that their tasks involved any mayhem.

J.S. Bach worshipped Handel but never got to meet him.
A sipper's lipstick will cause bubbles to collapse/deflate
due to the woman's fatty molecules and waxy petrolatum.
The # symbol—solid FIDE notation—means checkmate.

Mozart insisted a fugue must always be played slowly.
Leland Stanford never graduated from secondary school.
Garlic and olive oil *alone* are sole ingredients of aioli.
Any foreign, remote region may be denominated *thule*.

Johann Sebastian Bach by two wives had 20 children.
As soon as you meet someone, you know why you'll leave her.
Concrete has been history's main material for building.
No animal creature is more monogamous than the beaver.

A loud uncorking of champagne bottle is amateurish:
the cork should properly be released with a subdued sigh.
The art of lambrequin drapery is distinctly Moorish.
Nutmeg contains a toxin that can induce a powerful high.

G. B. Shaw was averse to watching his plays on stage.
Dosage is a highly secretive step in making champagne.
The sacred ceremonial herb in Ancient Rome was sage.
A chronic asthmatic can very badly be affected by rain.

A male calling card is long, narrow; a woman's larger.
Only Temple permit-carrying Mormons may enter a Temple.
Duplicating a driver's license is most common for a forger.
Swiss cheese is vegetarian-friendly, but, less so, Emmental.

Softness in dress cannot bear the weight of ornaments.
Actors shouldn't have viewpoints—follow the script!
Less preen oil allows for deeper dives with cormorants
A socialist worker should always refuse to be tipped.

A single flat blow cracks an egg most cleanly.
Serbians have ever been poorer than Croatians
Any open public use of toothpicks is unseemly.
The French describe vulgarians as "*béotians.*"

B15 is the world's largest iceberg: 4,250 sq. miles.
At 33, Mary Pickford played Little Annie Rooney, age 12.
Eclectic architecture is always a mélange of styles.
A membrane grows more rigid and thicker in a cancer cell.

Simple sunlight is every human's salvation.
Washington, Jefferson, Lincoln: all non-orthodox Christians.
A "lavender marriage" is averse to copulation.
Herbivorous were all horn-faced dinosaurian ornithischians.

All native people opposed America independence.
Louis Agassiz said whites only descended from Adam & Eve.
Self-aggrandizement motivates investigating descendants.
Shantung is a fabric that always comes in a silk plain weave.

TRUISMS II

Eggs in all types of cookery dislike severe heat.
The emotion of jealousy flatly contradicts love.
Alaskan pollock is used for imitation crab meat.
Lizzie Borden at trial constantly wore a glove.

Regnery Publishers lack all standards of accuracy.
The Pacific Railway Act of 1872 stole no end of Indian land.
Costa Rica is the only nation to disarm unilaterally.
The index finger is considered the most important on the hand.

All last-minute invitations epitomize vulgarity.
Shah Jahan's dead wife never saw the Taj Mahal.
Anonymity is the conspicuous virtue of charity.
A mere fertility god (name means "lord") was Baal.

Novelist Cormac McCarthy never once bothered to vote.
Whenever you accept a pardon, you have admitted guilt.
Adolf Hitler popularized the fashion of the trench coat.
A pinball machine shape remains—but also fails—a-tilt.

Jesus never once personally baptized a single person.
A gentleman never wears a tuxedo before six o'clock.
Sexual deviants mainly perpetrate the crime of arson.
Batters at home plate never advance on a pitcher's balk.

Disney's *Bambi*, is virtually devoid of all dialogue,
with about only 900 words used in the entire movie.
The Australian Shepherd is held the best sheep dog.
The Rwandan Hutu was always poorer than Tutsi.

The French Revolution began as a *grabelle*, salt tax protest.
Only a rube sends personal letters on business stationery.
Pro team owners—why?—raise championship trophies first.
Stockholders are ever protected when times are inflationary.

No cologne worn by a man should cause comment.
Golfers avoid jeans, tee-shirts, flip-flops, and sandals.
The transition to clarify gender identity is pure torment.
Nothing more clarifies who is a friend than scandals.

No serious Christian should ever die wealthy.
A cummerbund should be worn with the pleats up.
The subfusc-world in jazz songs is never healthy.
Tyrus Cobb always stole a plate showing cleats up.

Ham comes from the section of a pig's ass (*fundus*).
Brown shoes are never worn to a wedding or a funeral.
No plea for forgiveness transcends the *De Profundis*.
Three letters don't exist in a row for a Roman numeral.

Proving the earth round was never a goal for Columbus.
Couples at a formal dinner are never seated side to side.
No recipe is more variable than that for *Charlotte Russe*.
Christ forgave carnal sins but abhorred the sin of pride.

Mozart discovered J.S. Bach after decades of neglect.
A bow tie should never be worn with a button-down collar.
No great chef is subject to the laws of what to confect.
A middle school teacher must perforce become a stentor.

TRUISMS II

There are no operations in Chinese medicine,
only herbs, acupuncture—physicians alter *Qi*
("*tchee*"), the body's natural essence, jettison
all invasive procedure, bodies all surgery free.

Sharing salt with Arabs indicates an unbreakable bond.
"Prompt side," downstage, is a preening actor's paradise.
Brunettes tend to steer clear of girlfriends who are blond.
While virtue may wear a veil, a mask is chosen for vice.

People tend to appear far more interesting alone.
No actual muscles are located in fingers and thumbs.
Headaches ever follow upon the Alpine *foehn*.
Cross tribal telephones were Native American drums.

When Garbo retired, the only souvenir autograph
she gave was to her black maid, the only living soul
allowed in her dressing room, a framed photograph:
"To Ursula from your friend, Greta Garbo." *Sole!*

The verbs in Chinese do not have different tenses.
Racism against Egyptians mars the book of Exodus.
Australia's Dingo Fence is longest of the world's fences.
Learning problems characterize people ambidextrous.

A bare cross, without the corpus of Christ, is not a crucifix.
Garbo movies carried the fashion wallop of a Paris opening.
The seeds of bur marigolds are referred to as "beggar-ticks."
Communication, not song, was signified by Swiss yodeling.

No true gentleman would ever color or dye his hair.
Bill O'Reilly "history" books are what emetics are to shit.
Four couples could sleep in "The Great Bed of Ware."
In the US during WWII no Smith was ever again Schmidt.

Psychiatrists can never order patients to do anything.
A champagne cork can pop out at 50 miles per hour.
All Italian mobsters and gangsters wear a pinky ring.
Pastries should always be made with unbleached flour.

Laurence Olivier, astonished, said actor Kirk Douglas
achieved stardom equipped with only two expressions.
Cathedrals began to use glass with the flying buttress.
A huge theme in Russian literature is deep confessions.

Adjustable hosels, not fixed, improve all golf clubs.
No one remembers Blanche Du Bois' husband was gay.
It is ignorant to appear over-friendly in British pubs.
Saying "*toi toi toi*" is a good luck superstition in ballet.

Hollywood sells dreams but is ruled by nightmares—
its stock in trade is illusion, but it manufactures fear.
To find best data points in statistics use least squares.
In Africa or Arabia, a sultana is the wife of an emir.

The most embarrassing shot in golf is a shank.
The bottom button of a vest should not be buttoned.
The clay "*pygg*," not a pig, explains a piggy bank.
A manservant may be called but never summoned.

TRUISMS II

L. B. Mayer, a once inarticulate ex-peddler of scrap iron,
never made a film in his life at MGM, didn't know how.
Stormy weather is by far the best hunting time for a lion,
its prey convinced by weather any attack he'll disallow.

Almost all kangaroos and wallabies are left-handed.
The one person Jesus called friend ("*hetairos*")? Judas.
A praying-like position distinguishes every mantid.
Most plants have leaves that are commonly caducous.

The most curious thing about people is *lack* of curiosity.
Comedian Red Skelton was an expert on Abraham Lincoln.
Old smoothbore rifles had a very weak muzzle velocity.
The dodo bird after the year 1690 met its final extinction.

Depreciation is a dodge the wealthy cheat on taxes;
rolling forward all business losses; hiring their kids;
claiming yachts as second homes. If income waxes?
Sell inherited real estate! Always be feigning skids!

Most figures of fun in P. G. Wodehouse are aunts.
Jesus believed mercy was more important than tithing.
The French refer to field sickles as "*croissants*."
Not a month passes in the Congo without an uprising.

Fritz Haber, a Jew, at huge incremental cost,
personally created the lethal gas Zyklon-B,
killing millions during the Nazi Holocaust
and, therefore, attenuating his own posterity.

A man is killed onstage in the musical *Oklahoma!*
Mark Twain believed redheads descended from cats.
The ancient Aztec currency was *cacao Theobroma*.
Bing Crosby hid baldness compulsively wearing hats.

No Southern law ever passed requiring slaveowners be moral.
Cormac McCarthy spent 28 years with never a royalty check.
Red (colored inside and out) is the rarest of all deep-sea coral.
Used *strictly* for dry measure (equal to 8 dry quarts) is a peck.

Favoritism plays a huge role in all college admissions.
Chinese say, "A girl can be ugly, as long as she has white skin."
Capriciousness is the fickle vice of all econometricians.
Only one image—a 1534 lead disc—exists of Anne Boleyn.

Southerners refer to diarrhea saying one is "running off."
Physician-assisted suicide is legal in the state of Oregon.
Turnips are said to be an effective remedy for a cough.
Huge trees permanently darken the floor of the Amazon.

Arthur Sullivan, composer of "Onward Christian Soldiers."
also once wrote a memorable lullaby to a rasher of bacon.
Three bones but no sockets are found in human shoulders.
Bird droppings on you indicate good luck to a Jamaican.

The Pilgrims did *not* believe in freedom of religion
and were intolerant of any "liberty of conscience;"
they expelled Roger Williams, for causing division
in the Massachusetts Bay Colony by his tolerance.

TRUISMS II

Japan adopted Chinese characters for their language
during the Tang Dynasty (618–906 A.D.). Before that,
Japanese was only *spoken*, script dismissed baggage
and no accepted way of writing. Language? Solely chat.

Espionage is cheaper than Research and Development.
Any woman entering Mount Athos is jailed for a year.
John Howard, a Quaker, invented solitary confinement.
The oppressed always rebel to overcome their fear.

The Eiffel Tower (thermal expansion) gets taller in summer.
Zoroastrians Ahura Mazda and Angra Mainyu are ever at odds.
Great Britain's preferred food bean is the scarlet runner.
Personal striving and struggle, not war, defines Qur'an jihads.

Soap consistently tends to make water wetter.
Jesus revealed his identity at pagan Caesarea Philippi.
Hoping to recoup losses always sinks a bettor.
The heart never desires what's unattracted by the eye.

Genocide will always be linked to Srebrenica.
All Oxbridge philosophers abhorred imprecision.
G. Puccini's favorite Tosca was Maria Jeritza.
Fear of rivaling the gods, initiated circumcision.

The IRA, avoiding rifles, use nothing but revolvers.
Paul Robeson was never allowed to sing at the Met.
The pioneer west was rife with roving quacksalvers.
Tart-tongued movie spinsters all sported a lorgnette.

Author Henry James never wrote a single poem.
Moses talked to a burning bush and Christ to a fig tree.
A cupola is smaller than, often crowns, a dome.
The Internet made fully redundant the travel agency.

A Medeco lock is absolutely impossible to pick.
Guiseppe Verdi composed *Aida* for Jenny Lind.
Three feet is the standard length of a mahlstick.
Red beans and rice are compulsively twinned.

Snobs pooh-pooh locust wood for the fireplace.
The collar of Wendy, the fast-food icon, spells "Mom."
Anyone thoroughly involved is "at the coalface."
American citizenship is given to anyone born in Guam.

There is, oddly enough, no Latin word for tea.
No president on Mount Rushmore looks in the same direction.
Much milder than Camembert cheese is Brie.
Studies shown that 5.1–5.5 inches is the standard male erection.

Leeches should never be pulled off—they fall naturally.
Vermeer, father of eleven, painted no canvas showing kids.
Renata Scotto badly feuded with tenor Luciano Pavarotti.
Auctioneers can prevent the fairest deal on absentee bids.

Brendan Behan detested drinking mere pints of bitter.
2.2 million Americans have no running water at home,
The $20 bill is the best currency for a counterfeiter.
As important as blood type is the signature of the genome.

The French Revolution, a failure, ultimately led to nothing,
with a self-crowned emperor more absolute than any king.
The most vivid manifestation of flirting is a woman blushing.
Controlling the clock is done in football by means of rushing.

Nobody has ever bet enough on a winning horse.
George Washington hated the habit of handshaking.
Irish folk medicine relies heavily on ulex/gorse.
Messages from God are what kept Shakers quaking.

Irked, the pompous Maria Von Trapp was not invited
to the film premiere of the musical *The Sound of Music*.
No international protection exists for things copyrighted.
Only 70,000 people in existence now speak Tungusic.

Leeches die if applied to an alcoholic's skin.
The state of West Virginia has the highest depression rate.
Camels are treated like children by the Bedouin.
Jamaican dreadlock hairstyle often uses the Polish plait.

Ms. Rachel Carson, author of *The Sea Around Us*
and *Silent Spring*, disliked boats and could not swim.
Robespierre considered pity a vice and treasonous.
Inbreeding was the cause of the royal Habsburg chin.

Not one person in a Horatio Alger novel, bootblacks
and newsboys, ever actually becomes a millionaire.
Fuel for jet engines and rockets employs paraffin wax.
Longer than human fingers are claws of a grizzly bear.

The best applesauce apple is a Rhode Island greening.
Serbian folk poetry is the closest modern link to Homer.
After six months is normal time for a baby's weaning.
A pseudonym is in all ways an inappropriate misnomer.

Gratitude badly longs to communicate itself.
The twigs of all cherry trees are poisonous.
Snobs never buy attire/wardrobe off-the-shelf.
St. Teresa of Avila defined faith as joyfulness.

Humans are not really designed for swimming.
Abraham spent his entire life in Canaan, a landless stranger.
Okinoshima in Japan, a sacred island, bans all women.
Policing demonstrations is never done by a Texas Ranger.

No others ever appear in Martha Stewart's books.
More tourists than residents are found in Venice.
For centuries Chinese were kidnapped for cooks.
Hourglass shapes were the original courts in tennis.

Crowds do not require leaders: driven by fear,
the desire is to rage and display as a *community*.
Cream cheese and lox make a Jewish "schmear."
Diplomats all use the scam of political immunity.

Prisoners sew mailbags four stitches to the inch.
Palestinians are banned from defending their families from
    violent aggression.
Boxers seek momentary comfort by engaging a clinch.
Simply pursuing another one is a singular cure for a compulsive
    obsession.

TRUISMS II

Avalon is old Welsh for an "island of the apples."
Pharisees and Sadducees had hypocrisy in common.
Small capes, its cognate, constituted the origin of chapels.
As few as 4% of Indians today identify as Brahmin.

Jeeves was a gentleman's gentleman, *not* a butler.
All Chinese dialects are mutually unintelligible.
During the Civil War, a Jew was the usual sutler.
As to voting in the U.S., every felon is ineligible.

No prisoner in Alcatraz ever received an early release.
Queen Victoria knighted Arthur Sullivan, not William Gilbert.
A daughter of your niece of nephew is your grandniece.
The hazelnut traces its name to the French abbot, St. Philbert.

Condoms were illegal in Ireland until the late 1970s.
Never pick or eat a completely all-white mushroom.
As many as a million American slaves were Beninese.
A mother must be walked down the aisle by a groom.

No police informant enlisted should ever be the top guy,
as it gives him superpower and invulnerable to prosecution.
Nebraska is the state most well-known for its rhubarb pie.
Distilled water should be used in every saline solution.

In Genesis, the Lord created light on the very first day,
but, oddly, He did not create the sun until the *fourth*.
Black hue and a ruling agouti gene make a horse a bay.
Five hundred miles fully comprises magnetic north.

Aunts everywhere basically are all alike.
Chinese characters are all pronounced with a monosyllable.
Impaling its prey is the habit of a shrike.
Every good choir is arranged by care as vocally appositional.

North America, a significant part of a great continent,
has never had those migratory songsters, nightingales.
St. Paddy's Day and Evacuation Day are concomitant.
Christ's parables are often explained by sliding scales.

Soak veggie seeds in tea, refrigerate before planted.
No more than $10,000 can legally be taken out of the U.S.
News on modern television is now reported slanted.
One need not be held as gay if he/she opts to cross-dress.

Bee keeping is never mentioned in the Bible,
although there are constant references to honey.
The closer the truth, the more serious the libel.
Ayn Rand said the virtue of society was money.

There are 800 uses for dates in Arabic cuisine
and 971 dinner scenes in China's *Dream of the Red Chamber.*
A bird preens with its bill strictly for hygiene.
There are more than 300 colors in the million-year-old amber.

Metzitzah b'peh is when a mohel uses his mouth
to suck blood from a baby's circumcision wound,
yet nothing in that ritual could be more uncouth
and nothing, regarding hygiene, more unsound.

TRUISMS II

Most all small island birds have become extinct:
All hippopotamuses are first cousins to whales.
Hunt's Point, S. Bronx, most dangerous precinct
in New York City, is what fills up the city's jails.

Presbyterians have no interest in crucifixes.
Cassowaries in New Guinea have at times killed humans.
Most primitive of all birds were archaeopteryxes.
No New Dealer's record for zeal compared to Truman's.

The original color of corn flakes was a sky blue.
Flag rallies thrive among American hate groups.
For heavy gravy, a quart needs 6 ounces of roux.
"Your Grace" is the standard salutation for dukes.

Essenes preferred starvation to eating with non-Essenes.
A female must remain perfectly still during bird copulation.
A Papal election officially conclaves, and *not* convenes.
A vile, unclean practice is how Islam considers cremation.

Jell-O, part pig gelatin, is strangely accepted as kosher.
The Celts believed apples contained the essence of divine wisdom.
Touching his cap when opening a door is law for a chauffeur.
No one's lungs are sterile of germ-free in our circulatory system.

England was the major winner of the Seven Years War.
Comedian George Carlin excoriated all euphemisms.
Most nations where rain forests exist are extremely poor.
The French government abhors all Americanisms.

Christ predicted Elijah would precede his Second Coming.
Thomas Mann: "There is no such thing as an apolitical artist."
Near Taos, New Mexico is heard a constant eerie humming.
Every incontrovertible nationalist is, at bottom, a fascist.

Only the bravest Aztecs could wear a jaguar skin.
July 4, 2023 was the hottest day ever recorded on Earth
and the *very day before it*, broiling, was its twin!
The only place you can see a Quokka is in the city, Perth.

Emile Zola declared gluttony most pernicious of sins.
South Korea is the world capital for cosmetic surgery.
Identical fingerprints never match with identical twins.
Death is also his if a death penalty results from perjury.

Tongans believe liver to be the finest part of a meal,
because that is where the animal's courage resided.
Spinning is more worthy than reciting prayer wheel
for the Tibetan Buddhists believe the merit is guided.

The Limpkin bird feeds on nothing but large snails.
Isaac Newton was knighted, not for science, but currency reform.
Most world medical schools have a majority of females.
Israel legally bans Arab books, bananas, and anything cruciform.

A primate's genome code is 98% identical to a human.
Einstein, offered it, refused to become president of Israel.
The world's most popular spice after pepper is cumin.
Post's Golden Crisp has the highest sugar (59%) in cereal.

TRUISMS II

Fermentation is only a variation of a yeast infection.
Basil is often held too sacred to be used in Indian cooking.
The drugs Librium and Elavil prevent a male erection.
All sweet desserts in Britain are referred to as "pudding."

A mohel's traditional symbol was to wear a red silk belt.
No food has not been rendered flavorless by British cookery.
"That man" was the Republican snipe for F. D. Roosevelt.
Forty or so nests for birders officially constitutes a rookery.

Submersibles, to fight deep sea pressure, must be round,
or oval, for dense water loves, and works to kill, angles.
Henry David Thoreau always set out to walk westbound.
It is compulsory for married Indian women to wear bangles.

Every U. S. sailor must always carry flashlight and a knife.
Joey Chestnut once ate 182 full chicken wings in 30 minutes.
Salt water and fresh water both can serve a spawning alewife.
A city's taxation is essentially what determines city limits.

The Irish potato blight killed over a million people.
No bird is lovelier than the keel-billed toucan (*ramphastus sulfuratus*).
Horseradish is instant kryptonite to the potato beetle.
No threating cloud can possibly match the rain-filled Nimbostratus.

Most toilet paper sold for home use in France is pink.
Newton's *Principia*: the most important scientific book ever published.
Yale's Bonesmen seek gain by means of "doublethink."
As much as 13,000 tons of New York City's daily waste is rubbished.

Elmer Fudd was based on egghead Robert Ripley.
A true, original civet is always cooked with hare.
A girdle for a diamond should be fashioned thickly.
The hump powers the forelimbs of a grizzly bear.

Banks maintain therapists known as "wealth psychologists"
who aid ultra-rich clients unable to cope mentally with fortunes.
ENT doctors love to call themselves otorhinolaryngologists.
Polygamy in the "afterlife" is still a popular belief of Mormons.

Light is the God of Creation's eldest daughter.
Protection has every right to expect allegiance.
Almonds are a poster crop for excess of farming water.
Mob law in action never has a single grievance.

The world's most common name is Muhammed.
Nutmeg is extremely poisonous if injected intravenously.
Root crops are never suitable to be replanted.
Deists have little patience with Christian thaumatolatry.

Excessive egotism is the main ingredient of treason.
Elbridge Gerry never pronounced his surname with a soft G!
Instinct is the deployment in an animal of its reason.
Fruits grow right on the trunk of a Brazilian jaboticaba tree.

South of the Thames in London always lacked cachet,
in the same way that Queens is never quite Manhattan.
Women, *never men*, are the central subject of ballet.
Yiddish speakers have a fascination with hyperbaton.

TRUISMS II

Parricide is the crime most abhorred by the French.
Treason is the crime most abhorred by the English.
Only hexagonal keys drive rods of an Allen wrench.
Cephalopods alone can be denominated an "inkfish."

Aggression is predominantly fear's defense.
During the American revolution, there were 30 newspapers.
A "groat" was once the now defunct four pence.
Mozart felt the finest thing in life was a scarlet cloak.

The place in China famous for oranges is Fukien.
Only one nation has purple in its flag—Dominica.
Catholicism was attractive to a devout Tractarian.
Rare as farmers among Indians were the Seneca.

English ivy does not flourish in in the glare of hot sun.
In Simenon's *LePerdu de St. Pholien* Maigret commits a crime.
Every government project shows a cost overrun.
We experience both pleasure and yet terror in the true sublime.

Drowning is the number one killer of children in the U.S.
In his work Edgar Allen Poe completely ignores Christianity.
The third figure in storybook fables is always the wisest.
Comedian Bill Cosby who raped women combated profanity.

Nazis are (boringly) always Hollywood's got-to "heavies."
No great fortune has ever been amassed via good deeds.
Dikes are walls; banks—natural or man-made—are levees.
Sterling silver pearls are the foundation of Navajo beads.

Marx insisted machines aided capitalism alone.
Indiana Jones movies are all about the art of looting.
A discus is technically hurled and not thrown.
To refute is scientific; aggression involves confuting.

Never in cameras of any kind leave a shutter tensed.
or even cocked, as it will shorten and damage its life.
A dead whale was not stripped but rather was flensed.
Nothing's more sporadic than a Beverly Hills wife.

Marlins often die from over-exertion during a fight.
No tax collector in the New Testament is worth a damn.
"Dewey" is the usual nickname for a man named Dwight.
Impartiality in Ivy League college admissions is a sham.

S. T. Coleridge was the guiding spirit of E.A. Poe's life.
No mutilated catch can ever win a fishing tournament.
Always corral food with the non-edge not to dull a knife
Nothing essential, but which is added, is an appurtenant.

Jesus' ancestry was utterly dysfunctional:
incestuous Tamar, Rahab was a prostitute,
Perez, Zerah, each a sadly tainted juvenile,
and David, murderer and adulterer, to boot.

A crow's greatest enemy is the great Horned Owl.
Vehicles in Montevideo are taxed by the number of wheels.
No formally set rule in the N.B.A. constitutes a foul.
The oldest American car firm (fl. 1879) made Oldsmobiles.

TRUISMS II

Antarctica was not discovered until 1820.
Most people's eyes are never an exact pair.
Swaziland's basic money unit is the *ilangeni*.
Challenge in the animal kingdom is to stare.

Amateurs should always sail with an overcautious reef.
The longest full book title—cf. *Narrative of Arthur Gordon Pym*.
Meat has to be cured or pickled in brine to be "bully beef."
Grace and elegance among society women is merely to be slim.

Competitive eating contests are a mockery of poverty.
Ernest Hemingway always wrote while standing up.
No beach on the planet should ever be private property.
No tightrope walker is seen looking down or glancing up.

The Araucanians of Chile were much better fighters
than the Incas of Peru or the wild Aymaras of Bolivia.
Mawkishness has ever been the bane of sportswriters.
The best malts are made in peaty Islay (pron. "eye-la").

Glenn Miller's arrangements always voiced a clarinet
lead on top of two delicate musical altos and two tenors.
Baritones always complete chords in a singing quarter.
Iron, manganese, and chromium are uranium congeners.

Neither the Mongols (ca.1279) who ruled China
nor the ruling Manchus (ca.1644) were Chinese.
Abortion is fully illegal and punishable in Malta.
Tropical crop trees alone undergo "pink disease."

A cow can be led directly upstairs but never downstairs.
E. A. Poe never solved his "The Mystery of Marie Rogêt."
Frenchmen mainly concentrate mainly on women's derrieres.
You don't contribute to your deductible by means of co-pay.

The jaw of a cat remains unable to move sideways.
Coughs in a theater audience presage/indicate boredom.
Side to side is the means of stacking breadthways.
Slaughter inspections must always be done antemortem.

Spinsters often dream about decorating a nursery.
The Catholic Church excommunicates all IRA men.
Leaving out any material facts—omission—is perjury.
Denial of one's ego is the essential tenet of Zen.

A house fly hums in the middle octave key of F.
The Irish leader voiced his surname *Par*nell. not Par*nell*.
More than 200 medications can make a person deaf.
Glory boy aviators all favor *le manoeuvre chandelle*.

Ovens and clothes dryers are rarely used in Japan.
Antioch, not Jerusalem, centered Gentile Christianity.
It is style for both women and men to wear a caftan.
The success rate is small pleading temporary insanity.

Noah's flood is described as being *five miles* deep!
Japan consumes mostly Bulgarian, not Greek, yogurt.
In pre-waking morning occurs most all REM sleep.
The Votyak people if Russia speak Finnic Udmurt.

TRUISMS II

"Pack my box with five dozen liquor jugs;"
"A quick brown fox jumps over a lazy dog."
The former is one letter shorter, so debugs
the latter, the common pangram demagogue.

Tanning hides in Jewish orthodoxy is an "unclean" profession.
Mormons, Quakers, Methodists, and Shakers are all slang terms.
Donald Trump is impervious to the concept of concession.
Darwin spent most of his life studying, not apes, but earthworms.

Coleridge called *Romans* "the most profound work ever written."
Sherlock Holmes judged E. A. Poe's Dupin a "very inferior fellow."
Cells that are frozen immediately die when someone's frostbitten.
A decadence has always had a connotation of the color yellow.

Marching armies always break stride crossing a bridge.
William Davenant might have been Shakespeare's son.
"Blue tongue," a livestock disease, is work of the biting midge.
In his lifetime, few poems were published by John Donne.

St. Paul's letters were in circulation before the four Gospels.
No quotes from the Apocrypha appear in the New Testament.
The United States has never fully embraced youth hostels.
Native American people badly suffer under constrainment.

Tolstoy, Chekhov, Ibsen, Zola, Joyce,
Conrad, Meredith, Lawrence, Hardy,
the Nobel Prize passed over as choice.
The same with Frost, Proust, Valery,

Henry James, Woolf, Graham Greene,
Proust, W. Stevens, Strindberg, Kafka
Vladimir Nabokov, J. Borges, Twain,
surely the occasion of ironic laughter.

Rouge, an artificial blush that mimics vascularization
in women, a subtle signal of sexual interest or arousal
during the period of their mid-cycle during ovulation,
has become a staple cosmetic, announcing a carousal.

A ship weighs less sailing east than sailing west.
Sweden represents North Korea in western negotiations.
As heavy as tons can weigh a Bald Eagle's nest.
Deafness is a congenital defect in the dog Dalmatians.

Ground chuck by law must be 70% lean.
Northern Chile is dry, southern Chile is mainly wet.
Irving Thalberg refused his name appearing on a movie screen.
No dogs, pigs, or rabbits have the capacity to sweat.

Earth's second most populous country is Bharat.
Tipping in China, not done, is considered a bribe.
An acrobat's tightrope must never be too taut.
The tribe of Levi was the family of Moses's tribe.

Harvard University, long a bastion of Unitarianism,
denying Christ as the Redeemer—academic penury—
is weakly, anachronistically, an advocate of Arianism,
a long outmoded and hateful heresy of the 4th century.

TRUISMS II

The color red on any nautical flag indicates trouble.
The word "*Hell*" means gentle slope in Norwegian.
Women find erotic on a man's cheek a bit of stubble.
W.R. Hearst demanded his editors avoid the word "Depression."

Really good olives are rarely provided in a bar's martini.
James Baldwin hated grits and never ordered fried chicken.
Gentiles think of Jews in a yarmulke as wearing a "beanie."
Arrowroot with more fiber than cornstarch is best to thicken.

General George Custer was addicted to raw wild onions.
Raisins in a food recipe usually indicate Jewish origins.
All European Jews are, factually, all distant cousins.
Live plants and wet items are never allowed in storage bins.

Billionaire Elon Musk has a fixation on the letter X.
The most dignified batik pattern is the *satrio wibowo*.
Male box turtle plastron's are concave, females convex.
Sub-Saharan Africa, oddly, produces the most albino.

Onions are indispensable in the making of rye bread.
Oil companies always stand in the way of environmental health.
The longest of wave lengths belong to the color red.
Crows, who avoid bird feeders, always, and only, eat by stealth.

No true *pissaladière* is ever served with tomato sauce.
The Nobel Prize is usually awarded to safe mediocrities.
Japanese are fanatical is their love (and use) of moss.
Not a single written word exists by philosopher Socrates.

No one defaces more books than librarians.
Joseph Conrad, master of sea tales, was unable to swim.
Free will is the cherished tenet of libertarians.
A queer need for detective novelists is using an anonym.

Patting an elephant's ear will lower his trunk.
Blood sausage never uses the green part of leeks.
Soft clothes or silken are anathema to a monk.
Pentecost is the same as Jewish "Feast of Weeks."

The Sermon on the Mount serves as Torah for Christians.
Galapagos seals are, as a matter of fact, actually sea lions.
The key components of each and every heat engine are pistons.
Touching foreheads is the act of kissing to native Hawaiians.

Sexy Anna May Wong, like all Asian starlets,
was not allowed kiss white men on the screen.
Among Christ's lineage, numbered several harlots.
The floors of ancient Egyptian temples were green.

The color of Earth from space is the color green.
Shrunken head: go-to emblem of Ripley's *Believe It or Not!*
The act of eels mating has never once been seen.
The most complex of all tie knots is the Eldredge knot.

Philip, Duke of Edinburgh abhorred drinking tea.
Japanese break a raw egg over each bowl of sukiyaki.
Buddha's sacred bodhi tree was actually a fig tree.
The light brown always has a hint of *yellow* in khaki.

TRUISMS II

Spaghetti in China (its creator) is 意大利細麵條,
which can be alphabetized as *Yìdàlì xì miàntiáo*.
Papiamento is the odd fusion language of Curacao.
Frogs, according to the Japanese, say "*kero-kero.*"

The best Panama hats, made in Ecuador, are woven
underwater as straw exposed to sun becomes brittle.
Jews may eat no creature whose hooves are cloven.
From the lethal Marburg Virus there is no remittal.

Alligator pears, eaten with salt in Peru, taste like butter.
Truman Capote often used women's rooms in restaurants.
In almost all nation's fables figures an honest woodcutter.
There are no fillings in any French or Spanish croissants.

There are always thirteen steps leading to the gallows.
South America lies distinctly far *east* of North America.
African cuisine serves soups with breadish "swallows."
Ivy League secret societies love the thrill of esoterica.

The Hindu Baniya cult of India never eat red food,
forbidding even veggies which can resemble meat.
Twenty-one days or so is standard for hens to brood.
Of all the meats on earth, the healthiest is crab meat.

Sinkiang, China prevails in the world for brick tea.
The crutch word "like" has polluted American speech.
Carthusia Perfume pervades the island of Capri.
Hornbeam trees are the most popular trees to pleach.

Heavy drug addicts give off an acrid, medicinal odor.
No well-born gentlemen can have an indifferent palate.
No political hack is not, first, a shameless freeloader.
Dark colors were rarely found on an Impressionist's palette.

Goodness speaks in a whisper, but evil shouts.
Balanchine opposed marriage and babies for ballerinas.
Gargoyles essentially function as water spouts.
Mobsters who dispose of bodies are called "cleaners."

No writer understood women better than Thomas Hardy.
Shrewdness in love usually goes with a meanness of spirit.
A distinct language from Italian is spoken in Lombardy.
Nothing of *pure* gold exists in anything less than 24-karat.

Cicero, the Roman, called a library the "soul" of a house.
The great courtesans of history have never been great beauties.
Far too dry to broil is the flesh of a woodland grouse.
Precise moral obligation, not mere work, is implied by *duties*.

Peruvian cotton, with its long fibers, is considered the finest.
Old Hollywood chose Westwood Mortuary, snubbed Forest Lawn.
No true socialist will ever use the expression "Your Highness."
A king in chess can neither be trapped nor captured by a pawn.

Poetaster Maya Angelou was granted a U.S. stamp
printed with words that she'd brazenly plagiarized,
and, although all her work is as musty as afterdamp,
in 2023, there she is on a 25¢ coin, fully canonized!

TRUISMS II

Women in Thomas More's *Utopia* are inferior to men.
A computer mouse stops working when it hits the console.
The very first extinct American bird was the heath hen.
No polar bears ever chose to migrate to the South Pole.

Dr. Seuss was mad for looping, gravity-defying *stacks*!
Royal shrimp, strawberry pop: killer Dick Hickock's last meal.
Actually, keeping our ears untainted and *clean* is earwax.
Inclined planes or rollers worked before the use of the wheel.

Men are never allowed in the Umoja village, Kenya,
Mosquitos have 47 microneedles to saw through skin.
Billie Holiday always wore a trademark white gardenia.
Conquerors F. Pizarro and H. Cortes were next of kin.

Israel refuses to disclose whether it has nuclear weapons.
Jacques Pepin: "Dishwashing should be done only by hand."
Avoiding bloodshed: the primary role of duellists' seconds.
An actual language of symbols is the art of the cattle brand.

England's Victoria Cross, highest award for gallantry,
is made from Russian cannons all seized at Sebastopol.
A São Tomé Grosbeak Neospiza is world's rarest canary.
When born, 90% fully grown are the legs of every foal.

The reverse of a turned pillow is always cooler.
The fish Jesus ate were, almost surely, only tilapia.
No formal education exists to become a jeweler.
No leaves exist bigger than on the palm tree raffia.

A strath in Scotland is a larger valley than a glen.
Chefs allow no wearers of cologne in their kitchens.
It is the clock, not the London tower, that is Big Ben.
Hinduism is the oldest of all the world's religions.

Saying "America," N. Americans never include S. Americans.
In Egyptian hieroglyphics, crows symbolize discord and strife.
Zolgensma (one use: $2.1 million) is costliest of all medicines.
President Donald Trump has faced 3,500 lawsuits in his life.

A mussurana snake will always kill a jararaca snake.
To be "Bourbon" whiskey, it must be made in a new cask.
Ten-feet wide is the standard firefighters' fire break.
Double walls are structurally required in any vacuum flask.

The oldest poem in existence is the Song of Miriam,
as recorded in 15: 20–22 of the holy Book of Exodus.
Muslims on Fridays in Ramadan wear eye collyrium.
Only heroes were able to ride the winged horse, Pegasus.

In the "Borough-English" form of ultimogeniture,
all goods and property belong to the *youngest* son.
St. Joseph is utterly silent throughout all of Scripture,
being spoken of, but of his ever once speaking? None.

1950s *Arizona Highways* photographs are far too bilious.
No Yale Univ. secret society building has any windows.
The U.S. female pro soccer teams are always supercilious.
Refried, black beans are less delicious than softer pintos.

TRUISMS II

Three women in Christ's genealogy were Gentiles,
Canaanites and a Moabite: Tamar, Rahab, and Ruth.
Repeatedly lifting of heavy objects can cause piles.
Grape brandy is commonly used to fortify vermouth.

"Bort" is the umbrella term for non-gem-grade diamonds.
For the best muffins, use yogurt, not buttermilk or milk.
123 decibels: the standard aural reach of a firetruck siren.
It takes 5,000 silkworms to produce 1 1/2 pounds of silk.

A drink to be called Scotch must be made in Scotland.
Oxen are usually yoked by the horns, pulling with their heads.
Any formal sari worn is never mechanically fastened.
All shoeboxes, as to angles, are examples of parallelepipeds.

The highest mountains on Earth are the most recent.
Jesus never once alludes to Joseph as his co-genitor.
Chewing gum in Singapore, illegal, is also indecent.
Motivation alone is the genius's only true competitor.

A falling object always falls east of a vertical line.
Red Delicious and Fuji apples taste flavorless in pies.
It was the bubonic plague put lids on the beer stein.
More Italians than native Argentinians live in Buenos Aires.

Guarani is spoken more than Spanish in Paraguay.
A sentence containing only a gerund is actually missing a main verb.
Fruit, not a seed, a parsley family member, is caraway.
Beggary, in the form of praise, is the beating heart of every blurb.

It takes seven Gentiles to hook a Jew in business,
and eight Jews a calculating Armenian to outfox,
and nine Armenians one Iraqi to best in trickiness
but it takes that lot together one Genovese to top.

Ants pause eight minutes a day, but they never sleep.
Only Joshua and Caleb reached the Land of Canaan.
In Thomas More's *Utopia* is an attack against sheep.
Some part of animal regalia is a must for a shaman.

Whiskey matures only in the cask, not the bottle.
A locust's prime food has always been green wheat.
All of Aquinas's philosophy was based on Aristotle.
In all salt marshes, sediment and detritus accrete.

"*Machupichu*" in Spanish is an offensive racist slur.
Ocean water freezes at a lower temperature than freshwater.
Hogs and cattle are poisoned eating seeds of cocklebur.
Censorship is a subtle implication of a Catholic imprimatur.

Dogs in their wild state growl but never bark.
Egyptian royalty always believed "F" names were lucky.
Nothing can equal Poland's population of the skylark.
Abortion is completely banned in the state of Kentucky.

Uruguayans, who believe artificial heat is unhealthful,
have no stoves or furnaces and no steam-heating plants.
Reliance on emotions in decisions is always unhelpful.
There are (2.5 million for each human) 20 quadrillion ants.

TRUISMS II

A tapir's skin is so thick that, in order to kill it,
it must be shot in the forehead or behind the shoulder.
Faith is an act of the intellect: one cannot will it.
A bride's ideal groom should be eleven years older.

St. Paul in Ephesians 6:5–8 says all Christian slaves
should be obedient and serve one's human master well.
It is held as wicked for Hawaiians to point at graves.
Inharmonic partial tones are the sound of every bell.

Cows grazing in a meadow will never eat buttercups.
Nothing provides better tannin than quebracho wood.
Pedophilia among the clergy is riddled with coverups.
Nothing healthy in any human commerce wears a hood.

Only 8.5% of Americans play the game of golf.
Crows despise all noises louder than themselves,
A bad play or performance elicits many a cough.
One foot is common height of normal bookshelves.

The ancient Romans feared and greatly hated kings.
Supermarket birdseed, cheap, is basically white millet.
Fictitious are V. Nabokov's (cf. *Pale Fire*) waxwings.
Patriot James Otis hated most a British soldier's billet.

Runway models always show a sour, grumpy look.
Modern Germans feel very self-conscious about Jewishness.
Pike are a freshwater fish; saltwater for the snoek,
a torpedo-like shape for both, yet the latter known elusiveness.

The Three Magi probably hailed from far Babylon,
a stronghold of major astral observation at the time.
White is the least employed of any color crayon.
Virtually priceless is the rare 1894 S-Barber dime.

Religious cranks thrive on the Book of Revelation.
A bluebird can perfectly mimic a red-shouldered hawk.
It took ca. three minutes for a Civil War amputation.
A common pedophile fetish is often nothing but a sock.

Vultures, Amazon scavengers, are never killed by natives
Most of the female population in Paraguay smoke cigars.
First-Day Stamp issues are all simulated commemoratives.
Regolith is the name for soil and rock on planet Mars.

On the morning of her wedding, Princess Diana
spotted her gown, a drop of her favorite perfume,
"*Quelques Fleurs*," and in an awkward manner,
covered the spot, a curse, she felt, boding gloom.

The stirringly patriotic "sceptr'd isle" speech,
was voiced by John of Gaunt, a man who spent
the majority of his life in Aquitaine, a breech
of candor that begs the question if well meant.

Salt, which makes ice colder, so also melts it faster.
In no language can be found the letter "Y" doubled.
Buffoonery is always befitting a TV quizmaster.
Emily Dickinson's mother all her life left her troubled.

TRUISMS II

Jaguars particularly hate—and constantly attack—dogs.
A full 80% of earth's sea floor has never been mapped.
No mention in the Hebrew Bible is made of synagogues.
Every inexact word for Gustave Flaubert proved inapt.

Milk should always precede butter when mashing potatoes.
Catholics never sing the altar call hymn, "Just As I Am."
A degree of nicotine can be found in un-ripened tomatoes.
The prose of Elbert Hubbard had the quality of buckram.

The Earth was officially created October 23, 4004 B.C.,
according to an Act of the English Parliament.
Coral itself *is* held to be one of the animals in the Coral Sea.
Mother's care of a child is life's prime determinant.

Chilean government. gets most revenue from nitrates.
A jaguar can hold its breath underwater for 20 minutes.
The Corvidae family of passerine birds never migrates.
Demarcation is completely arbitrary in all city limits.

A Ramadan fast must be broken by eating dates.
Population of bacteria culture doubles every 2 minutes.
Candy corn was the favorite snack of Norman Bates.
It is a serious six-step move pouring a glass of Guinness.

Sous vide theory: cook meat low at its final resting temp.
Each Skull & Bonesman gets a grandfather clock at initiation.
No longer considered a narcotic plant is industrial hemp.
Family descent traced through a maternal line is called enation.

Micah 5:2 in the Hebrew Bible prophesizes Christ.
No body skeletons were ever found on the RMS *Titanic*.
Gadgets sold on TV all cost "$19.95, bargain-priced."
Death in crowds is always the result of sudden panic.

St. Augustine never once identified his mistress
of 15 years, nor the name of the one son they had.
Disquiet is perpetually the feline state of estrous.
Four times a year are the moves of a usual nomad.

Every banker is by very definition a usurer.
The Holy Koran is incantatory poetry, not prose.
No derivation can explain the term Hoosier.
Women's nylons were far sexier than pantyhose.

Nothing irks a Jew like the use of B.C. and A.D.
There are 580 characters in Tolstoy's *War and Peace*.
No man-made water pump can equal that of a tree.
Sheep's wool is natural—strictly artificial is fleece.

Herbert Spencer provocatively walked against
worshippers heading toward church on Sundays.
On the Chilean altiplano the sun is most intense.
The Boston Marathon is always held on Mondays.

Protestantism pays little attention at all to angels.
The quality of Sunday morning radio is horrendous.
No American appliance stores ever sell mangles.
Most fungi molds are multinucleated, filamentous.

TRUISMS II

Nietzsche had a special hatred for Christian thought.
Red oak is far softer and less expensive than white oak.
Brits before adding water put loose tea in a teapot.
Deuteronomy forbids dissimilar animals being yoked.

Convictions more than lies are the enemies of truth.
No PETA person can also possibly be pro-abortion.
Born a Gentile was Jewish Scriptural heroine Ruth.
Arthritis is the sly gift of a ballerina's life of torsion.

Cainites, a gnostic sect, revered the apostle, Judas.
Drug addicts make addictive fentanyl *from* fentanyl.
Respiratory problems decrease by taking sambucas.
Identical twins are very rarely completely identical.

Dutch men are the world's tallest people.
Tesla claimed he could illuminate all of Earth.
There are always ten stripes on a potato beetle.
Of the mineral Kyawthuite, there is a dearth.

Unions are not allowed in Argentina, Algeria,
Turkey, Russia, Panama, Ecuador, Myanmar,
Egypt, India, Zimbabwe, Kazakhstan, Arabia,
Bangladesh, Paraguay, Colombia, and Quatar.

Calvin's Geneva was a blueprint for the Third Reich.
Actor Henry Irving judged Shakespeare superior to Christ.
No United States employee is ever allowed to strike.
Loud rapping is traditionally the signal of a poltergeist.

George Moore's novel *The Brook Kerith* claims
that Jesus, spiritually disenchanted, had regret.
Secret society members love adopting alias names.
The Our Father urged us to forgive (*not forget!*)

Noam Chomsky dismissed the pure behaviorist
B. F. Skinner as a mentally deficient amoeboid.
War is a common solution to a hyper-nationalist.
His weak father was a lifelong bugbear to Freud.

When Quaker George Fox stated "Verily," it stood.
Sleuth Mr. Moto's favorite drink was a tall glass of milk.
The tastiest honey is from Tasmanian leatherwood.
Agave fiber, organic, is the source of pure vegetable silk.

Andrew Wyeth never let his models have an opinion.
Jokes in *The New Yorker* confounded A. N. Whitehead.
Praying with folded hands has no Scriptural sanction.
All cultures and nations consume some form of bread.

Joe Biden, an old man, wears aviator glasses to look cool.
There were 60 million slaves (1 in 3) in the Roman Empire.
Any region rare or remote is often referred to as *thule*.
Only one player in 123 years of MLB has struck an umpire.

Ministers often identified George III with cruel Pharaoh
and struggling American colonists with the Hebrew.
Richer in vitamins and minerals than meat is bone marrow.
A taboo is to pass ají chili sauce hand-to-hand in Peru.

TRUISMS II

Dante Alighieri had no knowledge at all of Greek.
Nevada and Wyoming, alone, have no roller coaster regulations.
The rarest hairline is said to be the "widow's peak."
Communication is in fact hampered, not helped, by abbreviations.

Etonians mainly attend college at Christ Church, Oxford.
Wodehouse's Jeeves is a gentleman's gentleman, *not* a butler.
Men during the simple act of hugging are always awkward.
General U.S. Grant during battle condemned the Jewish sutler.

Dogma, by definition, crassly rigidifies all thought.
"Something's wrong with the mouth:" said of all portraits.
It is impossible to *untie* a double fisherman's knot.
Solely constructed to be *defended* is the nature of a fortress.

U. S. State Fairs have always marked the end of summer.
The Hemlock Society recommends death by drugs/plastic bag.
Lead (origin of the occupation), is never used by a plumber.
The nation of Nepal has the only non-rectangular national flag.

No memoirist's account is not completely revisionist.
Zion, say Mormons, will be built in the United States.
The 1933 Double Eagle is the jackpot for a numismatist.
Madjools, hard to grow, are the crown jewels of dates.

Everyone's weight-loss journey is completely different.
John Updike compared a vaginal interior to a ballet slipper.
Apache tribes, in all matters, were perpetually itinerant.
It is an astral error to call a "constellation" the Big Dipper.

No figurative art is ever represented in a mosque.
Aristotle Onassis was never mentioned at Jaqueline Onassis's funeral.
Completely now obsolete is the public telephone kiosk.
The word *nulla* was used to specify zero and not a Roman numeral.

The country of Australia is wider than the moon.
The Kaaba, now all black, was once multi-colored.
Originally, 3 p.m. was the standard time of noon.
Raw food in the fridge should always be covered.

Avocados are, in fact, berries, not vegetables.
Band music's set in flat keys, orchestral in sharp keys.
The Chinese breed geese as watchdog-sentinels.
Unique as fingerprints are kneecaps of human knees.

Headphones can increase the bacteria in a person's ears.
The best genealogist in all fiction was Anthony Trollope.
Women comprise 70% of lawyers and judges in Algiers.
Terminology in L. R. Hubbard's *Dianetics* is codswollop.

J. P. Sousa believed the marches he wrote divinely inspired and in all his letters he wrote on only one-half side of a page.
Overweight women in Pacifica are generally most desired.
Gender plays no part in the bones of every human rib cage.

Petrol is much cheaper than water in Algeria.
Froot Loops are all the same flavor despite different colors.
Direct eye contact is held as rude in Nigeria.
Imams are holy leaders but in Islam *all men* can be mullahs.

TRUISMS II

The waitstaff at Fortnum & Mason's still wear tail-coats.
Americans always mispronounce the word *mischievous*.
The Old West pioneer food staple was buckwheat groats.
New England Yankees are and were, financially, risk averse.

No gorilla field-studying woman isn't fully neurotic.
In readings, Dickens allowed *no one* to sit behind him.
Television is a religion for the illiterately hypnotic.
Vigor is enthusiasm, but energy is the meaning of vim.

No worse weeds are found in any garden than docks.
The title of beadle in England is not an honorary one.
No distinction in the Trinity existed for George Fox.
Light takes eight minutes to reach Earth from the Sun.

The priesthood of Levi was predated by Melchizedek,
which sanctioned Christ, being of Judah and his tribe,
to be High Priest and Messiah, in fulfillment, by beck,
as both Psalm 110:4 and Revelation 5:5 so proscribe.

Derricks, the tall lifting cranes used on today's docks,
take their name from a 17th-century Tyburn hangman.
Most gambling casinos have neither windows nor clocks.
Once in freshwater, food is discounted by all salmon.

One must be casual about money to buy organic food.
Selfridge's Dept. Store, by fiat, doesn't sell furniture.
Insurance firms and wily lawyers constantly collude.
Totalitarianism demands a follower be a worshipper.

Judge Thurgood Marshall, although both were black,
detested his dim replacement, Judge Clarence Thomas.
Utterly meaningless was the invented word, Kodak.
The premise of a political vow is ever broken promise.

Queen Elizabeth of York, the wife of Henry VII,
Henry VIII's mother, is queen on the playing cards.
Many discern Divine Guidance in a clock's 11:11.
Woven into the fabric are the patterns of jacquards.

Taking College Boards, it us inadvisable to guess.
The Robber Bridegroom: smut by the Brothers Grimm.
Rafters offer less support than a solid roof truss.
A hyponym is in fact more specialized than a hypernym.

Psalm 119:36 warns against the waste of watching T.V.
To aid in a crime is to assist, to encourage is to abet.
The Eiffel Tower was constructed to battle wind, not gravity.
Poet and tunesmith of "America the Beautiful" never met.

One in every five people in the world is Chinese.
U.S. Marines roll up (and down) their sleeves twice a year.
Abortion remains utterly anathema to the Maltese.
Silverware is anything silver, but cutlery alone is flatware.

"Full gender neutrality" allows both sexes anything.
The Irish go in big for sentimental sampler quotes.
Most common Punjabi surnames are Kaur and Singh.
Animal feed constitutes 90% percent of grown oats.

A thatched reed roof can last 300 years, straw fifty.
No writer laid out maps for a reader like A. Trollope.
"Cautious" is the most risible euphemism for thrifty.
Red organs—male, white—indicate a female scallop.

Aimee Semple McPherson, the Canadian Evangelist,
admitted an affair with goofy comedian Milton Berle.
Charging fees for being silent is one ploy of an analyst.
There are no hereditary peers for the rank of an Earl.

It is always fully folly to walk in front of a beehive.
Acoustics at Wagner's Bayreuth were incomprehensibly bad.
Two refrigerators were the size of first hard drive.
"Beautiful" is the common response to songs that are sad.

Fastidiousness is the prime characteristic of the dilettante.
A "pollywog," unlike a "shellback," has not crossed the equator
Only a sparkling Italian wine may qualify as a *spumante*.
An executor's role is effective only after the death of a testator.

Marzipan is a bastard Teutonic innovation for marchpane.
Berlioz's "Symphonie Fantastique" is pagan and debauched.
The best remedy for altitude sickness is the drug cocaine.
In the Garden of Gethsemane, Jesus *needed* to be watched.

Acorns are a traditional Native American food.
Persons who enjoy meetings should never be chosen to lead.
It is only the deceitful who, by definition, collude.
There are never exactly a hundred legs found on a centipede.

Gertrude Stein's bizarre novel, *Ida*, is inexplicable.
Thawing any food in warm water is never safe.
The Squire SS100S Stronghold padlock is unpickable.
No 19th-century novel was ever missing a waif.

Wallace Stevens, a "confector of satisfying fictions,"
loved to mock himself in poems with ironic names—
Dr. Homburg; Canon Aspirin; Professor Eucalyptus;
and Ariel—in which they dabbled in aesthetic games.

Hybridization dilutes the scent of roses and lilacs.
American men wearing Bermuda shorts resemble toddlers.
No horns are more treasured than that of an addax.
It is a taboo in England to whistle in the shop of cobblers.

Ezekiel had wheels for eyes, ate a scroll,
cooked his food over human excrement,
laid on his side 430 days, his wife's soul
he never mourned, and all his hair he rent.

Yahweh's commands to Hosea all appear insane.
All writing in any form is ideologically motivated.
You act below your dignity whenever you *deign*.
All fashion is ephemeral as it is inevitably dated.

The wish is forever the father to the deed.
Sighting an owl in Kenya brings instant foreboding.
A neep is a rutabaga is a turnip is a swede.
Muzzle-loading is much riskier than breech loading.

TRUISMS II

Whichever way water may flow it always marries turf.
Much of feminism constitutes a theology of male evil.
Waves, when they are not crashing, are in fact not surf.
Rational thought consistently finds dogma medieval.

Music, as it is played, is theory that ratifies itself.
Sauerbraten is soulless without added gingersnaps.
Money or riches gained dishonestly alone is pelf.
Continuous motion is the law in all football snaps.

A platypus has never killed a human, despite the fact
that the odd creature has a toxic spur on its back ankle.
Good luck accrues to anyone touching a hunchback.
The severest insults are those that slowly fester, rankle.

A ship's cook traditionally shines the ship's bell.
Rock and ice are the primitive forms of bread and water.
The dressed skin of only a large animal is a fell.
No one not arrested may be entered into a police blotter.

The Portuguese Navy is the oldest navy in the world.
In Scotland, actors must not wear green shoes on stage.
A cat registers maximum comfort when sleeping curled.
Value in the United States has not purchase in old age.

Human body fat could produce a full seven bars of soap.
All sheep are indistinguishable from one another.
Slackline walking is less difficult than walking a tightrope.
Habitat loss dooms the existence of the piping plover.

No U.S. President and Vice President can ever ride together.
While Joseph Conrad wrote in English, he thought in French.
A bird's tail is the primary projection of the flight feather.
Vegetables are blanched to pale, but only the fearful *blench*.

Italians do not employ a spoon when forking spaghetti.
The greatest wars in the world were fought over pepper.
Legends of St. Francis were compiled in 1476 as *fioretti*.
India, Brazil, and Indonesia are modern lands of the leper.

One's right elbow on the table is seen as vulgar in Chile.
Poll taxes have consistently been a secret form of racism.
The lily to medieval minstrels was the "daffadowndilly."
Facial blandness in a 9-month child is a sign of autism.

On the Mount of Olives, pious Jews all want to be buried.
Men dressed as women was against the law in the 1950s.
St. Paul declared it was good for man never to be married.
Corruption in English literature is seen inevitable in cities.

Canaan, not "promised," was *stolen* by the Hebrews.
No place is more Catholic than the island-state of Malta.
Only the tunnels of moles are used by (adapting) shrews.
Wood alone—oak or maple—constitutes a Wiccan altar.

General Westmoreland dopily claimed the Tet Offensive
in January 1968 was a crushing defeat—*for the Vietcong!*
The lust for money in every politician is hypertensive.
The "mother grapevine" of the U.S. South is scuppernong.

TRUISMS II

Milton Berle's segue line from joke to joke was "I was . . ."
There are no photographs of humorist Mark Twain smiling.
The elemental excuse for almost all children is "because."
Accommodation and compromise occasions reconciling.
\
The Romans all used their urine to whiten their teeth.
Ford Madox Ford claimed Joseph Conrad hated the sea.
Encircling stands as the symbolic bond of the wreath.
Cameroon and Nigeria find it impossible to agree.

Most of the cash from England's Great Train Robbery
in 1963, worth $7 million today, has never been found.
Women were never active in ancient Greek society.
Atmosphere for painters is affected by a background.

There is no outstanding French-Canadian novel.
The Eiffel Tower serves not a single utilitarian purpose.
In every U.S. state, spanking at home is lawful.
Eating peanuts backstage is held as bad luck in a circus.

The Statue of Liberty is hopelessly out of scale.
The Gospels may be inspired but not dictated by God.
Never replicated are the tails or flukes of a whale.
An unfair advantage is considered "constructive fraud."

Having an enemy, alone made a Prussian feel alive.
Hard core feminists show teach men the nature of disgust.
Books, subject to Hawaii's humidity, never thrive.
Iridium, the most corrosive-resistant metal, cannot rust.

Curtailment begs to see us succeed only by what we cede.
Hunter Thompson's first novel, *Prince Jellyfish*, never saw print.
Anubis, a sacred creature, say scholars, was an Egyptian canid,
the African jackal, tall ears, long snout, a dreadful golden squint.

Cornelius, a Roman centurion, was first of converted Gentiles.
A California condor, flying, rarely flaps its (110 inch) wings.
The great 20th-century Irish writers flourished strictly as exiles.
Antonin Dvořák's "Serenade" was composed solely for strings.

F. W. Woolworth, who founded five-and-ten-cent stores,
paid for his N.Y. building in cold cash—all $13.5 million.
The oldest playing-card game in Great Britain is All Fours.
Any seat behind the horse or motorcycle rider is a pillion.

Celebrities all feign smugly to "know" each other.
Strop a knife blade to sharpen at about a 20° angle.
Envy yearns, jealousy hates, each the other's brother.
Capitalism, at bottom, is the fine art of the strangle.

There are neither forests nor rivers in Malta.
Dueling is legally allowed in Washington and Texas.
Charles De Gaulle was offended he was not invited to Yalta.
Manipooraga is the chakra linked to the solar plexus.

An ostrich's eyes are bigger than its brain.
Country singers all feel obliged to record "America the Beautiful."
Strangers are "from away" to people in Maine.
An anti-bacterial function is the structure of the human cuticle.

TRUISMS II

Vanity is the stretching outreach that identifies a midget.
Nicholson Baker, who wrote about Updike, seldom reads him.
A *bit* corresponds to a binary digit, a *ban* to a decimal digit.
The felt hats of most *noir* detectives always had a snap brim.

Mad ambition predominantly antedates all celebrity.
Saturn could float in water because it's mostly made of gas.
No prowess in a left-hander can be termed dexterity.
Rare is the fishing lure that can fool a Large Mouth Bass.

Techno-utopians tend to believe all humans are flawed.
The more serious the offense, the fewer steps apart in dueling.
An orthodox Jew is forbidden to mention the word "God."
The need to socialize is the ugly downside of vanpooling.

Students in Japan all attend school 243 days a year.
Emily Dickinson's solitary companion for 17 years
was Carlo, her Newfie dog, named from *Jane Eyre*.
Balance relies on the vestibular system in our ears.

No Mafia boss or *capo* ever *directly* orders a hit.
It was Paul Dombey's daughter who mattered, not his son.
Toxic cyanide can be found in every stone fruit pit.
Rumor and gossip are the primary causes of any bank run.

A snapped sweet birch branch smells like fresh root beer.
Young people are never seen in California's Palm Springs.
Claude Debussy, who could not swim, composed *La Mer*.
Asian cultures dispense with wearing engagement rings.

Beets benefit in earthy taste by hot cooking in ashes.
Buster Keaton had only one day of formal education.
Some sexy women have distichiasis: double eyelashes.
Heartiness belongs in Irish pubs, fit for compotation.

Never named are protagonists in *The Tell-Tale Heart*,
The Yellow Wallpaper; Rebecca; Roxana by Defoe;
The Power and the Glory, most of Sam Beckett's art;
Saramago's *Blindness; Boys and Girls* by Alice Munro.

Shaking hands with women is forbidden to Orthodox Jews.
To have to *search* for happiness *breeds* unhappiness.
John O'Hara's pleas for a Yale honorary degree? Refused.
Never picking up a tab rates very high in shabbiness.

Evelyn Waugh pronounced that it was *neurosis* in the air
in New York City that all natives there mistook for energy.
Men, not women, make 90% of developmental software.
Saturated fats and nitrates are a major cause of lethargy.

An Ultracapacitor can deliver energy a hundred times faster
than an equivalent weight battery and be charged as quickly.
No low in showbusiness is lower than television quizmaster.
Turtle breath can be held for 7 hours with an Olive Ridley.

Men out at sea read an inordinate amount of books.
There is no special word for "adopted" sons or daughters.
Nuttiness in lima beans is unsurpassed in Fordhooks.
"Adverse possession," proven, allows rights to squatters.

TRUISMS II

Japan tops the list of most sought for dining destinations.
Grieving Dani women in Indonesia cut off a fingertop.
Protest, never attest, is the deep soul of demonstrations.
A horse's shoulder alone may be hit with a riding crop.

Chef Julia Child thought vile canned tuna fish in water.
Almost 90% of the world's population lives in the north.
32,000 pigs are killed a day in the Smithfield N.C. slaughter.
Heedlessness connotes a mood in those who sally forth.

A "buttload" is a real unit of measurement—ca. 126 gallons.
Clambake (1967) is the all-time low in Elvis Presley movies.
Raptors and birds of prey alone have—not claws—but talons.
Three carats (for chromium cracks) are hard to find in rubies.

Just as the destruction of Jewry provided the necessary
rise and expansion of Nazism, so the ethnic cleansing
of Germans was a precondition—collateral accessory--
for the Stalinization of Poland, the parallel depending.

Shandong cooking fixes heavily on seafood.
Taiwan cuisine tends to skew much sweeter.
In Zhejiang food, fish. and rice always collude,
and chilies in Sichuan convey numbing heater.

Nothing not a secret interested writer Patricia Highsmith.
In India, nothing is more popular than Elvis Presley movies.
Pith helmets are made of the spongy cork called *sholapith*.
Any accumulation that is foul is, technically, a "colluvies."

Ultimately comic are the geometric configurations of sex.
The world of sports memorabilia is rife with hucksters.
The nave for catechumens, all unbaptized for the narthex.
Social acceptance is low for female orchestra conductors.

Consent is the central mode of feminine culture.
Red Sox star Ted Williams never kissed anyone on the lips.
Toxic bacteria die in the stomach acid of a vulture
Eastern Orthodox Liturgy never mentions the Apocalypse.

Ellison's *Invisible Man;* Yevgeny Zamyatin's *We;*
Notes from the Underground; Camus' *The Stranger;*
The Aspern Papers; The Road by Cormac McCarthy;
Ayn Rand's *Anthem;* Stresser's *Code Name Danger.*

Inverts have a psychoneurotic paraphilia for islands.
Gambling losses are not deductible from one's income.
Scottish Gaelic alone was originally spoken in the Highlands.
Iconography of Shiva is linked mainly with the lingam.

The Temple of Jerusalem was built by Herod the Great,
an Idumean, descendant of the Edomites, God's enemy
and of Israel Nation, the offspring of Esau, the cut-rate
twin brother of Jacob and a man of ignominious destiny.

The Maltese tongue, a dialect version of Arabic,
is the only Semitic language written in a Latin script.
Radical thought speaks the vocabulary of a heretic.
The true punch of a letter is always in the postscript.

TRUISMS II

Dying is the one thing in life you don't have to do:
it is, in every mortal instance, *always done for you!*
The best-selling color of women's sweaters is blue.
The cowardly hunter ever cravenly employs a battue.

Thunder and lightning petrified James Joyce.
The most intense of wars are always civil wars.
Legal contexts always opt for the passive voice.
Killing whales is still a business in the Azores.

Gold, a dubious investment, yields no revenue.
Surrogacy, illegal, is a punishable crime in Italy.
A grizzly bear claw necklace honored the bravest Sioux.
No Balkan treaty has not been negotiated bitterly.

Hatters, breathing fumes, often become mentally ill.
Louis Armstrong took laxatives every day of his life.
Rhizomes make savagely invasive the lovely cranesbill.
The Jewish Sadducees believed there was no afterlife.

Obese people have proven very hard to kidnap.
The head shots on Lincoln and Booth were exactly the same.
A dreadlock necessity is a fashionable rastacap.
Philip Roth's character in *Everyman* is never given a name.

In Christianity, Easter always falls on the first Sunday
after the first full moon on or after the Vernal Equinox.
Most suicides occur in the month of March, on Monday.
It is the dry seeds in Crotolaria that make the rattlebox.

No fiercer fighting fish than the broadbill swordfish exists.
Cooked cornstarch texture is more velvety than flour-based roux.
Liberals to even the sanest of Republicans are bolshevists.
The first plant to re-green after Hiroshima atomized was bamboo.

No high leap of a fish outjumps that of a mako shark.
Cornstarch, virtually flavorless, abets a Chinese kitchen.
The hypocenter for almost all pedophiles is a public park.
For ages, the prime fertilizer was the guano of a pigeon.

J. P. Marquand's Mr. Moto, is not a Japanese family name,
merely part of a surname, such as Yamamoto or Matsumoto.
No ownership is fully guaranteed by the deed of a quitclaim.
No sleek tail fins have ever outmatched Chrysler's De Soto.

The Prodigal Son's envious brother was also a prodigal son.
Black mothers invent names to make their kids seem original.
Many Revels wore blue, Union gray at the battle of Bull Run.
Southeast Asia is the ancient origin of the Australian aboriginal.

The truest personal journeys are ones that are made within.
There is always in the provocative a deep need for a curtain.
Christopher Hitchens felt being called "Chris" unmanned him.
Having to persuade yourself of something proves it uncertain.

The Chief Priests, enemies of Jesus, were Sadducees,
while the Hebrew Scribes were primarily Pharisees.
With a whopping 90% fat, there is, by way of grease,
the nutritional equivalent of Vaseline in cream cheese.

TRUISMS II

Wall Street's private knowledge fleeces public ignorance.
The state of Illinois has sent the most governors to jail.
Circumstantial evidence rides on the wave of inference.
The position of aircraft pilot is almost exclusively male.

A human cremation yields roughly about six pounds of ashes.
By *Mizraim* in the Old Testament, the Hebrews meant Egypt.
Surprisingly high is the mineral content in refined molasses.
Clepe (to name, call) in Middle English has given us "yclept."

The 1848 pan-revolutions began in Palermo, Italy.
Genius worship: the infallible sign of an uncreative age.
Ulster's nine counties are unified by way of bigotry.
$25,605 is the salary of 16-year-old Congressional page.

Empires by definition compulsively strike down rebels.
Pacemakers—implants—will blow up during a cremation.
Mary Cassatt's finished work was primarily in pastels.
Gay identity was once identified by the green carnation.

The frail Trillium is considered the flower of bisexuality.
Socialism found its feet in the 1848 European revolutions.
Nothing is more debilitating than other people's creativity.
Guilty personalities find a compulsory need for ablutions.

Onan was put to death by Yahweh, not for masturbating,
but for law breaking, the threat to disrupt family lineage.
Excessive optimism is, ironically, extremely enervating.
Good looks give an individual a perpetual advantage.

No penguin has never witnessed a polar bear.
The U. S. Marine Corps never experienced a mutiny.
Old women insist female strength is lost by hair.
No processed meats can stand up to close scrutiny.

The Statue of Liberty, pre-oxidized, was reddish brown.
Britain has not a single law *fully* protecting free speech.
The sentence "Blessed are the meek" employs an adnoun.
No braided basket does not involve the use of the pleach.

Every country where child poverty exists is corrupt.
Hasidic Jews are forbidden to use any electronic device.
A gallstone can painfully block the pancreatic duct.
The human scalp is by far the preferred domain of lice.

The Hays Office allowed no double beds in movies,
no race-mixing, no lustful kissing, no risqué speech,
no superfluous use of liquor, nude dancing floozies,
suggestive ogling, ridicule of religion or its breach.

No bull is ever tortured or killed in Portuguese bullfights.
Jesus only one time healed a fresh wound (Luke 22:47–53).
The Western Taipan has the most lethal of all snake bites.
Unctuous manners invariably (and secretly) mask villainy.

On November 11, Brits all pause silent for two minutes.
A plowman looking back always cuts a crooked furrow.
In the United States cannot be found true (finch) linnets.
A donkey—but not a mule—is the very same as a *burro*.

TRUISMS II

Maine is the only United States state to border one state.
Elijah was the prophet who meted out Yahweh's reprisals.
Paranoia nixes a bridge or highway across the Bering Strait
Airport departure levels are higher than that of arrivals.

Prince Henry "the Navigator" never boarded a ship or set sail.
Our Mutual Friend, a solecism, should be "our *common* friend."
A solid white color is virtually never found on a Clydesdale.
Nylon monofilament often badly weakens a "fishermen's bend."

A single angel slaughtered 185,000 Assyrian soldiers
(see 2 Kings 19:35) in the course of a single night.
Women are said to love male large muscular shoulders.
A human being's most elemental dream is about flight.

Cunning is the dark sanctuary of incapacity.
A full fifty-seven percent of the Earth is fully uninhabited.
A stated policy in *Mein Kampf* was mendacity.
Brightness in diamonds is not linked to the many-faceted.

The Emancipation Proclamation freed only *Southern* slaves,
left slavery untouched in the border states, and that depended
upon a Union military victory, ignoring all bondage enclaves
elsewhere that, only later, the 13th Amendment fully rescinded.

In 1914 Trotsky was cast as an extra in early U.S. movies.
The W in the acronym WASP is gratuitous and redundant.
Mahatma Gandhi's face appears on bills of all Indian rupees.
Dead plants compost best on conditions superincumbent.

Hyphenated Americans are immigrants and latecomers.
No ethnic group exists here called "British-Americans."
The full population on Cape Cod triples during summers.
Advice is inevitably variable with alternative medicines.

E. Nesbit, a passionate defender of girls in her books,
opposed the cause of women's suffrage, she claimed,
because women could swing Tory, with like outlooks
thus hurting the Socialist cause, thus brutally maimed.

The avocado, a fruit, ripens only after it is picked.
East Jerusalem is the capital of the State of Palestine.
Policies at the Korean DMZ will never derestrict.
At Oxford tutorials, one is expected to drink wine.

A bad reputation for jamming followed the Sten gun.
The most common crime in the Depression was theft of coal.
Mockery was the main method of H. L. Mencken.
A rowlock is a fulcrum is an oarlock is a pivot point is a thole.

Just as the destruction of Jewry was necessary for the rise
and expansion of Nazism, the ethnic cleansing of Germans
was a precondition for the Stalinization of Poland, all lies
to the contrary, proving secretly whatever fate determines.

Voltaire thought Judaism was the root of all religious evil.
More than a full 60% of Americans are clinically obese.
Gasoline engines are forty percent less efficient than diesel.
To be called "Morris" is the bane of people named Maurice.

TRUISMS II

Cruelty always lurks at the base of people who tease.
The correct term for chicken cacciatore is "*alla cacciatora.*"
Asian cuisines give no attention on menus to cheese.
A lamprey's suction rasp is fierce; not that of a mild remora.

Jesus never one mentions the great metropolis of Rome.
To convert knots into stature miles/hour, multiply by 1.51.
Americans dislike "house," cornily prefer to say home.
Insect blood is nearly always green—it lacks hemoglobin.

Agatha Christie's novels betray an anti-Jewish bias.
The simplest of all emulsion sauces is a vinaigrette.
An ascetic penitentially sleeps on a pallet or palliasse.
No creature on earth has a crazier eye than an egret.

Belgian "french fries"—the best—are cooked in ox fat.
No modern girl or woman has ever been christened Jezebel.
JFK who went bareheaded killed the fashion of the hat.
Daulatdia in Dacca, Bangledesh is the world's largest brothel.

Christopher Hitchens who referred to Christianity,
coldly, as a "bastardization of primitive Judaism"
and vilified both major faiths for their inhumanity,
was a Jew baptized a Christian, a double schism.

Reader's Digest is backed by the conservative, low-brow CIA.
Remorse is sorrow for what one did, regret for what one didn't.
Wimbledon in England was originally a club to play croquet.
No medical use has been approved of the species peppermint.

Palestine, cruelly, is no longer named on any 21st c. maps.
Amount of hydrogen a fat contains determines its saturation.
After dinner, Germans invariably take a shot of schnapps.
Survival is scant in most cases of lower limb amputation.

Of two Gomers in the Hebrew Bible, one's male, one female.
One should always start cooking dried beans in cold water.
Nowhere does harmful bacteria flourish more than on a handrail.
Gray is of the color black its grudging but arrogant daughter.

The Declaration of Independence that he helped write
was a document that Robert Livingston never signed.
It is the vacuum in a jar makes the jar lid far too tight.
A seller always praises the feet of the horse that's blind.

France outlawed all slavery in 1807, the British in 1833,
but it took the U. S. December 6, 1865, 13th Amendment.
Brittle wood makes for bad lumber from any Sequoia tree.
Intention is what in abstruse legalese is called "intendment."

20 catches in a game is the NFL record for receptions.
The entire Hebrew Bible is a long polemic against Egypt.
Objectivity—fact—is perpetually altered by perceptions.
The passage of time ever makes a mockery of any secret.

Mormons preach good Negroes become white in heaven.
A human crime is the compulsion to blab in a committee.
The only prime number that is followed by a cube is seven.
Three states can claim to own the province of Sioux City.

TRUISMS II

A lavender marriage is a lesbian marrying a homosexual man.
Islam is a plagiarism and mutation of Judaism and Christianity.
Severely dry skin on an individual will never quite properly tan.
War, for its death and destruction, is man's ultimate profanity.

Arthur Rimbaud was the first to export coffee from Ethiopia.
Israeli Jews are a *part of* the diaspora, not an escape from it.
Every map should depict an altruistic region named Utopia.
How high? Sea level to summit. How tall? Base to summit.

Thomas Jefferson believed that a huge mountain of salt
existed way out west, 180 miles long and 45 miles wide.
All clerestory windows owe full fealty to a ribbed vault.
The Mediterranean Sea is not subject to the forces of tide.

A Côtes-du-Rhone is the perfect wine with a Daube.
True hares (*Lepus timidus*) do not exist in the United States.
Lack of reason is much more likely the larger the mob.
Ignorance trumps intellectual heft in U.S. Presidential debates.

To serve Guinness Stout in a non-tulip glass is a crime.
Ackee fruit is poisonous if either overripe or underripe.
Four o'clock p.m. is considered proper English tea time.
No photograph has ever been clearer than a Daguerrotype.

The number 80 in French is complicatedly four 20s.
Radio waves, if not absorbed, travel on and on forever.
Only in 1943 were minted zinc-coated steel pennies.
One or some or every or all are covered by *whatsoever*.

Ipswich, Massachusetts has more "First Period"
(UK) houses in the U.S. in what was originally
seen as British colonial North America interior,
built well, continually, and showing no fragility.

No married couple doesn't harbor ineradicable resentments.
Mohammed forbade drinking wine but recommended vinegar.
A good reporter is ever vying for the dangerous assignments.
Preliminary drawings for frescos are usually done in sinopia.

Cold is the enemy of homemade mayonnaise.
Oafs who say "between him and I" think they're speaking posh.
Heathens always call Christmas "the holidays."
French slang for Nazis was *caboche* (rascals) or, short, "bosch."

"Phase oil," an unhealthy artificial melted butter,
is the fat secret of the fast-food restaurant industry.
Eight letters alone are the legacy of Jacob Hutter.
States' Rights is a dysphemism for white supremacy.

The most successful D-Day landing was on Utah Beach.
Ernest Hemingway used language as *a style* of writing.
Wood commonly used to smoke herring is copper beech.
Groupers swallow their prey and never go in for biting.

Native Americans, sadly, are rarely honored as role models.
Cartoon characters only—always—have three fingers.
It will take 450 years for nature to dissolve all plastic bottles.
The smell of cooking kidneys never disperses but lingers.

TRUISMS II

Adolf Hitler's favorite author was Arthur Schopenauer.
Crêpes are eaten on February 20, i.e., Candlemas Day
in France, celebrating the annual feast of *Chandeleur*.
Any illegal alien to the US who expresses fear can stay.

The craft of journalism, by the relentless culling of time,
is always dated and is the writing form that is first to go.
Nothing in foods or nature can duplicate the taste of lime.
Sixty percent of sound can be absorbed by muffling snow.

No United States man-of-war has ever faced a mutiny.
The dear sister of the copper bowl is the balloon whip.
Loudness of volume inevitably compromises euphony.
Naval pedantry insists on "vessel" to describe a ship.

Queen Victoria of England had a fifty-inch waistline.
The slang word "pete" in thievery parlance means a safe.
Moonshine, a misnomer, is but the reflection of sunshine.
Condescension is implied in a special favor to *vouchsafe*.

Gutenberg printed only 135 Bibles on paper, 45 on vellum.
On pennies, Lincoln—alone of presidential coins—faces right.
Every last human movement is controlled by the cerebellum.
It is the blackness at the back of a mirror that controls the light.

Fructose is the #1 source of calories in the United States,
mainly coming from (HFCS)—high fructose corn syrup.
80% of one's body muscles are worked using roller skates.
History was altered by the mere invention of the stirrup.

Zombification characterizes all catwalk fashion models.
The Brink's robbers all wore Captain Marvel masks.
Huge sums are given for straight-sided Coca-Cola bottles.
No one can explain the linguistic origins of Basque.

"Coast-to-Coast" radio show: 60% commercials, 40% bullshit.
Clairvoyant Edgar Cayce studied textbooks by sleeping on them.
Caraway seeds are the *sine qua non* of Scandinavian aquavit.
Legal citations prefer *idem* ("the same") to its cognate *ibidem*.

Beer in a can, peculiarly, is never drunk through a straw.
Pharisees believed in resurrection, the Sadducees denied it.
Dubiety is the controlling emotion of every father-in-law.
The Solomonic solution—a settlement—is always divide it.

Isak Dinesen ate only oysters and drank only champagne.
Malaysia and Indonesia are filled with niggling differences.
Fair compensation is legally required in eminent domain.
A Holy Trinity is denied by practicing Jehovah's Witnesses.

Dasani, not spring water, is filtered *tap water*, bottled.
Boxes of packaged cereals cost more than their ingredients.
Blotches are implied in the description of anything "mottled."
The most offensive form of arrogance is, by far, expedience.

Memory's fluencies make recollection an act of fiction.
The most lotteries won have been in the state of Indiana.
Country music singers as a group have terrible diction.
Commercially non-navigable is the river Susquehanna.

TRUISMS II

SAD ("Standard American Diet") as an acronym is apt.
U. S. meat packing is manned by cheap immigrant labor.
The causal deaths of Romeo and Juliet is that they co-act.
The trunk of a young fir is usually used for a Scottish caber.

Any *parfum* is far more expensive than perfume.
It is properly the Book or Revelation, *not* Revelations.
Most Nobel Prize winners have been born in June.
Deductibles is merely a synonym for depredations.

A mirror's mystery is its dark backing, needed to see.
Hebrew Zealots opposed the use of Greek in the Holy Land.
Matthew 21:12 to 23:38 is a complete refutation of Jewry.
A distinct vulgarity is ascribed to people constantly tanned.

President Biden has allowed in 12 million unauthorized
illegal immigrants, revised employment-based visa rules,
increased the number of diversity visas, all fully revised,
with free shelter, medical, driver's licenses, and schools.

Arthritic oldsters revile the cap of any childproof bottle.
IKEA is properly pronounced "ee-kay-uh," not "eye-kee-ah."
Lichen offers many dyes, the best being Scottish crottle.
At least nine formal spellings exist of the word *diarrhea*.

Getting re-elected is the sole work done by U.S. Senators.
Chinese mantises are the number one predator of humming-
 birds.
Latino men show a tendency to boast of being progenitors.
"Enigmatologists" is the puzzler name for makers of crosswords.

Every crowd, always leaderless, is a deranged community.
Kissinger, who went unscathed in Watergate, was fully guilty.
Supreme Court Justices can now accept gifts with impunity.
Flammability is completely synonymous with inflammability.

Washington Irving proposed renaming the United States,
in all seriousness, either "Appalachia" or "Alleghania."
World War Three may well begin over the China Straits.
Sarmale (cabbage rolls) is the favorite food in Romania.

Tarpon is never a consumer item in U.S. fish markets.
Brigham Young in all photos faced left, never right.
Summum bonum for stock traders is "hitting targets."
Amish may own private property—never a Hutterite.

Hyperbole invariably has its deepest roots in truth.
The Gutenberg is less scarce than the Bamberg Bible.
Obsolete now is the useful public telephone booth.
Parentage among most African families is intertribal.

All inventors are, by definition, explicit critics.
Confucius abhorred the use of knives at dinner table.
Rhythm in Homeric verse depends on enclitics.
The root of all Seven Deadly Sins is being *unstable.*

Alfred Hitchcock said blondes made the best film victims.
Chinese food, for chopsticks, has always been bite-sized.
Nature in all of its many aspects follow circadian rhythms.
A hint of accusation is at the base of anything surmised.

Bogart and Hepburn while filming *The African Queen*,
from germ fears, not once entered in the African waters.
Camouflage is almost always ecru brown and sage green.
Washington is resolutely facing left on U. S. quarters.

Worry is the direct opposite of the state of trust.
No one ever calls the zipper, a (more properly) slide-fastener.
Warm butter used in flour always ruins a pie crust.
$16.44 is the official hourly pay of every U.S. ambassador.

No person can ever be successfully verbally described.
McDonald's clamshell packet was an environmental nightmare.
No official in Nigeria does a thing unless he/she is bribed.
Scandalous, secret, sly, or sordid all go by the idiom "backstair."

An average individual spends at least 25 years asleep.
Christ in Matthew 22:30 promises humans angelic life.
Rectangular pupils offer wide field of vision for sheep.
Being a scold or virago is the connotation of a fishwife.

The oldest word in the English language is *town*.
96% of candles sold are purchased by girls or women.
Coulrophobia—threat—is morbid fear of a clown.
Casino profits—bets, wages—are made for skimming.

All the early *Tarzan* books are full of the "N-word."
No Gin and Tonics, Cape Codders, Rum and Colas,
Screwdrivers, or Scotch and Sodas need to be stirred.
Warm red skin back of a knee may prove an embolus.

A sponge can hold more cold water than hot.
Theater relies on the voice; cinema depends on the face.
Chinese terracotta soldiers all wore a topknot.
Prison sentences in the U.S. are often meted out on race.

The month of August has the highest percentage of births.
Director Mike Nichols, an alopecia victim, wore wigs all his life.
Mawashi—knit sumo belts—enhance the wrestlers' girths.
Trumpeting in an elephant is ever a sign of both anger and strife.

The darker a canelés rum pastry, the tastier it is.
In Maine, the town of Vienna is pronounced "*Vy-yenny.*"
Considered utterly useless is a classroom pop quiz.
Twenty-five years is the lifespan of an American penny.

Oceans account for 96 percent of the Earth's space,
and the "high seas" (open areas governed by no state)
64 % of the ocean's surface area—fishing free place—
as well as 90% of the high seas volume and biteplate.

St. Paul opened all of his epistles by mentioning his name,
but not so in Hebrews, which we conclude he did not write,
for his Old Testament quotes were in Masoretic, the same
way, whereas in Hebrews they're found in Greek, each cite.

A "hand" as a unit for measuring horses is four inches.
Christmas brandy in Norway must be the temperature of snow.
Persistent hoarseness may indicate cancer in the larynges.
Regional dialects are quite common in the world of the crow.

TRUISMS II

Red food dye, banned in cosmetics, is a carcinogen.
Water is pure in all the 106 Wallace bubblers in Paris.
All tennis players must dress in white at Wimbledon.
In all likelihood, gas constitutes the pole star, Polaris.

A once blackened name can never weather itself bright.
C'est ne pas du gateau: the French phrase for hard work.
Christian faith was the first tenet of a medieval knight.
No affection, joy, warmth, nor levity resides in a smirk.

The tough 1965 movie, *Who's Afraid of Virginia Woolf*
opens with a film shot of the moon and ends with the sun.
Ghibellines were noble, a merchant was mainly a Guelph,
A ton weighs 2,240 lbs.; 2,204.6 is the weight of a tonne.

Sacrifice is the quintessence of commitment.
Fauchon in Paris has the best madeleines, eclairs, and macarons.
Singapore is the largest port for transshipment.
Slang—and being improper—was the original state of Afrikaans.

Couverture chocolate is the best: cocoa butter, no fats.
To the Togo, West Africans, ambition is seen as a disease.
Madness was once aligned to the manufacturing of hats.
Touching a person's head is insulting to the Burmese.

Self-reliance means you find strength to save yourself.
Women never have their money ready at a check-out counter.
Martin Luther's mother thought him afflicted by an elf.
Its eyes migrate to hunt in a buried, camouflaging flounder.

Edgar Lee Masters disliked Lincoln, thought him a eunuch
who tepidly opposed slavery, a weak, shameless imperialist
in the pocket of greedy northern bankers with designs punic
and completely beholden to every last Yankee industrialist.

Without a show of mercy, there can truly be no truth.
Process servers may appear in any disguise, except a cop.
Onigamiising is the Ojibwe Indian name for Duluth.
Every Bertolt Brecht play was a manifesto for agitprop.

Erectile ads are often featured on sports talk shows,
since men with low libidos are consumed by games.
A bed's coverings—not pajamas—define bedclothes.
20th-century Russian painters despised gilded frames.

The slave trade mostly flourished in Mandinka territory.
Woman rarely hold doors for the following person to enter.
The fish's cheeks are the best tasting part of a John Dory.
A human's eyes—even a beauty's—are slightly off-center.

Seating arrangements in class can greatly affect learning.
20 horses were needed to transport the RMS *Titanic* anchor.
Most English public schools fostered the life of an urning.
Greed is considered meritorious in an investment banker.

Plato thought art to be a copy of a copy of a Form.
Type O blood people have the lowest risk for heart attacks.
Only in Scotland can be found the citrine cairngorm.
Palm trees alone are the single best source of vegetable wax.

Peter Llewelyn Davies so hated being identified
and mocked as J. M. Barrie's storied *Peter Pan*
that out of despair, at 63, he committed suicide
by madly throwing himself under a passing train.

Traffic in Lagos, Nigeria is a prefiguration of hell.
Hooded traffic lights exist because people are cheats.
Tone sounds better from a sand (not wax) -casted bell.
Outdated and antiquated in autos are all bucket seats.

Rednecks consider writing poetry an act of a cotquean.
The more white showing, the less valuable a skunk skin.
Greeting with a kiss is characteristic of an Argentine.
A Tudor exile lied about six digits to smirch Ann Boleyn.

Mark 6:2 clearly shows that Jesus Christ was literate.
Purple is the favorite flower color of all bumblebees.
Men holding doors feminists consider as inconsiderate.
Sexual cannibalism is the gourmet treat of all mantises.

Browsing deer will never go near the (toxic) foxglove plant,
whose nectar-rich flowers are the favorite of hummingbirds.
Not leaving the Dutch Republic was a habit with Rembrandt.
Germanic compound nouns always result in string of words.

Praise comes from equals, flattery from inferiors.
Matthew's Gospel is saturated with the Hebrew scriptures.
U.S. Presidents are generally named on U.S. carriers.
Leviticus is structured on 76 sinful bans and hard strictures.

Napoleon was not French, but a Corsican.
Alexander was not Greek, but Macedonian.
Abraham was not Hebrew, but a Chaldean.
Buddha was not Chinese, but an Indian.

Tom Brady, who could have demanded $30 million salaries
took $10 million, so the NE Patriots could hire better teams.
The avocado is the fruit with the most (322 whole) calories.
Beautiful girls all look less attractive in gowns than in jeans.

Private equity funds, a gross perversion of capitalism,
aren't subject to regulations by the S & E Commission.
Use of the adjective *philistine* is bigoted, pure racism.
Primarily oral were the languages Basque and Galician.

U.S. highest casualties on D-Day were at Omaha Beach
due to failed intelligence—crack Nazi battalions waited.
Only a single gene separates a nectarine from the peach.
Liverpool fans consider Manchester United most hated.

New Hampshire registers no motorcycle helmet law.
There are, scandalously, no brilliant female composers.
Stalemate in professional chess ever ends in a draw.
The liberty of tenants is always protected as estovers.

Male bees, "drones," have no father, and receive 100%
of their genetic code from their mothers, which in turn
means that each female has two grandmothers, so lent,
but only a single grandfather, all met with unconcern.

TRUISMS II

No Yankee cornbread ever employs use of sugar or eggs.
Women never figured strongly in any Shirley Temple films.
Alaskan King Crabs can have pounds of meat in their legs.
No lava is as hot (2,732° F) as the vitrifying heat of kilns.

Jews in scholarship never use or rely on the Septuagint.
Most professional chefs lose the sense of heat in their fingertips.
Mosquitos, ants, and mice detest the smell of peppermint.
The English love the taste of malt vinegar on their fish and chips.

The American national bird—scandalously—is inedible.
All TV animation is outsourced to the country of Korea.
No secret smile from a perfect stranger is ever forgettable.
Orthodox Islam in the republic of Iran is predominantly Shia.

The French constantly dip their croissants in coffee or tea.
No blowhard doesn't like making church announcements.
The most commonly used letter in English is the letter E.
Thug Al Capone was nailed not by cops but FBI accountants.

All good bone meal fertilizer must first be "steamed."
Bossa Nova beat starts all patterns on the second bar.
High priestliness is implied in Jesus's robe unseamed.
Small-scaled trout (cooked intact) are all called char.

Writer Lauren Berlant formally referred to herself as "they."
From the 2008 economic fall, all cryptocurrency was born.
In nutritional terms, a true superfood is proteinaceous whey.
The Jewish *shofar* was invariably fashioned of a ram's horn.

Grass, which is a cool weather plant, despises heat.
Banks never save, unlike its lame patrons—they invest.
A 4:4 or 2:4 measure is the standard reggae beat.
Cowardliness in a pervert drives him mainly to molest.

The greatest colonizer in the history of the United States
was Mormon Brigham Young who brazenly staked claim
to approximately one-sixth of the western USA, the fates
be damned, without let, without hindrance, without shame.

Bees always seek to land on the spotted nectary of a bloom.
Tradition says the Holy Kaaba stone was originally white.
Male energy (handle) and female (bristles) make a broom.
True fact: Barcelona, Spain has officially banned the bullfight.

True mercy is open and accessible to all pleas.
Tolstoy execrated his own "tedious, vulgar *Karenina*."
There is no sequence whatsoever to memories.
Once, a routine part of delivering a baby was an enema.

A pinch of baking soda fluffs up mashed potatoes.
Heroic Joan of Arc stood only four feet, eleven inches.
California produces 95% of United States tomatoes.
The front belly of a horse proves the best for cinches.

The best paper for ink line drawing is Strathmore vellum.
Thoreau's walking reputation is inflated—he loved trains.
A good-for-nothing in South Africa is called a "skellum."
A columbarium, not a mausoleum, houses all cremains.

Elijah Muhammad taught that Mr. Yacub, a black wizard,
created on Patmos the white race of devils 6,600 years ago.
All gravel that birds swallow act as "teeth" in the gizzard.
Southern girls prefer to refer to boyfriends as their beaux.

Woody Allen won't watch his films after finishing them.
One kiss is seen as sexy, a foreign double-cheek kiss chaste.
A popular mode in mystical literature is the apophthegm.
No sentences in the original Book of Mormon were spaced.

Crocodiles, while they can move very quickly,
are unable to move for long distances on land
as the hot pain of a lactic acid building thickly
in their muscles soon begins to take command.

Mr. Toishi Ichiyanagi, Yoko Ono's first husband,
whom no one ever hears of, was also a composer.
The top of a two-buttoned jacket must be buttoned.
A blazing fastball defines best in a baseball closer.

Shakespeare never identifies the nature of Iago's evil.
69% of all U.S. veteran suicides are inflicted by guns.
William Smith & Son is unsurpassed for a sail needle.
A common greeting in Tibet is sticking out of tongues.

The so-called "Promised Land," claimed by Hebrews,
belonged to Canaanites, Hittites, Amorites, Jebusites,
Perizzites, and Hivites, was illicitly stolen by the Jews,
depriving the tribes of their homeland and their rights.

Połtawska in Polish is pronounced "pole-DUS-ka."
Źdźbło is actually pronounced "zee-DEE-bzu-war."
The word *Żółtko* is pronounced as "zo-wy-ed-ska."
Przestepstwo is pronounced "pushshepre-EMP-svar."

Memories never have any sequence, succession, or shape.
Atychiphobia, fear of failure, is a specific phobic disorder
Victims report—a U.S. fact—only ninety percent of rape.
Psychologically *disorganized* are collections of a hoarder.

13,000 nuclear weapons are stockpiled in the world,
held by nine aggressive countries: the U.S., China,
the U.K., Israel (undisclosed, but ready to be hurled)
Pakistan, India, France, Russia, and North Korea.

Chicken gizzards should go uncooked for a white stock.
Burgundy is the most terroir-conscious of French wine regions.
Chicken gizzards should be roasted for any brown stock.
Julius Caesar's 10th was the most elite of all Roman legions.

Both a stopper as well as a spout is the use of a spile.
An albatross can stay far out at sea for entire years.
To survive an attack, gouge the eyes of the crocodile.
Nobody can retain one's balance without one's ears.

Post-traumatic stress disorder was once identified
—without pretentiousness—as simply "shell shock."
Gerard Manley Hopkins found nature prettiest pied.
In no gambling casino can one ever find a clock.

TRUISMS II

There is no such thing as Spring on cool Cape Cod.
White semi-dry wines pair best with Asian foods.
No etymology connects the word "good" with God.
In the hot summer months is the time a hen broods.

The rare U.S. Flowing Hair Silver Dollar coin
(1794) is the most valuable coin in numismatics.
A cow's muscle-less back yields the tenderloin
At the heart of every single game is mathematics.

Chefs refer to the genitals of crabs as the "apron."
Damp peat is useless to anyone trying to keep warm.
Taste improves by hormonal changes in a capon.
Amazon rain forests are fertilized by any dust storm.

Petrels and shearwaters can catch naps as they fly.
Aisle seat armrest buttons on an airplane are hidden.
DaVinci's Mona Lisa has no eyebrows over the eye.
Zebra can't carry cargo and are unable to be ridden.

Social networks exist for the epistemologically lonely.
No eye contact on a Manhattan subway is standard code.
Love alters and beautifies any creature who is homely.
No pre-nuptial agreement ever fails badly to incommode.

Painter Andrew Wyeth hated to be caught working.
Loss is never uninvolved in something you have won.
All U.S. state workers feel entitlement to be shirking.
A long log in the Civil War was called a "Quaker gun."

Wherever grief looms, women all accumulate blankets.
Playing any kind of game involves pursuing a theorem.
A specific sexiness adhibits to a woman sporting anklets.
The first month of the Islamic calendar is Muharram.

The full ocean floor of the Earth has yet to be explored.
Ants always rest for about 8 minutes in a 12-hour period.
A flying osprey always carries a caught fish face forward.
Innumerability is invariably invoked by the word myriad.

Only wind coming out of the west is called a "zephyr."
No lineal descendants of Shakespeare were alive after 1670.
A pianist in a bar or a café was called in slang "professor."
The highest sex-offender risk is designated "level three."

Start cutting peat only when yellow flag irises flower.
because by then all the oils in the bog will have risen.
Both lime or lemon juice can make a true whisky sour.
Catholic baptism calls for oil and balsam as a chrism.

Burning at the stake was punishment for heresy,
a crime against the church in Europe. Witchcraft
was a felony in colonies such as Salem, its legacy,
hanging, for the dastardly crime against statecraft.

The Apocrypha, although a product of Judaism,
are not a part of the Jewish canon of the Bible.
The sailing world never refers to a "helmswoman."
London, England is the capital for cases of libel.

Half of the deaths of the Israeli bombings of Gaza.
in 2024—with 40,000 victims killed—were children.
Florida exceeds all states in the use of the toll plaza.
Silence is the greatest selling point of any building.

Hot water will turn into ice faster than cold water.
In Bresse, France, only 12 chickens occupy a henhouse.
The highest GDP per capita in the world is Qatar.
No book/volume in Hawaii is ever safe from a booklouse.

The strongest muscle in the body is the tongue.
In sailing, wind is always coming from the *side*.
Glossopharyngeal breathing offers aid to the lung.
January 6th is the formal ending of Christmastide.

Erotic model Bettie Page never felt sexual arousal
while she was being photographed in lewd poses.
Horses all go counterclockwise in a U.S. carousel.
Every single variety is edible in the world of roses.

Facebook's business model is to monetize loneliness.
Hot-air hand dryers spread germs, not remove them.
Chemical penicillin is secreted in a bread's moldiness.
Wisdom for Benjamin Franklin lived in the apothegm.

Julia Child swore by regular salt and white pepper.
Jacques Pepin preferred black pepper and kosher salt.
Armadillos have often been associated with a leper.
Completely non-existent in nature is pure cobalt.

No one ever hears, ethnically, of an "English" restaurant.
WWI German officers took pride sporting a facial scar.
The essential Renaissance virtue was to appear nonchalant.
Etymologically, the name of Caesar informs the word *czar*.

The left ear, higher than eye level, points downward
and is more sensitive to sounds coming from below,
whereas the human right ear, lower, pointing upward,
is more acute to sounds that coming from above bestow.

It is the fat in a crawfish where the flavor resides.
Novelist Len Deighton starts reading all books on page 100.
Emerald green beetles are a source of cantharides.
The history of capitalism is a tale of the openly plundered.

Religion for Protestants involves only the Bible, alone.
New York Times best-sellers are mostly lowbrow trash.
An oosik is Native Alaskan for a walrus's penile bone.
Corn without lima beans is an unsuccessful succotash.

The phrase Judeo-Christian when spoken is never reversed.
It was common for Elizabethans to be able to read but not write.
The Island of Dolls in Mexico is reputed to be cursed.
In the country of India, widows all traditionally wear white.

Baby orcas are born tail first in order to harden their tail
and fin better to prepare them for immediate swimming.
Stuffing is greatly improved by using bread that is stale.
A prose style is always detectable as written by women.

Legendary assassins are always identified by three names.
The Wendy's girl logo necklace subliminally reads "Mom."
Chauffeurs as archetypal cultural ikons are named *James*.
The 51st state to be included in the U.S.A. is likely Guam.

The Soviet Union never experienced the Great Depression.
Stand in front of a "pulling guard" in football at your peril.
Replacing it with yet another is the sole cure for obsession.
Susan Sontag said a hint of the feminine makes men virile.

Horses and ponies are the boyfriends of adolescent girls.
Nothing is more horrific than the phrase "harvesting organs."
The most expensive and sought after are South Sea pearls.
10 to 15 miles below the earth are found most hydrocarbons.

J. Edgar Hoover made it a point never to laugh aloud.
The *annus mirabilis* of Hollywood films was the year 1939.
Early January is the best time to see a Magellanic Cloud,
"Runge's Phenomenon" best illustrates the curval spline.

The axe forever forgets what the slain tree remembers.
Mussolini" "A crowd does not have to know; it must believe."
A King Herod edict cursed the 28th of all Decembers.
Nothing's more cryptic/inscrutable than a magician's sleeve.

Lewis & Clark's corps preferred dogmeat to elk, venison,
with beaver tail and buffalo hump a special gourmet treat,
all the while as they scoured the plains a major benison
was finding 122 new animals and 178 new plants to eat.

Hollywood film director John Ford loathed all child actors.
Lee Harvey Oswald during capture was never given a lawyer.
Uselessly added to kids' old pencil boxes were protractors.
Sid, his half-brother, gets no notice compared to Tom Sawyer.

Bialys are never boiled before they are baked.
The Frick Museum allows in no children younger than ten.
A canoe to have superb flowing lines is lap straked.
The Egyptian personification of air and breath was Amen.

Antarctica's Thwaites Glacier, slowly calving, in five years
or less could raise global sea levels by several feet or more.
It is impossible correctly to discern sound without two ears.
A drawee takes the check from he who wrote it, the drawer.

New Haven pizza, the acme, is always cooked *well done.*
Recruiting cheating in college football is a perpetual scandal.
The only number that can't be divided by another is one.
Audiences always stand for the "Hallelujah" chorus by Handel.

Salt, its preservative, is used in the making of all cheese.
The term "organic seafood" on a product is a total fraud.
"Sleaze" in the world of fashion is strictly done to tease.
The sport of foxhunting in Britain in 2005 was outlawed.

In China, 18 is good luck because it sounds similar
to the phrase *Yīdìng huì zhīfù*, i.e., "definitely get rich."
Laughter in the matter of sex is always an inhibitor.
My Friend Flicka was banned for calling a dog a bitch.

TRUISMS II

Agbogbloshie in Accra is toxic electronic wasteland.
Any worthy item 25 years old may be called antique.
Iron in a soil is best enhanced by use of green sand.
Deforestation in Myanmar makes a crime of cutting teak.

No Roman emperor ever gave up his throne willingly.
A hustler buying used books to sell, not read, is a cretin.
Lichen is composed of two organisms: fungus and algae.
Receiving a gift with a single hand offends any Tibetan.

In Tibet, never touch an individual's head or hat.
Avoid milk and fruit juice when taking penicillins.
Nothing is weirder than giving movie stars *eclat*.
Predatory fish are an avoided food by Brazilians.

Jefferson washed his feet in cold water every morning.
No flexitarian dieter is not a total pain-in-the-ass.
Every 19th-century shop/store chose to have an awning.
Never found in its natural state is the metal brass.

Weeping hard was Katharine Hepburn's go-to emotion.
Bitter orange is essential to an authentic Sauce Bigarade.
Forks/Knives (not chopsticks) are used by a Laotian.
Finnan haddie not made with smoked haddock is a fraud.

Indians measured distances by travel time, not miles.
The traditional mold for Paskha is a clay flower-pot.
Iron deficiency anemia is a significant cause of piles.
Zero is the meaning of nil, nowt, naught, and nought.

Jack Ruby had been hired to kill Lee Harvey Oswald.
The physician at Oswald's death was never identified.
RFK, although the attorney general, was never called
to be on Warren Commission, guilty of a need to hide.

The U.S. Constitution not once mentions Christianity.
Mark's is the oldest, most vivid of the four Gospels:
Matthew, Luke, and John all copied from him liberally.
The dogma of the Trinity is abhorrent to Pentecostals.

Any gloss in a formal document states "hereinafter."
40% of the world's oil comes from the Indian Ocean.
Indifference is the natural environment of laughter,
the reaction of which has no keener foe than emotion.

Lobster *Newburg* was originally called Lobster Wenberg.
Toilet breaks are not permitted King Charles' Royal Guards.
Equally both French and German is the town of Strasbourg.
100% plastic are all decks of Las Vegas casino playing cards.

A person needs to be tall to have a career in politics.
Locke-Ober's lobster stew is made of strictly knuckle meat.
Surprisingly, not insects, but arachnids are all ticks.
Europe's last leper colony was located in Spinalonga, Crete.

Shoshone were hated by Sioux, Blackfeet, and Crow.
Bostonians add a bit of coffee when cooking baked beans.
JFK's hatlessness to the hat industry was a death blow.
Purse-seining is the only way fishermen catch sardines.

Sunny days depress Woody Allen, rainy ones cheer him up.
Desert-bred Arabians have one vertebra less than other horses.
For humans and cattle all parts are poisonous on a buttercup.
60% of second, 73% of third marriages end up as divorces.

The *N.Y. Times* is the only paper with no comic strip.
Garlic is a must in any dish of Mushrooms Provençal.
The lower lip is oddly unaffected in a case of cleft lip.
Hebrew bias links Beelzebub with the Canaanite Baal.

London's grey skies are perfect for photography.
No large household staff is not fussily territorial.
Irene, by Victorians, was pronounced "*eye-ree-nee*."
Canopy is a basic need for all animals arboreal.

Jimmy Carter's Camp David Accords on Sept. 17, 1978,
was a cruel disaster for every Palestinian and Jordanian.
Casseroles, to be appetizing, need an added makeweight.
Martin Luther's pet dog "Belferlein" was a Pomeranian.

The U.S. Marines never accepted blacks until June 1, 1942.
Brigham Young instigated the Mountain Meadows massacre.
Yves Klein, a monochromist Catholic, adored the color blue.
The Grand Inquisitors virtually lived to torture a blasphemer.

Diluting extra virgin olive oil is a common practice.
During rainstorms, most Manhattan penthouse ceilings leak.
The Teddy-Bear Cholla is the fiercest-spiked cactus.
A bird's diet is dictated by the shape (nose/mouth) of its beak.

Singer Taylor Swift at every performance demands
a Grande Iced Caramel Latte with two Sweet
'n Lows and a great Grande Iced Americano—brands
matter—some sugar and soy milk, *complete!*

Every Fascist mind thrives on ceremonies.
Syria has for ages had an age-old competition with Iraq.
Eaten on Chinese New Year are abalones.
Walnut in the U. S. has long been the favored gunstock.

The twenty-seventh day of the month of Ramadan,
for practicing Muslims is the holiest night of the year.
Never as a call, but as a response, is an antiphon.
It is said there's more power, when uttered, in a prayer.

The Comanches, known as the "Lords of the Plains,"
were the fiercest Native Americans on the frontier.
Government must aid in fiscal policy, said J. M. Keynes.
Birch oil goes into sarsaparilla, sassafras root beer.

Tyrone Power was the one love of Lana Turner's life.
Nebbiolo, ripening in mist/fog, is to me the matchless wine.
Dame Trot and her cat are always troubled by strife.
Mary Shelley was a teenager when writing *Frankenstein.*

Japanese fear numbers 19, 33, and 42 which sound
like *repeated hard luck; terrible trouble;* and *death.*
Apothecary weights only measure by the troy pound.
Clarity, in any form, always determined by breadth.

TRUISMS II

Pablo Picasso in 92 years never once visited the USA.
Rabid fans of any kind, irrational, border on insanity.
A mother is often the girlfriend of any man who's gay.
Joan Crawford answered all here fan mail personally.

Less than 1% of North Dakota is covered with trees.
Joan Crawford who hated Jean Harlow called her "Cow Tits."
Eastern Asian nations have no appetite for cheese.
Tungsten carbide, for any masonry, make the best drill bits.

Political power is always born of asexual drive.
Washing eggs before easting, killing "bloom," is harmful.
93-degrees is standard temperature for a beehive.
Any and all authority to an extreme feminist is patriarchal.

All advanced processor chips are now made in Taiwan.
Clark Gable refused in GWTW to try a Southern accent.
Corn syrup is made from number #2 corn, yellow dent.
A tabernacle in Old Testament is synonymous with tent.

There is a great deal of narcissism in one's self-hatred.
MLB broadcasters belong *nowhere* in the Hall of Fame.
To the Aztecs, a *cuauhxicalli*—stone bowl—was sacred.
An actual business exists selling people a domain name.

Actors Richard Burton, Greta Garbo, John Barrymore,
and Cary Grant have never won an Academy Award.
The first floor in the US in the UK is the ground floor.
The American CIA and the FBI are never in accord.

Red pigment in tree leaves acts as a sort of sunscreen,
and brown the result in fallen ones of leftover tannins.
A Neo-Nazis code for Adolf Hitler is the number 18.
Only a single area code (406) services all Montanans.

Jesus Christ died in the 1,998th week of His life.
Oak, hickory, and beech leaves are the last to change color.
Cezanne followed Courbet's use of a palette knife.
The somber mood of almost all Penitentes painting is dolor.

Tulip poplar tree leaves start changing color in August.
L. B. Meyer demanded MGM film mothers all be saintly.
The Girl with a Pearl Earring's stare was seen as immodest.
A raised *digitus minimus manus* is the epitome of dainty.

No father on radio and TV sit-coms is not a cretin:
Archie Bunker, Homer Simpson, Fibber McGee,
Throckmorton P. Gildersleeve, dumbo Peter Griffin,
Fred Sanford, Frank Costanza, Chester A. Riley.

Beatle George Harrison always railed against materialism
yet was the first person—the very first pop star, in fact,
—to write the 1966 hit "Taxman" in favor of hedonism,
from the album *Revolver*, complaining about income tax.

All human beings have an innate resistance to obedience.
The straight lines of the Greek temples were actually curves.
H. Kissinger made decisions not by morality but expedience.
Appetizers begin a meal, preceding a meal hors d'oeuvres.

Turkeys in trees, refusing to descend, indicate snow,
as does the situation of sheep facing downhill to feed.
Nothing better than its *canelé* goes with a Bordeaux.
L.B. Mayer, functionally illiterate, could barely read.

"Did you eat rice yet?" 밥 먹었어? (*Bab meog-eoss-eo*)
supplants the greeting "How are you?" in South Korea.
J. Locke and H. Grotius birthed democracy. We also owe
J. Burlamaqui, Puffendorf, Montesquieu, and Beccaria.

Rabbits actually thrive on eating the "death cap" toadstool.
Roosevelt was accompanied by 200+ hangers-on at Yalta.
Only a witness's evidence is admissible by the "hearsay rule."
Seawater is drunk straight (filtered) on the isle of Malta.

No one, reversing names, refers to the Navy/Army game.
Stars twinkle due to great turbulence in the atmosphere.
Cruel is the slang usage of the popular adjective "lame."
The salah is a special form of worship in Islamic prayer.

The word Christmas is now reviled when used in public media.
Numbers 13: 1-3 proves God the Father a sneak and a spy.
Not in France, the French Revolution was contrived in America.
It is the *caring* for the plant that crucially matters in bonsai.

Applewood is by far best for a rod in the act of dowsing.
A test tube with Edison's last breath is in Henry Ford Museum.
Grazers eat grass—eating leaves, shrubs, plants is *browsing*.
Built above ground, unlike a burial vault, is a mausoleum.

Perfume, selling as *le parfum*, always costs $100 more.
Old women living alone were the main scapegoats as witches.
Time, now considered a dimension, leaves us with four.
The Hebrew prophet Amos inveighed mainly against riches.

American colonists, more Stuart-minded than Georgian,
believed it was King George III made laws, not Parliament.
No tree or plant in every Spring doesn't fail to bourgeon.
The penal cost of a war lost always calls for disarmament.

Pluto is named after the astronomer Percival Lowell.
Every edge is a boundary between two squares on a cube.
America's greatest decoy carver was Elmer Crowell.
The key to television was Farnsworth's cathode-ray tube.

Ninety percent of what Sir Isaac Newton obsessed about,
alchemy, Biblical prophecy, astrology, etc. was rubbish.
Of the same family—actual cousins—are salmon and trout.
The main vice of clubs is that its members are all clubbish.

Jesus Christ is mentioned not once in Carl Sagan's *Cosmos*.
The Chinese never drink cold water or keep salt on the table.
Boys are the exploited "chocolate slaves" of the Ivory Coast.
Unreliable is every painter's brush if it isn't made of sable.

Peace in the human equation is but the laboratory of war.
Dublin's Gravediggers Pub pulls the best Guinness pint on earth.
An ethnic, racist, and sexual slur is the vulgar word *squaw*.
Too much or too little amniotic fluid can cause a breech birth.

TRUISMS II

No fresh fruit/veggies may be imported into the USA.
Moirologists—hired mourners—is a specific niche for actors.
Raspberry chocolate purple enhances a true cabernet.
Anonymity is the primary virtue of the greatest benefactors.

Anthony Bourdain's *Medium Raw* prefigured his suicide.
Neutral Portugal during WWII was thick with spies—of both sides.
No book reviewer does not look for some detail to deride.
For leather jackets nothing surpasses full grain cow leather hides.

The Nazi swastika was skewed at a 45-degree angle,
so, its perimeter was that of a diamond, *not* a square.
Either to destroy and to smooth out defines a mangle.
The *Légion d"honneur* outranks the *Croix de Guerre*.

The nation of Burundi punishes and imprisons all gays.
American sports franchises are almost all owned by Jews.
A stare is always baleful, because a stare is to appraise.
Nothing positive is ever conjoined with jazz or the "blues."

All Vietnamese *pho* eaters complete their dish at table:
a dot of chili paste, some chili sauce, squeeze of lime.
Providing drainage is essentially the reason for a gable.
Israel's destruction of Gaza was a *national* war crime.

Nerds always give sports scores backwards: i.e., "13 to 40."
Half the NFL demographic are rabid female football fans.
Alexei Maximovich Peshkov, bitter, took the name "Gorky."
It is almost always brainless types who relish being tanned.

Night Train, a hobo pull, was widely considered worst wine ever.
Rudy Vallee was asked to replace Ed Sullivan on TV but declined.
The size of 20 normal wine bottles compose one Nebuchadnezzar.
Yellow is the international code color of the officially quarantined.

Pythagoras' five perfect solids are the cube, tetrahedron,
the octahedron, the icosahedron, and the dodecahedron.
Abraham's tomb is what makes holy the site of Hebron.
Brains make up 1 percent of the body weight of a dugong.

Outer planets, Jupiter, Saturn, moves stately and slow,
but the inner, like Mercury, move rapidly in their orbit.
No insertable spoke can be wed without its spousal felloe.
To include some but exclude others is the point of argot.

Beer lines in pubs should be cleaned at least once a week.
Old Avon paperback books had shiny isinglass-like covers.
Except for scoring, pinochle is the same game as bezique.
No progress is made, purposely, as a hawk in wind hovers.

Any spy or mole is, by definition, a born traitor.
Once is happenstance, twice coincidence, thrice enemy action.
Stalin's purges depended fully on the compurgator.
Haphephobes in the extreme have an intense fear of any taction.

The Israeli Lobby sends cash to every U.S. congressman.
E. O. Wilson: "Ten thousand trillion ants occupy Earth."
Consonants predominate in the native language Wakashan
American early pioneers sought to build in an open garth.

TRUISMS II

Dodge Ram trucks lead the list of the worst drivers.
Members of Opus Dei believe in physical mortification.
Early U.S. invaders in Vietnam were called "advisors."
Only traveling by foot is, technically, a peregrination.

Kim Philby, a British spy for the Soviet Union, said,
"To betray, you must first belong, I never belonged."
The source of the Nile is not a single fountainhead.
A woman raped is under any circumstance wronged.

There is a severe paucity of public toilets in London.
Air conditioning is basically banned in Switzerland.
Anything corresponding, in logic, is called "one one."
The back half of cows, for Kosher Jews, is jettisoned.

Singer James Brown demanded he be called "Mister."
Cows eat grass a foot high; 6 inches for grazing sheep.
Mental health is strong when one sister loves her sister.
The sole food preservative in Guyana is bitter cassareep.

Irving Thalberg, the so-called genius at MGM studios,
nixed all proposals to produce, judging the job a pickle,
stating of *Gone with the Wind*, as worthy cinema goes,
"No U.S. Civil War picture ever made a plug nickel."

Anyone can beat a Polygraph Machine by taking Valium.
Air, which is invisible, can exert great forces of pressure.
Composer Andrew Lloyd Webber owns the London Palladium.
Discontinued as a variety in English cheese is Blue Cheshire.

All "nativist" paranoid types are fanatically right-wing.
Darwin on the H.M.S. *Beagle* constantly read *Paradise Lost*.
A golfer's bad drive is always born on the backswing.
No human artistic design can compete with natural hoarfrost.

No Indian cook shares her secret recipe for Murgh Biryani.
F. Scott Fitzgerald in his fiction always slighted Yale University.
Dubious pasts characterize most traveling workers in a carny.
Mountain climbers are mainly lost by acts of fatal inadvertency.

It took five years in 1941 to build a single battleship.
Both male and female reindeer, uniquely, grow antlers.
Flaneurs have always favored a shoe's toe-cap wingtip.
Alcohol and drug disorders proliferate with gamblers.

The numbers on a standard roulette wheel equal 666.
Spectators are crucial in sports in what happens in games.
Consecotaleophobia is the morbid fear of chopsticks.
France leads the world in the largest number of surnames.

It's an animal's canines that fatally bite, incisors browse.
All casino games are statistically against you from winning.
To defeat someone through trickery or deceit is to chouse.
Sheep, goats, and deer famously deliver offspring, twinning.

Brigham Young refused to allow his hair ever to be cut,
as he claimed it made the ends bleed. It was singed.
Good conduct online is officially denoted "netiquette."
Most good nutrition in potatoes resides in their skins.

TRUISMS II

A back-row dancer in a chorus line was a "showgirl;"
but the front-row girls, all shorter, demeaningly, "ponies.
North Indian cuisine is much less spicy than Mughal.
Rabbits, to avoid sexual play, replaced the word conies.

A double-minded person is unstable in all his ways.
Never put a rear-facing child seat in the front of a car.
Harold Pinter never spoke on "meaning" of his plays.
The one and only cat that loves the water is a jaguar.

The flatter the wing, the much faster goes an airplane.
With sails, the harder a wind blows, the flatter the sail.
Most all entertainment is same sex only in Bahrain.
Christian Dior preferred his fashion colors to be pale.

The U.S. Navy in 1941 kept Blacks as merely messmen.
Seppuku, ritual suicide, must be performed Japanese soil.
In an open chess board, knights are very weak chessmen.
Its throat—via etymology—is the function of a gargoyle.

Only true Samurai, who believe the soul rests in the belly,
can alone perform the Japanese suicide ritual of *hara kiri*.
A respondent in a court of law is technically an *appellee*.
The toilet pan in a house is, ironically, the most sanitary.

Academy Award statues are never allowed to be sold.
Chrome on cars in the 1940s was called "brightwork."
Earthquakes—inside its fault lines—can create gold.
The Turk—thus, the slight—has no friend but the Turk.

To make leather, divest an animal skin of all hair and fat
and simply immerse it in a dilute solution of tannic acid.
Bing Crosby, balding early, was never seen without a hat.
The Pacific Ocean, ironically, is and was never placid.

Horace Mann believed kids' early books should teach
whole words, skipping the alphabet and sounds of letters.
Only a single gene separates a nectarine and a peach.
Try to keep your pieces in the center in Chinese Checkers.

"Nothing is certain" is the number one cancer cliché.
Virtually every U. S. President was excessively libidinous.
Mormon tea has no flowers nor leaves nor any bouquet.
All lilies, hibiscus plants, even asparagus are hexapetalus.

Hugo Butler, MGM originator of the Andy Hardy movies,
17 of them, was a card-carrying Communist who despised
bourgeois values, of the very sort that established a pattern
that all warm cozy, American families have always prized.

Elvis Presley never performed outside North America
and never once in Alaska, Delaware, Idaho, Montana,
New Jersey—OK, once in a German inn (for esoterica)—
New Hampshire, Vermont, Wyoming, or North Dakota.

Halcion (chemically *triazolam*) induces suicidal thoughts.
A food salt brine is ready when a raw potato can float in it.
The most prized healing stone or mineral is crystal quartz.
Minute (small, pron. *maɪˈnjuːt*) defines the "time" minute.

In the U.S. Congress, the Republicans side is on the left,
ironically, while the Democrats are located on the right.
Jews may consume only beasts whose hooves are cleft.
In New England, family cooks are free on Wednesday night.

Spices begin to lose their strength after being ground.
Jesus' body was laid face down in the tomb, not face up.
No planets, because they spin, are ever perfectly round.
The German Wehrmacht ran solely on steel from Krupp.

French painter Henri Rousseau, a customs inspector,
painted only on Sundays, which was his only day off.
Hoarding, at bottom, is an iniquity in every collector.
The surname Rolfe in England is pronounced "Roff."

The mantle—or the head—of an octopus is its trunk.
There is no universally accepted way of setting a table.
No reporter is not also a cheap gossip and a *quidnunc*.
The Statue of Liberty is less a sculpture than a stabile.

Pure piety has never been powerful in Anglicanism:
it has never produced—could never—a St. Francis.
Tribal knowledge in every nation exists in aphorism.
No arranged marriage is made exclusive of finances.

The hospital on an ocean liner is always midship, low.
All Venetian gondolas are required to be painted black.
No bed in the UK is without its chamber pot—a "po."
Gossip columnists in Hollywood constitute a claque.

Paul Morphy, America's greatest ever chess champion
was never crowned so: no such title existed at the time.
Life as we know it explicitly began in the Precambrian.
No human design can equal or surpass hoarfrost or rime.

Study of molluscs is malacology, of shells conchology.
There are no White Castle restaurants on the West Coast.
Faulkner never wrote a novel with straight chronology.
Any herbivorous animal can make a delicious pot roast.

A lobster with both claws missing is called a "pistol."
Shallows usually form on the inside of a rover's curve.
Moses' brother Aaron was a fanatical lover of crystal.
163.4 mph is now registered as tennis's hardest serve.

Always alternate high nitrogen layers (green matter)
and carbon layers (brown matter) when composting.
All conversation in a beauty parlor is strictly natter,
whereas, music hall and burlesque lingo is riposting.

John F. Kennedy throughout life rarely read a novel.
Greta Garbo was at her prettiest in 1931, at age of 26.
No two Stradivarius violins have ever been identical.
Harvard University structures are mainly all of bricks.

Poets are particularly vulnerable to clinical depression.
Chaulmoogra oil given intravenously for leprosy helps.
An 18th-century woman's fan constituted facial expression.
There are no existing toxic or deadly seaweeds or kelps.

TRUISMS II

Memorial Day, until 1971, was called Decoration Day.
Washing butter is the best way to make it more pliable.
Never underestimate the soothing power of the ordinary.
The greater the truth, in England, the greater the libel.

Alexander Selkirk, the original island castaway off Chile
and Daniel Defoe, the *Robinson Crusoe* author, never met.
Any William, ashamed to age, will still call himself Billy.
Pomposity in society is invariably denoted by a lorgnette.

Marinara sauce, named ironically, has never seafood in it.
Playing card queens are named Judith, Rachel, Argine, Palas.
Named for the very food it eats—hemp, flax—is the linnet.
Red is considered the rarest color in the Aurora Borealis.

There were never dining rooms in Venetian palaces.
Farting is a commonplace with people doing yoga.
Asian & Indian artwork is a playground of phalluses
Romans rarely wore anyhing underneath their toga.

Actor Mickey Rooney maintained nothing of civility
with any of his ex-wives (eight) after divorcing them.
There is always a touch of feminine in a man's virility.
Falling stock prices always lower skirt lines of the hem.

An average laying hen drops 260 eggs in a given year.
Greta Garbo never personally answered the telephone.
The talents of a toreador are the gifts of an auctioneer.
Only a half-grown quahog may be called a cherrystone.

No comedian in its all-star cast was allowed to ad-lib
in the film *It's a Mad, Mad, Mad, Mad World* (1963).
Jehovah created woman out of man's *thirteenth* rib.
The sacred Bo Tree of Buddha was actually a fig tree.

Stevedores work in the ship, longshoremen on the docks.
Vladimir Putin's grandfather was Lenin and Stalin's cook.
Not one Las Vegas casino allows any windows or clocks.
After the queen, the most powerful chess piece is the rook.

Only three million Venetians in life have ever existed.
Pregnant women all look as if they are leaning backward.
Growth and development of corn is ever wind-assisted.
Celebrity and fame in Hollywood is strictly manufactured.

Only 8% of Americans are affected by the stock market.
Green Bay Packers fans despise the Minnesota Vikings.
Every last Jewish household that exists is a matriarchate.
A curmudgeon's glory is based solely on his dislikings.

Most varietals are an indiscriminate blend of grapes.
To bard is another way of instructing to make lard.
Joseph Van Aken was the greatest painter of drapes.
A fencer solely in a defensive stance is *en garde*.

The harp on a symphony orchestra is always far left
and both string bass and double bass on the far right.
A good host must never plan any outings for his guest.
It is illegal in all 50 U.S. states to stage a cockfight.

Comedian Buster Keaton, sax player Johnny Hodges,
television host Ed Sullivan, composer Nelson Riddle,
Soviet Andrei Gromyko, actor Daniel Craig, stodges
all, had stone faces unbudgingly stiff as a bull fiddle.

A "programmer:" a low-budget B movie for double bills.
It's barrel wood that makes Cabernet Sauvignon so costly.
The flat Maldives archipelago is completely bereft of hills
Always returning home, and monogamous, is the osprey.

Lightning bolts are 5x hotter than the surface of the sun.
Cole Porter's song "Night and Day" is a Jewish melody.
Soleil et lune, anglicized, gave us (cf. cake) Sally Lunn.
A woman named foreperson for a jury is the "forelady."

"Original sin" has never been, as such, a sin at all
but rather the weakness in a human *leading* to sin.
A crack in concrete or brick is technically a spall.
The pelt of a small animal is formally called a skin.

The Four Seasons singing quartet, all Italian boys,
took their name from a New Jersey bowling alley.
A "*shhhh*" is audible at the heart of all white noise.
Contaminants can accumulate is lobster tomalley.

Faking injury ("diving") in soccer effeminizes players.
No one—even pallbearers—refers to caskets as a "pall."
White Leghorn chickens are by far the best egg layers.
A full 27 New Testament books are attributed to St. Paul.

An American flag upside down is a national distress signal.
Karl Marx declared believers in an after-life ignored this one.
Bad or "forced" poetry, sadly, is the downside of a hymnal.
70% Americans defended MacArthur when fired by Truman.

As with the words "fish"," "sheep," and "offspring,"
the most widely accepted plural of "Lego" is Lego.
The soul of a watch is a balancing wheel hairspring.
Pushing, not pulling, is the action of a Dutch hoe.

Only a fraction of world shipping containers are inspected.
Wm. Thackeray thought A. Pope the greatest English poet.
No animal is not badly traumatized that has been vivisected.
Virtue doubles in a giver who will anonymously bestow it.

The John Birch Society always hated Richard Nixon.
Cows produce 18% of all methane emitted in the U.S.
Open hostility in Sicily fosters serious malediction.
Heterosexual lust often has a penchant to cross-dress.

A perfect lobster chowder should age at least 5 hours.
Jonathan Swift held his every birthday as a day of mourning.
Titan arum is by far the worst smelling of all flowers.
Red next to yellow in snakes are the colors of fatal warning.

"Vegemite," a spread of used yeast dumped
by breweries, while it is popularly smeared,
is best when with butter it is double-humped,
when it will never go eerie, or "off," so tiered.

TRUISMS II

Joe DiMaggio was only a *fourth* ballot Hall of Famer.
March 25 in old New England was first day of the year.
A "Down Easter" is popular slang for every Mainer.
In Great Britain, 805 individuals are a hereditary peer.

Men plant maple trees for their children,
according to old New England tradition;
oaks are planted for their grand-children;
Elms? For great-grandchildren, in addition.

Actor Eddie Murphy once said he never understood
a word that the black hipster James Brown ever sang.
The Hebrew tabernacle was made from shittimwood.
A combination of ? and ! constitutes an *interrobang.*

Only in Massachusetts is a milkshake called a *frappe.*
Walking anti-clockwise is taboo among Mongolians.
The British refer to a bathing hat as a "jelly bag cap."
Our largest dinosaurs thrived among the Patagonians.

Snakes are only able to see two colors, blue and green.
George Washington was the first donkey owner in the U. S.
In England, a synonym for inferior is, oddly, *puisne.*
A required school subject in Armenia is the game of chess.

Bias in writing of history is, inarguably, inevitable.
Charles Dickens gave 472 dramatic public readings.
The amount of Black people in Montana is negligible.
Violins in orchestras often signify special pleadings.

Matthew Brady's Civil War photos were all staged.
North Korea, with no blacks, does not let them in.
Desperate narcissists in hotels often pay to be paged.
Carved from a single rock is the royal palace of Yemen.

The *best beef* animal is a steer 30 months old,
confined to a small stall and fattened on corn,
except perhaps for a heifer, if the truth be told
30 to 50 days pregnant, and just before its born.

Teacher strikes are official illegal in Massachusetts.
One in 1,666 kids is born with no XX or XY chromosomes.
Student tuitions were never charged by Confucius.
Only one person (Irene Adler) ever bested Sherlock Holmes.

General Eisenhower scorned Jewish friendships.
The Socotra dragon tree of Yemen produces a red saps.
Fingerprints in court are never foolproof forensics.
Paris has the most extensive collection of world maps.

Trans exclusionary radical feminists bully trans people.
Iowa's the only state bordered by two navigable rivers.
Sterile are all parts of any given flower's calyx or sepal.
French *qavre* ("quick") gave us our word for "quivers."

The Nobel Prize committee is generally held to be
narrow-minded, Eurocentric, biased, and politicized.
Nothing castrates any reporter so easily as flattery.
St. Paul declared Christians need not be circumcised.

TRUISMS II

Chili con carne is a Texan, not a Mexican, dish.
There was never a *city* called Galatia: it is a region.
Lifting a lady's hand to kiss it is considered oafish.
Demons in Scripture are given the name "Legion."

Hair always grows more quickly in the sun.
A fastball in MLB is invariably followed by a curve.
Henry Clay utterly despised Andrew Jackson.
An amuse-bouche is a *single* bite-sized hors d'oeuvre.

Old U.S. Marine bugles were all in the key of G.
A sperm whale spouts merely air, nothing else.
All modern plans are descended from green algae.
Only animal skin with fur can be called pelts.

Jesus never prayed the "The Lord's Prayer,"
asking to "forgive us our trespasses," since
He never sinned. The prayer, is never called
the "The Lord's Prayer" in the Holy Gospels.

Charles Dana Gibson would never sketch a man
not clean shaven nor a girl with her hair in bangs,
Shakespeare praises no character named Anne.
Chinese ghosts and zombies are called "*changs.*"

Lean ground chuck is the most flavorful grind.
Tradition has it illiterate dowsers best succeed.
The thin layer on a fruit is skin, but thick is rind.
A centipede is venomous, but never a millipede.

Celebrity is an elusive and unstable currency.
Dogs always sleep on the spot you want to step.
Nobody in the 17th-century spelled correctly.
Trendy in the 1960s was "hip," in 1940s "hep."

A champagne glass should be two-thirds filled.
Suits, not sport coats: law in all Trump organizations.
Ballpark hot dogs are steamed, and rarely grilled.
The fiercest of all ancient people were the Thracians.

The Arabic language contains 4,000 verb roots.
Savings versus investing have always been at loggerheads.
Fear any nation where authority wears boots.
Strict constructionists in the 1860s were all "copperheads."

No Supreme Court proceeding is ever filmed
and all cameras are banned from their premise.
Beer, wine, cider, and *sake* are never distilled.
Grass must be cut at 8 mm. for Wimbledon tennis.

A condor will virtually never flap either massive wing.
Charlie Chaplin claimed to have slept with 2000 women.
Edward VIII, the abdicate, was never crowned as king.
Avoid eating any, all, dairy with an acidic persimmon.

The arch phrase *"Bon appetit!"*—enjoy your food—
is lowbrow and what a common waiter would say.
Serbs despise Bosnian Muslims, who are viewed
as hated remnants of the Ottoman Empire in its day.

One third of a sperm whale's oil lies in its head.
Donald Trump considers baldness is a sign of weakness.
The best lubricant for nuclear reactors is black lead.
Computer systems proceed under ongoing obsoleteness.

The most effective remedy for fury or anger is delay.
Mae West refused to be photographed with a younger woman.
Utterance is held as more virtuous when we pray.
Black light, as it contains phosphorus, reveals a glow in urine.

Until the 1980s, English Customs officers believed
travelers carrying condoms were all suspect persons.
The Bay of Pigs fiasco was fully CIA misconceived.
The smallest rip in any sailboat sail always worsens.

There were as many as 10 Howdy Doody TV puppets.
Hitler never accepted a decision he thought imposed on him.
Haydn's "Concerto in E-flat Major" he wrote for trumpets.
A hippo can neither breathe underwater nor is able to swim.

Ford Maverick Hybrids 2024 are very hard to find.
Browsers needn't travel as far as grazers do for food.
Sentinelese island tribal people are famously unkind.
The first pancake that one makes is never any good.

Moloch, the pagan god, had a penchant for child sacrifice.
There was a bit of the angelic in the Witch of Endor (cf. Saul).
St. Paul in his epistles *quotes only once* the words of Christ.
Sublimity, as such, alone can be found in something small.

A dowser's secret is in the mind, not the wand.
Written Japanese depends on Chinese characters for terseness.
Investments are always high risk with a junk bond.
No waters can outdo that of the Drake passage for fierceness.

Civil War soldiers, when shooting, always fired low.
Ayn Rand, spitefully, never put any children in her novels.
Osage orange wood Indians most preferred for a bow.
The Gobi Desert is the *locus classicus* for dinosaur fossils.

Every Southern accent in movies sounds ignorant.
Most prey species can run faster than most predators.
Every early Methodist preacher was an itinerant.
A debtor's memory is much worse than a creditor's.

Disney artists, treated like workers on an assembly line,
were personally never allowed to draw an entire scene.
Franz Kafka habitually wrote all his stories at bedtime.
Players and TV prefer tennis courts be blue, not green.

Homosexuality is criminalized in Ghana.
Proxime accessit dux wins no accolades.
A modern rodeo was an ancient gymkhana.
The most valued card is the Ace of Spades.

Hiroshima had 120,000 casualties, Dresden *130,000!*
Methyl anthraniolate is what flavors grape Kool-Aid.
Isinglass is created from sturgeon membrane hausen.
Senegal and Angola most fed the African slave trade.

TRUISMS II

Cutlery to be used first is placed farthest from the plate.
Irish coffee is only made properly with Demerara sugar.
The luckiest number in Chinese culture is number eight.
A disaster is to add any thickeners to a pressure cooker.

Mark's Gospel never mentions "The Lord's Prayer."
Woodrow Wilson had an emotional crush on his father.
Begging is the sole income for the order, Poor Clare.
Swaddling clothes for infants are technically a swather.

Miners consider themselves the elite of laborers.
It is illegal to be gay in 76 countries in the world.
One's own family constitute most alcoholic enablers.
Cork oaks and coastal live oak trees are all gnarled.

A writer is not allowed to copyright a book title.
The Nobel Prize for physics is always awarded first.
A successful play is said to succeed any bad recital.
The Island of Dolls in Mexico is supposedly cursed.

A profile is rare on all 17th-century gravestones.
Stacked rope on ships uncoils from the *middle.*
No pain is as excruciating as passing kidneystones.
Alice of Wonderland was named for Alice Liddell.

There can be no true culture that is international.
Always refrigerate a bottle of vermouth after opening.
Nitrites and acids are completely incompatible.
To sell, customers, not products, demand focusing.

A whale eats, *not* by swimming with open mouth
but by *lying still*, deep, with its mouth wide open.
Maryland sympathized with the American South
during the Civil War and was the most outspoken!

It is a scarcely believable fact that no character
in a Dickens' novel reads anything by Dickens!
Solicitors handle UK law, courts need a barrister.
Scriptural word for coming alive is "quickens."

Old seafarers commonly used to measure rope
by spreading both arms and calling it a fathom.
Theodore in 642 A.D. was a Palestinian Pope.
During sex, Lilith refused to lay under Adam.

Table tombs in graveyards stand for wealth, prestige.
Sitting U.S. presidents are all targets for free-form resentments.
Lime juice is what kills potential bacteria in ceviche.
The "third" is the most idiotic of Congress's 27 amendments.

The Durupinar boat-shaped formation in Turkey,
many conjecture, is the landing spot of Noah's Ark.
A *preparation method* named the product, beef jerky.
Forward vision is impossible for a hammerhead shark.

All North Korean products are banned in the U.S.
Richard Wagner wept entering the Cathedral of Sienna.
Taking college boards, one is advised never to guess.
Russian women love to dye their tresses with henna.

Condors change all their feathers every year.
Hungarian smoked sausages are always sold in pairs.
1585 to 1592 are missing years for Shakespeare.
Ants who detect sound with antennae have no ears.

Mathematics is ignored in the Nobel Prize awards.
John Waters' mustache is Maybelline eyebrow pencil.
Skeptics insist that "group mind" explains Lourdes.
Farmers, using silos, never use the valid word "ensile."

The average height of land is 2,770 feet above sea level.
Standard depth of the world's oceans is 12,140 feet.
A slang term for addictive Seconal is the "red devil."
After his presidency, JFK said he'd run for a Senate seat.

Instead of curbing alcoholism, Prohibition *increased* it.
Bitcoin has no value, so its price is inherently unstable.
To ferment beer, one always has to Brewer's Yeast it.
A bell attached to any sleigh is technically a cascabel.

Sysco is the largest food distribution in the world.
John Brown claimed to have hypnotic power over beasts.
All shillelaghs are definitively knobbed and gnarled.
No individual more than Friedrich Nietzsche hated priests.

All the World Trade airplane hijackers carried knives
with 4" blades, *which were all legal to carry on board!*
Only eight feet above sea level stand the Maldives.
Steuben glass blowers make objects they cannot afford.

Moose and European elk are exactly the same species.
Balthus the painter deliberately set out to unsettle viewers.
Human waste is the most dangerous of all animal feces.
There can be found in all modern Indian cities no sewers.

Voluptuous Mae West never used four-letter words.
In England, the upper class all keep separate bedrooms.
The largest stateless nation in the world are Kurds.
Unsavoriness has always been a connotation of poolrooms.

Himokawa Udon is the most telegenic of all noodles.
Babe Ruth always stepped on first base coming in.
Puff pastry is not used in traditional German strudels.
Far less nutrients are in potato's flesh than in its skin.

Richard Wagner needed silken garments to compose.
There are in existence no modern underground cities.
Oppose as a word is the complete opposite of appose.
Muddle is the crippled personality of all committees.

Nothing in the United States was more *un*-American
than the House Un-American Activities Committee.
One single parable alone redeems every Samaritan.
Kansas City, Mo. Should be called Missouri City.

Tap water is completely undrinkable in Dubai.
A jealous mate and an opposite sex best friend are fatal.
Mincemeat is no longer an ingredient in mince pie.
Injuries relating to the buttocks are referred to as "natal."

TRUISMS II

The darker the roux, the nuttier the flavor.
Jews are banned from praying at the Temple Mount.
Cross Donald Trump once, you're out of favor.
Honeybees, seeking landmarks, are able to count.

In the Elizabethan age, years began on March 25th.
Thoreau on trips to Cape Cod, never slept on a beach.
"By this means," not "here" defines the word *herewith*.
One gene alone separates a nectarine from a peach.

Sleeping on any and all Cape Cod beaches is banned.
Jane Seymour was the favorite of Henry VIII's six wives.
Both the letters "e" and "t" comprise the ampersand.
A *protection* from illness and infection are actually hives!

The best knives on the planet are hot-drop forged.
R. Nixon, W. Wilson, C. Coolidge: all were food phobic.
Its head is invisible when a tick is fully engorged.
No Iroquois of the Native American tribe are acrophobic.

Shortening words comes naturally to every Australian.
Abstention in its purity is a central vow of a Sannyasi.
All U.S, presidents with a beard have been a Republican.
The most common Italian surname in that country is Rossi.

A single flat blow best cracks an egg most cleanly.
NHL goalies all have fanatical pre-game routines.
Ignoring clients at, and by, RMV is done routinely.
A single species of fish does not describe sardines.

Jacqueline Kennedy always weighed exactly 120 pounds.
Dumfounded, grammatically, is preferred to dumbfounded.
"God's wounds!" is the root of the vile curse "'zounds!"
Zero voltage results in an electrical device that's grounded.

Italian pasta doesn't contain salt because it interferes
with any gluten development which makes it possible
to roll pasta into sheets. To make certain it adheres
salt is added to flavor cooking water, so dissolvable.

The odd angularity of Boston's Fenway Park, quirky
right field chiefly, is the toughest MLB field to play.
The Ganges, the most polluted river, is always murky.
"*La Fete de l'Ane*, Jan. 14, was once a French feast day.

An ounce of white roux has the thickening power
of as much as four ounces of a brick (darker) roux.
Daylilies are most hummingbird's favorite flower.
Americans, unlike Brits, despise having to queue.

At midnight is the standard time for electrocutions.
The Social Register records pedigree, not achievement.
Subduction gives a symmetrical curve to the Aleutians.
Going through it is the fastest way out of bereavement.

Explain the lyric: "Blue skies, all of them gone,
Nothing but blue skies from now on." *Logic?*
Shaun, Eoin, Ian, Hans, Ivan, names for John,
include Juan, Janek, Gianni, Yahya, and Yonic.

TRUISMS II

A bride wearing a green dress brings misfortune.
The name Bouvier, of humble roots, means "cowherds."
Nothing's thornier than to figure out gross margin.
Scientifically linked to ancient dinosaurs are all birds.

Methane gas is twenty-five times more powerful
a greenhouse gas than the chemical carbon dioxide.
The Mursi of Ethiopia consider lip plates beautiful.
Chaucer's Wife of Bath, with two spurs, rode astride!

When shaking a can of mixed nuts, larger nuts go to the top.
It was illegal in 17th-c Massachusetts to celebrate Christmas.
Pedophiles notoriously, repetitiously, habituate a bus stop
Acme, Inc. in old comic books is the name of every business.

Applewood is the best for successful dowsing.
Camel milk is held to be healthier than cow milk,
Excessive eating or drinking, alone, is carousing.
When damp and inside out is the key to iron silk.

A block of ice thaws faster under cold running
water—a fact—than in a 200º Fahrenheit oven.
Religious cults take a cruel delight in shunning.
A *covenstead* is a meeting place for a coven.

Apples, Malus genus, are part of the rose family,
Mufflers on vehicles are located ever on the right.
The poorest country on the planet is Burundi.
Bathroom sink stoppers are often turned too tight.

The *Mayflower* exiles, denoted as separatists,
called themselves "saints," but never *pilgrims*.
Experience alone is knowledge to empiricists.
Weather changes is a major cause of megrims.

In Switzerland, Swiss cheese is termed Emmenthaler.
"Dixie" was penned by an Ohioan in a NYC boarding house.
Lengthy speeches are a major vice of a stonewaller.
Humidity below 60% will generally eliminate a booklouse.

Smoking cigarettes initially was thought effeminate.
Rudyard Kipling refused to write in anything but black ink.
A doubled consonant (cf. "thi*nn*ess") is a geminate.
The exudation on hippos—a natural sunscreen—is pink.

Apache chief Geronimo's real name was Govathlay,
but Mexican settlers called him "Jerome" in Spanish.
Stone Mountain is considered holy ground by the KKK.
Thick eyebrows, square jaw make women look mannish.

The richest country in the world is Luxembourg.
Blue stars in the sky are the hottest, red the coolest.
Prince Philip Mountbatten was born a Battenberg.
Accord was the first job of the "second" of a duelist.

The most common German surname is Müller.
Rhode Island could fit into the state of Texas 270 times.
If it is neither fried nor twisted, it is not a cruller.
The only "music" at the soul of rap is obvious rhymes.

TRUISMS II

Italians do not like to have women pour wine.
The nether, technically, is not part of a millstone.
Cows collectively alone can be qualified as kine.
Les Québécois insist that visitors be francophone.

Ignoramuses say "eye-ran" for Iran, *Hollowe*'en
for Hallowe'en, and "dackery" for the drink daiquiri.
Many hotels name the 13th floor "M," not # thirteen.
Jesus was much less fond of Judaea than of Galilee.

Irving Berlin only played in the key of F-sharp,
the black note that fell easily under his fingers,
with an added moving key board, a semi-harp,
that supplied all other keys for range and ringers.

Continents are wider in the north than in the south.
Corn always has an even number of rows on each cob.
Drought, voiced differently, means same as drouth.
Kaiser Wilhelm saw virility in a Prussian *pickelhaube*.

Claret is the British term for red Bordeaux wine.
Pornography is paradigmatic template for rapists.
Rope's of many twisted fibers, fewer have twine.
The Ulster Unionist Party execrates all Papists.

Most Broadway Show titles are invariably a spondee:
Carousel; Dames at Sea; Guys and Dolls; Hairspray;
As Thousands Cheer; On the Town; The Gay Divorcee;
The King and I; South Pacific; Brigadoon; Cabaret;

The Lion King; 42nd Street; Top Hat; Oklahoma!
Babes in Arms; A Chorus Line; Broadway Folly;
Man of La Mancha; Call Me Madam; Saratoga;
Kiss Me, Kate; The Sound of Music; Hello, Dolly!

All airplane "black boxes" are in fact always yellow.
Most, if not all, polar bears are strangely left-handed.
The coffee flavor was never a great success in Jell-O.
A snake is less liable to predation when it is banded.

Kubrick originally intended to end *Dr, Strangelove*
with the General Staff involved in a crazy pie fight.
"Of which," "of what," not where, defines *whereof.*
A wainwright is always, culturally, a wheelwright.

Bandleader Cab Calloway called white people "pinks."
Udon and Himokawa is about noodles, ramen about broth.
Silk is high temperatures and hot water always shrinks.
An individual full of wrath (noun) is—adjective—*wroth.*

All his journal pages were written in reverse by Leonardo.
Jesus was born in Nazareth, but in Bethlehem theologically.
Most savage torturers favor foot-whipping—the bastinado.
Logical synthesis seeks to conjoin opposites philosophically.

Fake pearls are all smooth and slippery, whereas real pearls
give a rough grating sensation; to evaluate them, to be brief.
—to ascertain imitation from the real things' rutty knurls—
rub a given rope of pearls roughly across your front teeth.

TRUISMS II

Most of the crass villains in the Bible have red hair.
An obese individual actually gain weight inside of his mouth.
Polaroids filter out *horizontal* light waves, source of glare.
One point south of due east on a compass is east by south.

Large eyes in a Swiss cheese mean more intense the flavors.
There is no correct way to wear a remembrance poppy.
To make a single crotchet you need eight demisemiquavers.
What secretes melatonin is specifically the pineal body.

The Japanese do not have a word for the color brown.
Toxic are Red 40, Yellow 5 and Yellow 6 food dyes.
Any English noun that counts plurals is a "count noun."
Gray is considered the rarest color in all human eyes.

A comminated bone fracture is the worst one can have.
Mathew Brady, photographer, used one T in his name.
A blue whale is pregnant a full year before it will calve.
A zebra, unlike horses, is completely impossible to tame.

Jehovah's Witnesses refuse to say the "Pledge of Allegiance."
The standard table napkin is formally 30 inches by 36 inches.
Nebraska is the only state without a test by a Board of regents.
Their proper collective noun is, formally, a "charm" of finches.

George Washington, who loathed shaking hands, only bowed.
90% of grapes used in the USA are Thompson seedless grapes.
Caning British private school boys kept them properly cowed.
Laughter as a response exist for chimpanzees and great apes.

Chinese chopsticks are longer than those used in Japan and Korea.
No windows existed on floors 7, 8, 108, 109 of the World Trade Center.
It was in the time of Christ that Pontius Pilate governed in Caesarea.
A miser, a hoarder, and a cheapskate may all be identified as a
    congener.

The Pirazzi family, who made violin strings for Paganini,
make the finest strings anywhere on this entire planet.
Linguine is flat and narrow, but wider is its cousin fettucine.
Juanita is Jeanette is Jean is Jane is Janeth and is Janet.

Gravity devours light—and may also emit light, as well.
Machines are never used to a handle caviar/sturgeon roe.
It was to rescue souls that Jesus once descended into Hell.
To push not pull is the purposeful action of a Dutch hoe.

The "Polo Lounge" at the pink Beverly Hills Hotel
was the center of all old Hollywood deal-making.
Personality is required in any director of personnel.
Browning creates extra layers of flavor in baking.

Dance bands were forbidden to play "God Bless America"
back in the 1930, and swing arrangements were ruled out.
China and the USA constitutes, symbiotically, Chimerica.
Epoxy is far better than cement as a standard for grout.

It is a tradition for all freed Reno, NV. divorcees
to throw their wedding rings into the Truckee River.
Natives of Vietnam are correctly called Annamese.
Irregular eating schedules are unhealthy for your liver.

TRUISMS II

Schocken Books publishes only in books written by Jews.
Merely saying "you" to a MLB umpire gets a player thrown out.
Fashion allows Scottish men *and women* to wear tartan trews.
No fish is voracious as surface-skimming, ever-hungry trout.

"The Girl That I Marry," as written, was meant ironically.
Pablo Picasso was never allowed or given a U.S.A. visa.
No one from the state of Maine does not speak laconically.
Provocation is an underlying motivation of every teaser.

No one can explain why stars are arranged in bundles.
Pluto the planet is white from methane, like fallen snow.
Rainforest s have fewer trees, more sunlight, than jungles.
More eyelashes exist above the human eye than below.

On planet Mars exists a volcano, "Olympus Mons,"
that is 17 miles high and 370 miles across its base.
Shrimp have two pairs of legs, with three on prawns.
A dominant nostril can be found on a human face.

Oscar Wilde found idleness necessary for a state of perfection.
Women's largest breasts are found in Iceland and Norway.
King Farouk (1920–1965) owned the greatest coin collection.
Anticipation to anyone imaginative is an aspect of foreplay.

All large moons in the solar system have been despun.
Songs about songs were a signature of Irving Berlin.
Wooden artillery composed a Civil War "Quaker gun."
Nutrients predominate not in its flesh but a potato skin.

All those end up earning it who marry for money.
Of xylem and phloem sap, we choose the latter: sugar.
Thieves prefer twenty-dollar bills in ransom money.
Pressure cooker food's tastier than that of a slow cooker.

Kansas is too far inland ever to receive a hurricane.
Charlie Chaplin never set foot in England during WWII.
Learning actually changes the *structure* of a brain.
Ancient Greek language had no term for the color blue.

A crow has the brainpower of a seven-year-old child.
Clover, alfalfa, timothy and orchard grass make up hay.
Palestinian and the Jew, for 2000+ years unreconciled.
Nowhere is the Bible is it stated we should kneel to pray.

Third political parties always fail in the United States.
Saki's punchlines are all masterpieces of understatement.
Dinners in Korean households feature lots of plates.
Hiring a ship to sail with cargo is called affreightment.

UFOs are circular because of particle acceleration.
Rosé wine is tasteless, worthless, after three years.
For Broadway shows gay men have a predilection.
Birthday wishes are trifling when observed in arrears.

Women own only one percent of the world's land.
Aztec emperor Montezuma wouldn't let anyone watch him eat.
From the ground to its withers is a horse spanned.
Alaskan pollock is the predominant source of imitation crab meat.

TRUISMS II

Marco Polo's Cambulac in China is now modern Beijing.
A sapiosexual is sexually attracted to intelligent persons.
Alarm pheromones—seeking help—accompany a bee sting.
All reports, accounts, explanations, and reviews are versions.

Lard has less saturated fat and cholesterol than butter,
and, unlike all partially hydrogenated vegetable oils,
it carries no trans-fat and should be used (no shudder!),
to make the best pie crusts and tortillas (no despoils!)

Thomas Merton's grim poem "Original Child Bomb,"
about the U.S. bombing of Hiroshima, August 6, 1945,
bookstores shelved among "juveniles" without a qualm,
assuming it was for little children of age four or five.

Bloodstock was Queen Elizabeth II's favorite subject.
Most celebrities intrinsically are never worth knowing.
Affect means to produce a change; the result, its effect.
Missouri River basin waters are the most overflowing.

The speed of sound—Mach number—is 761 m.p.h.
British toffs will never ask "Pardon?"—they say "What?"
Any two-handled drinking vessel is ritually a *quaich*.
All over-iced (concealing taste) American beers are rotgut.

"Strike" and "Ball" should properly be "Straight" and "Wide."
Einstein in Switzerland was refused a job teaching high school.
Having not a thing to do with a Spring season is a Spring tide.
Inadmissible is every U.S. court is the banned "hearsay rule."

One high tide faces the moon, while the other faces away from it.
A ball player can reach first base faster running than sliding.
Having to be flared or collared is the fashion of every grommet.
Harshness, neither drollery nor wit, is the nature of chiding.

Salting a grapefruit always makes it taste sweeter.
Women have never liked the humor of W. C. Fields.
A vessel ready to sail flag-waves a "Blue Peter."
A lemon pre-heated in water squirts out greater yields.

No person praised in it should be allowed to blurb a book.
All divorced persons are banned from the royal HMY *Britannia*.
The largest and most valuable of all salmon is the Chinook.
The loveliest world road is the Transfagarasan in Transylvania.

Barometer high—heave short and away.
Barometer shifting—reef tackles prepare.
Barometer low—let the sunken anchor stay.
Barometer steady—set sails without fear.

The eaten "roe" of the sea urchin are actually its gonads.
There can be found in Jane Austen's six novels no kisses.
Livestock is the sole of resource of the Bedu, or nomads.
Idaho is the redoubt of most extremist American. Militias.

The French pronounce the English word "cut" as *curt*.
Eggs of caged hens are more likely to harbor salmonella.
An effective face mask (zinc, calcium) is plain yoghurt.
A rare delicacy is Asian cuisine is jellyfish subumbrella.

TRUISMS II

Raymond Chandler pictured Philip Marlowe as Cary Grant.
St. Paul had extraordinary little interest in the historical Jesus.
Gibberish on religion or morals, alone, technically is *cant*.
Ecstasy as a danger has always been connected to Dionysius.

Searing meat does not seal in its juices; if anything,
it dries it out juices and forces it to lose its flavor.
Michael was the baptismal name of Martin Luther King.
Charity is the impulse of an unconditional waiver.

The only underlying purpose of any census is taxation.
Europeans, and most countries, never refrigerate eggs.
Vernation structures leaf buds; with veins, it's *ve*nation.
Anti-inflammatory properties exist in the oil of nutmegs.

Marinades may flavor meat but will never tenderize it
Artichokes, with phytochemical cynarin, can discolor skin.
The British with a foreign word ever try to Anglicize it.
Shunning temptation means to avoid an "occasion of sin."

There has never been a great film without close-ups.
Norman Mailer believed contraception diminished manliness.
A new defensive polymer, from sunlight, self-destructs.
Poet William Blake said wisdom comes from excessiveness.

Corn is one of the least nutritionally complete grains.
Most *The New Yorker* cartoons are utterly meaningless.
It was held as raffish for WWI soldiers to carry canes.
Conflict of the inner ear and eyes causes sea sickness.

The New England Patriots gave away QB Tom Brady
--winner of seven Super Bowls—for absolutely nothing.
Any utopian situation (with shepherds or no) is Arcady.
Effective in cards, if only done *sporadically*, is bluffing.

White Leghorn chickens lay eggs all white-shelled.
Plymouth Rocks and Rhode Island Reds lay brown.
Bleach and rubbing alcohol are always a lethal meld.
Coulrophobia posits a terrifying threat from a clown.

"Cleanskin" is a term for inexpensive wine whose label
does not indicate the winery or the winemaker's name.
The often referred-to sleigh bell is, technically, a cascabel.
Two hundred times sweeter than table sugar is aspartame.

Avocados are not vegetables, but rather fruits.
The lines of rubber tire treads are known as *sipes*.
Two fingers are used in Polish military salutes.
Essentially a martial instrument are all bagpipes.

The country of Australia is wider than the moon.
Froot Loops, with different colors, all have the same flavor.
Spiritual color of wisdom in Buddhism is maroon.
Walking by way of seeking alone is he way of a wayfarer

In every Muslim prostration—Sajdah—forehead, nose,
hands, knees, and toes must be firmly on the ground.
None can serve in the U.S. Army who has missing toes.
Jewish shabbat starts minutes before sunset, not sundown.

TRUISMS II

There is literally a blind spot in every human eye:
it is located 15 degrees on the nasal side of the fovea.
Any shiny object is attractive to a (Pica pica) magpie.
A morbid fear of buttons is called Koumpounophobia.

Suspicion in its inflexible neurosis that despises facts.
English Plum Pudding uses no plums, only raisins, currants.
It is indisputable that Luke wrote the Book of Acts.
Most parents' behavior inevitably channels their own parents.

Jesus' hometown, Nazareth, is not mentioned in the Talmud,
or the Midrash or in Josephus or in the entire Old Testament.
Sycamore trees, used to make buttons, are called buttonwood.
British aristocracy considers a use of euphemisms inelegant.

Arkansas is the largest rice producer in the United States.
Vitamins B and C are destroyed by the process of boiling.
A colloquial reference to virginity is the term "V-Plates."
A necessary expertise among climbers is rope "coiling."

To conspiracy theorists, any lack of solid evidence
confirms that all is well-hidden, and everything rigged.
Search for self is the highwater mark in adolescence.
Anonymity's the main reason UK lawyers are wigged.

The best of all white wine comes from Burgundy,
whereas the best of red wine hales from Bordeaux.
In Werner Heisenberg's "principle of uncertainty,"
what's said of one property of the other less we know.

Greta Garbo, John Barrymore, Charlie Chaplin, Alfred Hitchcock,
Cary Grant, and Gloria Swanson have never won an Oscar.
The cradle of Christianity was, not Rome, but the city of Antioch.
A charge of rape was once brought against poet Geoffrey Chaucer.

Brown sugar will not harden if stored in a freezer;
on the other hand, flour can readily be frozen hard.
Caesarean describes not the birth of Julius Caesar.
Topps 1952 Mickey Mantle is the top baseball card.

The singular joy for Nikola Tesla was love of pigeons.
Mohawk Indians have no fear atop windswept girders.
Meat from dairy cows, ill sought in American kitchens
or restaurants, becomes dog food and fast-food burgers.

Add yeast to water, but never add water to yeast.
A lighter color in maple syrup proves a higher quality.
Any Catholic priest who marries remains a priest.
Socialism has always valued liberty less than equality.

All hoarders of survivalist food rations own shotguns.
Swiss eat American-style burgers with a knife and fork.
No one exceeded Will Shakespeare in scatological puns.
The most rebellious Irish have come from County Cork.

During World War I, every German soldier swore a belt
that proudly proclaimed "*Gott Mit Uns*" on its buckle.
Both salt and fresh water can be inhabited by the smelt.
Poisonous to dogs is the plant (woodbine) honeysuckle.

TRUISMS II

Chapter 53 of the book of Isaiah—accepted
as part of the Holy Scripture—is prohibited
from being read in Israel. And why rejected?
It foretells the coming of Christ as exhibited.

JFK, uniquely, called his youngest brother "Eddie."
No humpback whale, misnamed, actually has a hump.
Mt. Everest's East Face/Ridge is notably unsteady.
Every heavy shell landing gives the sound of *crump*.

The benefit of using dandelion over standard rubber tires
is that for autos dandelion rubber can be grown in a year,
while a traditional rubber tree, slow to develop, requires
up to seven years to grow, its latex no better for wear.

DaVinci, Gandhi, and Leo Tolstoy never ate meat.
The human face is the prime source of movie drama.
Nothing is not fully edible in the entire plant of a beet.
China jails any supporters of the 14th Dalai Lama.

All fish have vertical tail fins, whales are horizontal.
Most silent films were produced by a hand-cranked camera.
Details are held inconsequential in any *tout ensemble*.
Democracy, in reality, is a complete and utter chimera.

Mignonette sauce is best enhancement of raw oysters.
Actor Erich von Stroheim farcically won the Legion of Honor.
Women are never allowed to enter Trappist cloisters.
No rain, no wind, and 50°F on race day pleases a marathoner.

Only a mere fifth of solid Aristotle's works are extant.
Richard Nixon's trousers always fell a trifle too short.
Weight, that it never wobble, is important in a sextant.
A stripper is obliged not dance as much as to cavort.

A group of flamingos is referred to as a "flamboyance."
Jackie Robinson didn't play baseball between age 21 and 26.
Women's lipstick, to Adolf Hitler, was a great annoyance.
A female personalized deity was the underworld's River Styx.

The heart of every shrimp lies in its head.
Recycling one ton of cardboard saves 46 gallons of oil.
Every Jerusalem has its living Tancred.
The highest water holding capacity is found in clay soil.

There are exactly 293 ways to make change for a dollar.
People used to say "prunes" when their photo was taken.
A larger knot in a tie always goes with a wider collar.
Aeration lessens strength in a martini when it is shaken.

No terrorist cannot quickly improvise a Molotov cocktail.
White House staffers columnists praise are usually "leakers."
"Cow hock" is undesirable in breeds, except for a Clydesdale.
South Korea accepts any/all North Korean asylum seekers.

Venus is the only planet that spins clockwise.
There are no words to the Spanish national Anthem.
Cold weather prevents flight with butterflies.
A tall man is considered three-fourths handsome.

TRUISMS II

The forage fish for Lake Superior salmon is the cisco.
America's first Christmas tree—Sorel, Quebec, 1781.
"Revelation through Concealment:" the art of Christo.
Shakespeare was the master of the scatological pun.

A cow without teeth farmers denominate a gummer.
President Andrew Johnson considered blacks ill fit to vote.
Boosting his/her happiness is subtext of a hummer.
Narrowness—for quick turning—is needed in a whaleboat.

Bare-knuckle champ John L. Sullivan refused to fight a Negro.
What fans called "The Tramp," Chaplin called "The Little Fellow."
250 vegetables and 170 fruits flourish in gardens of Monticello.
An orange tinge on the rim is a telltale sign of a good Merlot.

Headphones can increase the bacteria in your ears.
Exotic medical operations are always tabloid fodder.
Regret—including joy—is the cause of all tears.
God and silver jewelry both require a hard solder.

A Nazi salute is the holy grail of shoulder rehab signs.
Wiretapping, a crime for laymen, for the FBI it's "monitoring."
Pictures and statues are never part of Muslim designs.
Homesteading is/was utterly dependent on subsistence farming.

Despite an arrest record of 75 years, Anthony ("Big Tuna,"
"Joe Batters," etc.) Accardo spent only one night in jail.
Coins grow in size/weight with value of the Czech koruna.
God twice miraculously supplied the Israelites with quail.

Horace Mann and Daniel Webster despised each other.
Israel slaughtered 40,000 Palestinian civilians in 2024.
A sister's period is delayed by having an older brother.
Chinese and Japanese connect death with the number four.

Mean sea level is *the same* in the Atlantic and Pacific.
Abe Lincoln never slept in the White House "Lincoln bedroom."
Very few ancient Egyptians could read hieroglyphic.
The ribs of the oil palm tree have best fibers for making a broom.

No one on earth since 1980 has had a case of smallpox.
The cost of the Apollo 11 moon flight was $25 billion.
No seed pod in the *genus Crotalaria* is not a rattlebox.
The *ceceo* factor predominates in all spoken Castilian.

"Be beige" is a covert CIA directive, which is to say,
avoid notice, desist from trying to look "interesting."
Rules allow drinking cocktails when playing croquet.
Vivisepulture resembles magnetic resonance imaging.

Water does not figure in the Tuareg version of creation,
only rocks, because they have lived with no sign of the sea
Scriptural/Biblical lines of descent go strictly by agnation.
A person of one-eighth African ancestry is seen as a mustee.

St. Thomas Aquinas is the patriarch of scholasticism.
Attar is the oldest perfume in all of cultural history.
Venom against Arabs (semites) is also anti-semitism.
Silver is the ideal metal for use in a surgical bistoury.

TRUISMS II

Literary agents serve the same function as a panderer.
The fulcrum of jazz, good and bad, is improvisation.
It is a vogue among gourmands to excoriate coriander.
Supporting evidence is irrelevant in a true asseveration.

Scratch any political hack to discover a moral bankrupt.
Head chefs tend to scorn sous chefs and chefs *de partie.*
Cheese makes an *au gratin* when potatoes are scalloped.
Kippers are used in Scotland when cooking a kedgeree.

Dom DiMaggio was a better outfielder than his brother, Joe.
The Octagon House in Washington DC is actually hexagonal.
Ravens give a low croaking sound; it's cawing with a crow.
There is technically no shape to a—line segment—diagonal.

Rivalry between father and son over the paternal mistress
is to the French a theme in art more distasteful than incest.
Staring upon the mythic Gorgon any defense was resistless.
Avoid whiplash on coasters by pressing back on the head rest.

The Catholic Church, annulled three of Sinatra's marriages,
conveniently—for a fee—so that he could marry a fourth!
Jealousy offers one's select enemy nothing but effleurages.
Death as the one constant in our lives is true magnetic north.

Conscience must forever have its correlative in conduct.
It is considered disrespectful to salute with your left hand.
Virtually anything touching liquid oxygen will destruct.
Kalaallisut and Danish are mainly spoken in Greenland.

Herbert Hoover irrationally feared the number 13.
So did FDR, who would never travel on that day
but, for Woodrow Wilson, the numeral was keen
and, for the lucky 13 letters in his name, A-OK!

It is taboo for any skier to announce his or her last run.
Tokyo is officially the world's culinary capital.
No one wrote a wife lovelier love letters than Hawthorne.
The textual. narrative of all dreams is irrational.

Grapes, raisins, and currents are poisonous to dogs.
Elizabeth P. Peabody of Salem would have made a great President.
No17th-c Pilgrim dwellings were built as cabins of logs.
Malaria, shingles, and pneumonia are notoriously recrudescent.

Arturo Toscanini, a mad womanizer, was virtually a satyr.
Only 10 of Emily Dickinson's poems saw print in her lifetime.
No hateful or peevish personality is not compulsive testator.
There are 1000 windows in the English palace of Blenheim.

Perfume bottles cost much more to fabricate than perfumes.
Dorothea Dix stated no Civil War nurse should be beautiful.
Windows jutting over moats were medieval castle bathrooms.
T, D, N, S, Z, and I are all retroflexive consonants cacuminal.

"Waldo" was R. W. Emerson's preferred name for himself.
Only as late as 1968 (!) did a Federal statue outlaw lynching.
The Atlantic is always trying to explain America to itself.
Autistic children are behavioristically addicted to pinching.

TRUISMS II

The narrative of very El Greco painting rehearses skew.
No shape resist water's crushing pressure than a sphere.
The Ancient Greek language had no term for the color blue.
Pink with women is good for every shade of skin and hair.

Any faith deprived of or wanting in ethics is a dead religion.
Planets, smaller, have less gravitational pull than stars.
No one thing understands space and time more than a pigeon.
Omissions are the *sine qua non* of all celebrity memoirs.

San Diego, California is the top migrant border entry point.
Protestant theologian Karl Barth despised Martin Luther.
Every bookcase made proves the validity of the butt joint.
The history of priapism starts with a Hollywood producer.

No chocolate, at bottom, does not have the taste of sin.
Finding peace of mind with little is the greatest wealth.
Sharkskin soup chefs discard everything but the fin.
Dishonestly acquired riches, alone, is considered pelf.

Indira Gandhi was assassinated by her two bodyguards.
Every local celebrity is an astonishing pain-on-the-ass.
The Hall brothers (Hallmark) created folded Christmas cards.
Top predator in the aquatic ecosystem is the largemouth bass.

In traditional old London, it was Lock the hatter,
Harris the chemist, Fox for cigars, Evans for guns,
locks at Chubb, Fortnum &Mason for food matter,
Berry Bros & Rudd for any wine and spirits runs.

The gift of a clock is considered very rude in China.
Nabokov's Humbert was likely based on Norman Douglas.
Never one unified state were North and South Carolina.
There is no architectural elegance at all to a flying buttress.

The vibrant undersense of Nature is God's best secret.
There are three versions of Ludwig Beethoven's *Fidelio*,
the score of which was an often reworked, frequently cut,
refractory and compulsively rewritten musical libretto.

Female ducks prefer a male duck with the brightest bill.
In India, Japan, and Peru women very rarely wear a bra.
Theology's inveterate debate—Grace versus Free Will.
Hotter than the sun by 9,940 Kelvins is Sirius the Dog Star.

Sinatra, hating bulges, carried no wallet or credit card,
only a set of folded C-notes with a golden band or clip.
Most women's skin-care products are essentially lard.
B vitamins and folic acid deficiency can cause cleft lip.

The oldest surname in world history is Katz,
the initials of Kohen Tsedek—a lengthy pedigree
that lists every Katz, synonym for priests, stats
state, extending from the line of Aaron, 1300 B.C.

Freud, elemental, understood the aim of life is death.
Fine graphite from China best sold as *yellow* pencils.
An appetite suppressant is the amphetamine meth.
Bristol artist Banksy's sole equipage are his stencils.

TRUISMS II

Anonymity's crucial to graffiti artists since it is illegal.
New England's Robert Frost was born in San Francisco.
Standard entrance to skater's jumps is the "spread eagle."
It was essentially 1970s gay clubs that invented disco.

Most suicides have a deeper homicidal ideation.
The quilts made by the Amish always feature a border.
Wearing only one shoe is grave taboo to a Haitian.
Bob Kramer's chef knives—perfection—are made to order.

Poet Ernest Dowson's cry for "madder music"
was an assault on conventional Victorian values.
Shamanism is the main religion of the Tungusic.
Zimbabwe elections lead in world voting snafues.

True socialists and radical always drink a budget wine.
Finland is the world's largest consumer of coffee.
It is fully impossible for all eight planets to ever align.
Dwellers in Islamic heaven exist eternally at age 33.

Only drones choose wines by way of Robert Parker points.
King James I believed drowning proved a woman not a witch.
The hips and shoulders are a human being's weakest joints.
A slip stich is in order whenever one needs an invisible stitch.

China leads the world in illegally appropriating patents.
42% of Americans—100 million—suffer from obesity.
Quakers who swear no oaths ate famous non-combatants.
Lack of sight is not blindness as such but in fact, cecity.

In 2020, Hispanic voters replaced Black voters
in the U.S. as the largest minority voting block.
Vitamin C and zinc militate against eye "floaters."
Every minstrel's man's joy was doing a cakewalk.

Tomasina turkeys are much more tender than the toms.
Women wear their belt buckles clockwise, right to left.
His First Symphony took a lifetime to finish by Brahms.
The major theme of Romantic poetry is feeling bereft.

Jesus is inferior to the Father, touching on his manhood,
but He is equal to the Father, touching on his Godhead.
The Holy Spirit, co-eternal, was neither made nor created,
Nor begotten; he proceeds from the Father and the Son.

Coca-Cola owns the design rights to the Coke bottle.
Myrmecologists, coming the ground, always walked stooped.
The determination of disruptive camouflage in mottle.
Pride, more than any other human fault, Jesus Christ rebuked.

A customary greeting when approaching a tent (*ger*)
in Mongolia is "*Nokhoigo Khorioroi*" ("Hold the dog").
Private and closed properties characterize Big Sur.
Any soil is unfit and useless for cultivation in a peat bog.

Al Capp's Joe Btfsplk's name is pronounced as a Bronx cheer.
An apostle—its definition—officially had to see the Lord in person.
Beethoven wrote his Ninth Symphony totally unable to hear.
The promise of a husband's first brutality is that it will only worsen.

TRUISMS II

Elizabeth David's *English Bread and Yeast Cookery*
should be given as a gift to every marrying couple.
At the Somme, 300,000 men were killed, a butchery.
Misfortune, when understood, makes a person supple.

Cheap-labor Republicans and assured-vote Democrats
have sanctioned illegal U.S. immigration since 1986.
Nothing's more manufactured than sincerity in diplomats.
Only for consuming noodles do Indonesians use chopsticks.

Males, 50% of the population, represent 80% of suicides.
Never accept any food in Mongolia with your left hand.
The main constituent in human body fat are triglycerides
J.P. Sousa formed a concert group, not a marching band.

It is illegal in the U.S. to import medicine from overseas.
The set of G. Herriman's Krazy Kat was Arizona territory.
A dilettante takes pride in being highly difficult to please.
The cheek is the tastiest part of the special fish John Dory.

A sweet sherry is ideally consumed at mid-morning.
Jesus often, oddly, repeated himself (cf. John 7:33–35).
Balinese believe tears shed impede a soul when mourning.
The favored concealed pistol for most carriers is the .45.

Cooking avocado, obscene, murders its flavor.
Notifications on computers appear in the upper right.
Every gun-rights maven is a desperate flag waver.
All human eyes have a blind spot, a scotoma in sight.

The material of Amish dresses is always a plain color,
never checked, striped, or printed, or with polka dots.
Not subject to Fed Reserve regulations is the Eurodollar.
Little improves the human body more than doing squats.

There is no such thing as inaccuracy in a photograph:
all photographs are accurate. None of them is the truth.
George Washington's is the most valuable U.S. autograph.
Brutus, tyrant slayer, was the favorite role of J. W. Booth.

There are thought to be more than 15,000 total ant species.
The U.S. is projected to be a majority minority country in 2045.
Aztec chinampas was a fertilizer of mud and human feces.
Physicians and insurance companies constantly inter-connive.

The human body prefers—digests—beef well done.
Sardonyx gemstones are the red sister of black onyx.
Shakespeare never met his contemporary Kohn Donne.
In 1996, illiteracy became, "officially," Ebonics.

Condoms and birth control are forbidden by the Amish.
Gila monster venom contains hormones regulating blood sugar.
"*Hygge*" is the cozy, comfort value held among the Danish.
High altitudes receive the greatest benefits pressure cooker.

An Englishman is not insulted—rather he's affronted.
Trees in their overspreading affection are like mothers.
Slippage is tthe danger of working tools when blunted.
Dopamine and serotonin are happy chemical brothers.

The Prophet recited, but he did not write the *Qur'an*,
nor was that apocalyptic book written in his lifetime
but was compiled from all his recitations thereupon
after Muhammad's death, his every word a paradigm.

Robert Frost always aimed for a "poetry that talked."
Cuisine magazine was bought by *Gourmet* from jealousy.
Any pitcher faking a throw to first base has balked.
No list or compilation does not subtly reek of cupidity.

Durags are associated with crime, thug, and gang culture.
With Islamic hospitality, the oldest are always served first.
Thermals, allowing it to coast not fly, comfort a vulture.
Need for approval is the most elemental high school thirst.

Author Norman Douglas, an open and active pedophile,
who had many friends of the pretense of not-knowing,
openly admitted using children for sex, seen in his vile
and blasé book, *Looking Back* (1933), proudly crowing.

A person speaking another language is a different person.
No pain exceeds the sting of a bullet ant (*paraponera clavata*).
Conditions of Huntington's Disease progressively worsen.
There is no medical or scientific explanation for a stigmata.

Fauré's *Requiem*, avoiding all horrors of death and loss,
concentrates uniquely on repose, acceptance, and release
—the true meaning of "requiem" means rest—a gloss
bringing serenity to the subject, elevating and of peace.

No chicken recipe is the equal of Elizabeth David's
"Poulet à l'Estragon" in *French Provincial Cooking*.
Much of tonal Thai (spoken) cannot be translated.
Every UK butcher has his version of black pudding.

A group of tortoises or turtles is called a "creep."
Modern automobile hubcaps invariably feature ten struts.
Humans are the only mammals that delay sleep.
Without bee pollination, there would be no Brazil nuts.

Gris is the official name for wine between white and rosé,
but it is called, as well, "Oeil de Pedrix" or "Partridge Eye."
On a side-cock or slant is the correct way to wear a beret.
A person is able to blink properly when wearing a glass eye.

Dairy cows are always less valuable than meat cows.
Levi jeans were originally called "waist overalls."
Women's square-shaped faces call for thick eyebrows.
The cliché name for cataracts is "Horseshoe Falls."

Gaiety is the frantic, slightly sad side of true happiness.
The Russian Orthodox church excommunicated Tolstoy.
One hundred fifty miles is the distant limit of subpoenas.
Sweden is ground zero for a population of Xanthochroi.

The most complicated knots to tie are the Turk's Head,
the Double Fisherman's Knot, and also the Constrictor.
Serial numbers on watches help identify many of the *Lusitania* dead.
The Roman officer for punishing criminals was the lictor.

TRUISMS II

No one fully understands what "gird your loins" means.
Beef cuts from a cow's shoulder are the least expensive.
The small metal fastener innovation made for stronger jeans.
Rain forest depletions in Brazil are the most extensive.

RMS *Titanic*, traveling at 20 knots in ice, was madness.
Cooked carrots provide more antioxidants when cooked.
The hardest crimes to track are those that are purposeless.
The Bank Tavern in Bristol, UK, is constantly booked.

The French use wine corks to tenderize a beef stew.
Brazil cattle ranching has virtually deforested the nation.
Setting sail on a Friday is an age-old nautical taboo.
Henry James' late style was complicated by dictation.

"While we are at home in the body, we are away from the Lord"
asserts St. Paul in his Second Letter to the Corinthians, 5:1–5.
A single root note is the main note on which is built a chord.
The Chinese find a metaphor for a flourishing life in a chive.

The U.S. banned circulation of the French 100-Franc bill
because it dared depict Delacroix's bare-breasted Liberty.
Jesus is never reported to have laughed, rode a horse, or become ill.
It is not equality that French women want, but reciprocity.

Sports team owners yearn that playoffs go seven games.
Broccoli has a much higher nutrient content if eaten fresh.
Akuma (devil) is banned in Japan for use in given names.
The most popular god in all the Hindu religion is Ganesh.

The Icelandic alphabet does not include the letter "C."
May 1st in the 1910s, allowing them, was "Straw Hat Day."
The greatest NFL quarterback of all time is Tom Brady.
Fermentation, not fruit, gives wine its aroma and bouquet.

More than 20% of Amazon rainforest has disappeared.
Kobe beef, a subset of Wagyu, comes from Tajima cattle.
All cranes, with lifting mechanisms, are double-geared.
Movable property (as opposed to real property) is chattel.

No professional chef will ever cook with salted butter.
Speech was given to humans to conceal their thoughts.
A faster green in golf firmly warrants a heavy putter.
White chocolate missing cocoa solids is feebly ersatz.

Almonds are actually a member of the peach family.
No one see a police car nearby without a twinge of guilt.
"Big Hair" bands were the opposite of being manly.
Soft and filled with eiderdown is a continental quilt.

Parsley will balance any over-garlicked dish.
No metal should ever come in contact with sourdough.
Standard edible roe replacing caviar is lumpfish.
The firmest snowballs are fashioned from corn snow.

There are 36 spokes in the average bicycle wheel.
"Cage-free eggs" means zero: birds were still packed in tight.
Abuse of baby cattle should prohibit the selling of veal.
A non-color, never appearing on the color-wheel is white.

TRUISMS II

A cable length—tenth of a nautical mile—is 600 feet.
"The Last Post" is England's military equivalent of taps.
Used to fight depression is the tryptophan in a beet.
Peach in the UK and USA is the most popular schnapps.

A foghorn sounding three times is a "sailors farewell."
Priming a job is needless: paints now contain primer.
The best branching plant for hedgerows is gromwell.
Ascending alone is inadvisable for any rock climber.

A person is permitted to ask questions of meaning
only if he has a language in which to phrase them.
More scream than song is the Irish funeral keening.
Israeli citizens are prohibited visiting Bethlehem.

Meek Woodrow Wilson went to war two years too late.
911 in France is 112, in China 110, and in England 999.
Jealousy, a paradox, is a combination of love and hate.
A pig more than 180 pounds is a hog: both are swine.

Lyric poets do their best work when they are young.
Eels, who enjoy density, always cuddle up in piles.
As many as 10,000 taste buds exist on a human tongue.
Varicolored diamonds on solids alone pattern argyles.

Memory to the Arab mind is the safest of repositories.
Safety says keep your belt buckle between rails on a ladder.
Didacticism is the inevitable blight of all allegories.
Madness, for toxic fumes, has ever been linked to a hatter.

"Covered wagon" is seagoing slang for a pie,
"Soap and flannel" slang for cheese and bread.
Biscuit with currants they call "Squashed Fly,"
and for meat pudding they say, "Baby's Head."

All four of the Beatles were baptized Catholic Christians.
Women in photos love placing a hand on a mate's waist.
Psilocybin fostered art by way of pre-Columbian visions.
Plain rice, along with oats, are completely lacking in taste.

Milk, according to the Qur'an, is the most sacred drink:
Allah describes seas of milk in heaven that never spoil.
Creativity is the first disastrous casualty of groupthink.
Carbon emissions is the prime legacy of mistreated soil.

Frank and Ava were both neurotically obsessive
—each reconciliation prefiguring the next break-up—
compulsively flirtatious and intensively possessive,
—each savage quarrel exceeding a need to make up.

An "Irish Hurricane" at sea is slang for a dead calm.
Jesus called not a single Scribe or Pharisee to become an Apostle.
Bones most prone to fracture are in the human arm.
It was strictly an Egyptian street food that Israel copied for falafel.

The short drop in hanging (1'–2') causes death by strangulation,
rope, usually 1½" manila, pre-stretched, and oiled with soap.
The long drop, 4 to 5 feet breaks the victim's neck—saltation!—
to avoid the bungee phenomenon of the prisoner flying back up.

TRUISMS II

The more keys on one's chain, the lowlier the job he has.
Lincoln walked with his head inclined toward his left shoulder.
Piano trios are the most common configuration of jazz.
A "cabriole" is in fact the technical name for a cigarette holder.

An oak is the very last tree to release its leaves.
Apophatic theology addresses what *not* may be said of God.
Pedophiles adore kids in Peter Pan collars and puff sleeves.
Would-be sophisticates work hard at being never awed.

Narcissists are in love with being misunderstood.
Caerphilly is pronounced "Cayerphilly," not "Carephilly."
A tight timber, there is no visible grain in bass wood.
Capitalism stands as open treason to Social Christianity.

Eucalyptus wood makes the very best didgeridoos.
NFL hockey players must end a fight when separated.
Al-Hakim bi-Amar is incarnation of God to a druse.
Law terms "cruelty" any marriage unconsummated.

Advent, while joyous, is liturgically a penitential season.
We are all shadowed by the dark, backward, and abysm of time.
The first sacrifice and forfeiture of every war is reason.
The U.S. appropriated French *disme* ("tenth") to name our dime.

The ranting roar of all rap music is worse than banausic.
The Christ of liberalism is a moral mentor, not God incarnate.
Most damage is likely permanent in any injury hypoxic.
No sin is not forgiven according to the Godly court appellate.

30 million folks can trace their ancestry to the *Mayflower*.
A goat needs a proper milk stand, locked in, to be milked.
Southerners love to cook with White Lily self-rising flour.
Carnival fun fair games are rigged so that you'll be bilked.

Sopranos, having he highest voice, always sing the melody.
Pedophilia has placed Catholicism on the intellectual back foot.
A woman who is foreperson of a jury is termed the forelady.
The liniment of Southeast Asia is oil taken from the cajeput.

In a Welsh penillion, harmony is improvised, to a harp.
Distributism, a third way, solves capitalism and socialism.
The Shun Classic 8-inch chef's knife will ever stay sharp.
The politically correct mind cravenly loves a euphemism.

Feminists take a dim view of wearing fluted sleeves
No recommended dietary allowance exists for vitamin K.
Courting each other, every lover crucially misperceives.
As far east as Cairo is the town of Kirkenes in Norway.

The plain Union Jack is never worn or flown by yachts—
H.M. ships wear it on a jack staff in the bows when at anchor.
Things of no importance register as aughts and naughts.
Investing, not saving, is the sole preoccupation of a banker.

In her classic book *Household Management* (1861),
Mrs. Isabella Beeton never mentions afternoon tea.
Federal Deposit Insurance can save you in a bank run,
Butter has a much lower smoking point than ghee.

TRUISMS II

The pithy heart of a cattail stem makes a tasty salad.
A banter-prone born next to you on a long flight's a living hell.
Fashion seen as a yardstick for validity is never valid.
Every female in the west (novels, saloons, etc.) is named Belle.

Americans brainlessly inject the odd word *like*
into each and every sentence in every possible way
as an adverb, adjective, enclitic, filler to spike,
used without thought, design, or meaning to convey.

Woe is in store for a girl three times a bridesmaid unwed.
The Spanish believe that cactus plants ward off evil.
A wet nurse in England is often shunned if she is a red head.
Torture by any nation is degenerate, unholy, medieval.

Freedom is contingent upon some degree of restriction—
regulation, or forms, are a precondition for expression;
the object of poetry is defamiliarizing—by depiction—
the familiar by an ingenious wit, of refreshening vision.

The traditional rod for most dowsers is a hazel twig--
used both to locate water *but also* estimate its depth.
A New Englander in the old colonies was a Whig.
The analytical, logical side of the brain is on the left.

Mouth-to-mouth insufflation is found in 2 King 4:32–37.
Most helmsman prefer to keep to the windward side of the tiller.
The points on every maple leaf number to eleven.
Hurting animals is invariably a childhood vice of a serial killer.

St. Paul condemns same-sex relations in Romans 1:18–32.
Mao Zedong's policies killed as many as 80 million souls.
The least common color in foods we eat is the color blue.
Never seen before were new psalms in the Dead Sea Scrolls.

In India, a superstition is to eat curd before leaving a house.
Stanford White, Charles McKim, and Saint-Gaudens: all redheads.
There is a brainlessness to simplicity of design with Bauhaus.
Chinese believe that overs are invisibly conjoined by red threads.

Woman predominates as the central focus of all primal myth:
moon goddess, immortal queen, universal matriarch, deity.
A lucky bond is said to be yours if married by a blacksmith.
The sole essence of a defining uniqueness is its haecceity.

American Anglicans have no sense of being in a diocese,
a titular head, national church, or worldwide communion.
The Danish and Finnish languages have no word for *please*.
The Civil War was fought not to end slavery but for union.

Food-eating contests are primitive, decadent wasteful.
Morra, the Italian hand game, causes constant fistfights.
Euphemisms, while seemingly not, are in fact distasteful.
Purity was held to be the high virtue in medieval knights.

People always refer to the operation "Tommy John Surgery"
after that MLB pitcher's elbow (ulner ligament) was repaired,
a rare procedure that a genius devised, a term almost perjury:
it should be named for Dr. Frank Jobe, a surgeon who dared.

TRUISMS II

Whole Foods for environmental concerns sells no live lobsters.
Mao offered the U.S. 10 million of its female citizens as a gift.
A strong loyalty to wife and family is a trait of killer mobsters.
Generally not needed are items that depressives mainly shoplift.

The most powerful spirits in the world, at 96% 192 proof,
is Polmos Spirytus Rektyfikowany, a Polish-made vodka.
There exists a 1.4-inch slope on any advertised flat roof.
Thirty-six active volcanoes can be found in Kamchatka.

Hungarians write their names hind side to, front side back.
Jesus would only ride a colt upon which no one else had sat.
The architecture of Las Vegas, NV, is comically gimcrack.
That angles are attitudes is evidence in anyone's cocked hat.

Whenever a war ends, retribution inevitably begins.
Robert Frost, painful fir him, never read "To Earthward" in public.
Bonding starts in the mother's belly regarding twins.
The current exchange for one dollar (1$) is 3,450 Mongolian
    tugrik.

The North Yungas Road from La Paz to Coroico, Bolivia,
at a horrific height of 15,000 feet—12 feet wide, no guardrails,
and limited visibility from rain and fog, guarantees hysteria
as "The Death Road," well-named by dint of such details.

The Maldives has the highest divorce rate in the world.
Bohemian (Czech) cuisine is all about goose and caraway seeds.
Finish carpenters greatly value any wood that is burled.
Counting prayers is a distinct oddity in people holding beads.

Literary agents are the least talented of book people.
No fluid, easeful gestures are ever seen in a robin.
No one wins more races in his dreams than a cripple.
Plodding is the equine connotation of a draft dobbin.

Dividers are used for measuring distances,
protractors employed for measuring angles.
parallel rulers for promoting line instances,
and confusing the lot only causes mangles.

Islam views all tattoos, unclean, as altering Allah's creation.
Anyone not from Maine is (coolly) considered "from away."
The English tend to be irked by one rising above his station.
Manet used black in his palette, a color abhorred by Monet.

In the book of Isaiah, the word "woe" is repeated 29 times.
All Thoroughbreds' birthdays, whenever born, is January 1st.
San Francisco is tops for the highest parking violation fines.
England's Ancient Ram Inn (cf. 1496) is said to be cursed.

Pres. Teddy Roosevelt talked *loudly* and carried a *small* stick.
One rakes quahogs, digs clams, pries mussels from wave-washed rocks.
Initially, Leon Trotsky was not a Bolshevik but a Menshevik.
It may take as long as two years fully to perfect one's dreadlocks.

Not one of Mao Zedong's aphorisms is original or insightful.
Baal, older than the Bible, is not one, rather a galaxy of gods.
D. H. Lawrence said he most liked writing when feeling spiteful.
No matter the game played, casinos always have the best odds.

Spitting water is the spiteful task of each and every gargoyle.
Improvisation and sense of rhythm is the secret to singing scat.
An omelet with Périgord truffles should be prepared in olive oil,
declares the Provence school—the Bordeaux school, goose fat.

Oddly enough, both Esther and Mordecai, both Jews,
were named for Babylonian gods—Ishtar and Marduk.
Any tight-fitting trousers of tartan are considered trews.
Jesus is a paragon of revolution in the gospel of Luke.

The followers of Gnostic teacher Basilides (117–138 A.D.)
claimed Simon of Cyrene was crucified instead of Christ.
A person of one-eighth African ancestry is called a *mustee*.
A ghost that freely announces its presence is a poltergeist.

Saint-Gaudens' Double Eagle coin is the U.S.'s most beautiful.
No Major League pitcher has struck out 27 batters in 9 innings.
Everything that Gertrude Stein ever wrote remains inscrutable.
You can't deduct gambling losses without reporting winnings.

Stridulations of beetles go fully unheard—they are all deaf.
Jesus never drank white wine: no mention of it in Scripture.
New musicians find it hard learning to play the bass clef.
"Separable fastener" was the original name (1917) for "zipper."

A Mormon to most folks is considered theologically unsafe.
No surgeon is not fascinated with the deftness of his fingers.
Anticipation is the one guaranteed assurance for "fail-safe."
The secret sorcery of perfume is that it voluptuously lingers.

No human pavane can perfect the "wheel" of dragonflies mating.
The first uncircumcised Christian was Titus, Paul's friend, a Greek.
Literal, direct, straight word-for-word alone is valid translating.
The United Arab Emirates have the longest (52 hours) work week.

The sublime, for Immanuel Kant, is a principle of disorder.
A dingy underwater creature sheds its skin and is suddenly a
    dragonfly.
Under Pres. Biden, 13 million illegals crossed the U.S. border.
A hard, plastic acrylic is the composition of a human prosthetic eye.

A bee loaded with pollen is unable to fly upside down.
Never buy a boat designed for fresh water for use on salt water.
In a glorious rainbow, you will never see the color brown.
On no consecutive mornings does one see the same daughter.

Neatness equals roominess in any cramped space.
Three parts water, one part chlorine bleach removes mildew.
Skin around the eyes is thinnest on the human face.
"Freak Street" (*Jhochhen Tole*) is now famous in Katmandu.

The tongue is the only human muscle attached to one end.
No revenge matches that of a lovely actress growing old.
The capacity to cope in life is basically to have to fend.
Customers love to purchase but literally hate to be sold.

On a boat, never trust a squall that you cannot see through.
Jesus always—only—referred to his mother as "woman."
The tower of Suurhusen is most scandalously out of true.
No one can explain the etymology of the word *yeoman*.

TRUISMS II

A vessel carrying three red lights is not under control.
More mention is made of Jesus than the Prophet in the Qur'an.
Condole is to show sympathy; giving comfort we console.
No fashion item is as elegant for men and women than a caftan.

If righteousness comes by the law, Christ died in vain.
If you win $10,000 at a casino, you take home $7,600.
The first daylight seen in the U.S. is in the state of Maine.
Deducibility in insurance policies is thievishly plundered.

Not one of Jesus's sayings in Aramaic has ever survived.
No white man in the U.S. has ever sung *Porgy and Bess* in public.
Agent-less writers sending work to publishers are despised.
Chalcocite is the most common mineral with copper, 34% cupric.

Of all fats, butter gives the best flavor, by far.
Queen Victoria's favorite food was a lamprey pie.
A cold, wet fog in North England is called a *haar*.
A wedding after 5:30 p.m. necessitates black tie.

Lead is the best ballast for any ship: it never corrodes,
deteriorates, and never loses its market value as scrap.
The devil of legend is easily summoned at crossroads.
$3 dollars a bag is a standard tip to an airport skycap.

Baseball's Billy Martin said 5 players hate you,
10 love you, and 5 cannot make up their minds,
and a manager's job, for the latter who rate you,
is to try to keep them from joining the 10 in kind.

In Cornwall, people pronounce pasties as "*pass tees*,"
and most all Cornish natives prefer to eat them cold.
Hiligaynon is the dialect spoken in Philippine Cádiz.
The most painful wrestling grip is a merciless toehold.

New England macho hunters as a competitive boast
all race to hang their deer carcasses from trees, early.
Nothing for vulgarity can match a Hollywood "roast."
The funniest of the Three Stooges, easily, was Curly.

Sift all pastry and cake flour, to aerate and lighten it.
Winds are named for the direction *from* which they blow.
Using wood shims on any stripped screw can tighten it.
No host was not a buffoon on any television game show.

Red raspberry Freezer Pops are paradoxically blue.
State lotteries recapitulate a bookie's numbers game.
Wakan Tanka is the one deity of the nomadic Sioux.
Prosody and syllabic meter greatly signify in a name.

Every punk mode is an apostolate of irreverence.
Oliver St. John Gogarty hated Eamon de Valera.
Great comfort is had in the abruptness of severance.
"Strangling Angel" is what Victorians called diphtheria.

W. S. Gilbert was crabby, sullen, full of dissension.
Arthur Sullivan, a much milder man, often quelled it.
Strings of operetta successes often eased the tension,
but, in the end, nothing quite ever fully dispelled it.

TRUISMS II

Danish traits appear in none of the characters in *Hamlet.*
Ponos in Greek and *labor* in Latin mean both "work" and "suffering."
A Denver Sandwich: slices of toast enfolding an omelet.
There is no known cure for the indisposition of advanced stuttering.

Japanese subscribe to the belief called *"ochobo,"*
where a small mouth is seen as more attractive.
Water tanks are "directories" for many a hobo.
The human liver first registers the putrefactive.

Frank O'Connor wrote many versions of the same story,
rewriting the same over and over but with varied design.
D-lysergic acid exists in the seed of the Morning Glory.
A condition of human feet is that they never quite align.

There are no people in the books of W.H. Hudson.
The No. 1 *Mad* magazine (near mint) sells for $9,000.
Speaking in public cell phones is literally a ruction.
The largest freshwater fish in the world is hausen.

John Lennon disliked his song, "Run for Your Life"
on the *Rubber Soul* album because of its misogyny.
Northern lights are best seen in Canada's Yellowknife.
The signifier ⚨ is the accepted symbol of androgyny.

Jeremiah is the most depressed person in Scripture.
In his total production, Shakespeare created 1,280 characters.
Swelling of the rotator cuff is standard pain for a pitcher.
The act of shaking hands is not done by English barristers.

Wars start at the top but are prevented at/from the bottom.
Every Hitchcock blonde in films is eventually humiliated.
John Keats wrote fall's most beautiful poem, "To Autumn."
The habit of American men wearing fedoras is antiquated.

A real estate agent's essential job is to say, "Look."
Feminists approve the gall of biblical Queen Vashti.
Egypt's King Farouk I claimed he never read a book,
as did Enrico Caruso, Edward VII, and Jay Gatsby.

M.I.T. hacks, not mere pranks, represent feats of engineering.
The Lystrans thought St. Pail was Hermes, the Greek messenger.
Armenian woman (by survey) are said to be most domineering.
The lion in both the bush and the plains is Africa's apex predator.

No human passion quite surpasses that of adolescent love.
Dante was only 9 when falling in love with Beatrice Portinari.
Van Gogh's "yellow period" was inspired by (digitalis) foxglove.
Largely in Botswana, southwest, is spread the desert kalihari.

Communism is Biblical, emulated by the early Christians.
"Butch Cassidy" was a Mormon outlaw named Robert Leroy Parker.
Legacies complement a major part of Ivy League admissions.
Than Scottish poet James Thomson no writer's work was darker.

No toilet facilities existed in the Elizabethan Globe theater
for 3,000 nightly patrons and no intermission between plays.
Lost tribes in Amazon/Indonesia live the lives of a brachiator,
Gaming tables prefer (clarity) the bright green fabric baize.

TRUISMS II

No prophetic OT book contains more dates than Ezekiel.
Japanese women hate to be seen with their mouths open.
Homoerotic is ever one step short of saying homosexual.
Six pack plastic rings for cans are invariably polypropene.

Aldous Huxley predicted climate change in the 1950s
in his alarming and prognosticatory essay, "Canned Fish."
Originality in every instance is abhorrent to committees.
Aloofness is rudeness, whereas uninvolved is standoffish.

Jesus often desperately wrestled with the will of his Father.
falling on his face in agony, yet ever showing submission.
Doubt is often too blind to see that faith is its twin brother.
All heroes of Russian novels ached to express contrition.

Aluminum baseball bats not only have larger "sweet spots"
but more evenly balanced than their wooden counterparts.
All undershirts worn must always be tucked in for Croats.
Most folks instinctively think of their souls as their hearts.

The English predilection for water cures is notorious.
A border around a map is technically called a neatline
A faithless husband is often, paradoxically, uxorious.
Every place that Washington slept has become a shrine.

Medieval educators consistently treated music as science,
not as a source of pleasure, insight or mode of expression.
Due diligence and pitfalls are often sacrificed in self-reliance.
The government in Nicaragua bans all religious procession.

The poet Alfred L. Tennyson wrote virtually no prose.
Hebrew Purim, named by pagan Haman, means lots or dice.
Never missing at a Scottish breakfast is a bowl of brose.
Moses was banned from Canaan who struck the rock twice.

There exists no Spanish word for bullfight.
Nervous illness is mainly the prerogative of social elites.
An honored guests sits always to the right.
To detox your liver successfully, drink the juice of beets.

Apostle Peter denied Christ (John 18:18) at a charcoal fire
but at a charcoal fire John 21:19) was also later redeemed.
Buddhism declares, "The source of all suffering is desire."
Jesus's garment, top-woven throughout, was unseamed.

Bouillabaisse is the dish that Marseille gave the world.
Dr. Johnson: "Shakespeare never has six lines together without
    a fault."
The shrill, wailing, blown sound of bagpipes is "skirled."
Any twitch of lameness in a horse shows it suffering from stringhalt.

Type O-Negative is the universal blood type.
Machines John Ruskin denounced as "intrinsically hideous."
All nations but the USA eat cowheel and tripe.
World travel is impossible for any who are overly fastidious.

Tact, not a virtue, is but a toady's buffering mechanism.
Cabbage leaves were once worn in men's hats for cooling.
A large overdose of quinine is associated with cinchonism.
Only as late as 1992 did the nation of Uruguay ban dueling.

TRUISMS II

Soap was not made commercially until the 14th century.
True godly worship should made with cathedral silence.
No written memoir is not constructed on episodic memory.
Stability in a golfer's putter requires good counterbalance.

"Crab" is the only dog to appear in Shakespeare's plays.
The Cambridge "Apostles" were exclusive, secretive, and Masonic.
Most people commit suicide on Sundays and Mondays.
Deep dissatisfaction in extreme pessimists and cynics is. Chronic.

The practice of Tao consists of subtracting: "If one doubts
his ability to advance an inch, then he should retreat a foot."
Cancer risk is lowered by sulforaphane in Brussels sprouts.
Gloves are disallowed to all athletes throwing the shot put.

Where there is no vision, there is no fantastical Illyria.
Lydia Maria Child suggested earwax be rubbed on a wound.
Mental conflict becoming somatic is "conversion hysteria."
For human tissue to be operated on, it first must be obtund.

Melancholy in a life can give a truer sense of values—
See Saint Paul, Dr. Johnson, Kant, Cesare Lombroso.
Moods are very much conveyed by one's eyebrows.
Inhabitants of Lesotho are, however, known as Basotho.

A demon possessing a person always possesses a name.
It is the size of water droplets and sun that color clouds.
To be neat in cross-stitching, use an embroidery frame.
Fluid, a brainless flow, is a perfect analogy for crowds.

Hannah (1 Samuel 1:1-20), Elijah (1 Kings 19), Job (1–42),
David (Psalm 6, 13), and Jonah (4) all suffered mental illness.
No rabid ultranationalist is not also a classic xenophobe.
A feminist rant in high cant is the epitome of shrillness.

The art of biography is very rarely as grandiloquent
as all arbitrary chapter-breaks contrive to make them.
All early teenage marriages define an "act precipitant."
No women like Botticelli's more beautified an anadem.

The Spanish National Anthem—as with nations Kosovo,
San Marino, and Bosnia and Herzegovina—has no lyrics.
As much as a full 63% is public land in the state of Idaho.
A hidden sexist bias lingers in the negative word hysterics.

Nothing like a straight line exists—look very closely
to note a flutter. Laser beams are even slightly curved.
Few Abraham Lincoln yarns were not told jocosely.
Compunction remains in the minds of the undeserved.

Giraffes will hum to communicate with each other.
Allodoxaphobia is the fear of other people's opinions.
Low-growing plants deep shade: ideal for ground cover.
Political hacks are the embodiment of servile minions.

The Heritage Foundation; American Enterprise Institute;
Oath Keepers; America's First Legal; extremist troops;
Center for Renewing America; Three Percenters, to boot,
plus the Proud Boys, etc., are all U.S. right-wing groups.

"Zillennials "as a group comprise the demographic cohort
on the cusp of Millenials and Generation Z ("Zoomers ").
Nepal's Tensing-Hillary is world's most dangerous airport.
Crinoline, making skirts lighter, ended the fad of bloomers.

Victorians ate arsenic to achieve a paler complexion.
San Diego Padres' slugger Tony Gwynn almost never struck out.
Most every Hungarian for paprika has a predilection.
Natural good looks in a man or woman are a social *passe-partout*.

Venus is the only planet that actually spins clockwise.
Ketchup was once used as medicine for diarrhea and indigestion.
Poisonous from milkweed are all monarch butterflies.
One's strong opinions are essentially created by autosuggestion.

"We repair what your husband fixed," says the plumber.
Igbo society view twins as a bad omen sent by the gods.
A mime performs without speech, not so a mummer.
Elizabethan orange-seller theater girls were mainly bawds.

The continent of Australia is wider than the moon.
Humans can't walk in a straight line without looking at something.
El Greco had an inordinate attraction for the color maroon.
Ted Williams demanded all baseball batters employ an upswing.

La Sabanata in Venezuela is the worst penitentiary on earth.
No mechanism exists to display metallic colors on a computer.
Upper berth rights include during day sitting on lower birth.
The lead within it is poisonous on all antique pieces of pewter.

Dali's flaccid watches, a mnemonic system
in collapse, was inspired by a meal with Miró,
when in hot sun a Camembert began to soften
and so melt in an eerie, semi-symbolic flow.

The real name for a hashtag or pound sign is an octothorpe.
Hawaii moves nearly three feet closer to Alaska each year.
Black *a capella* vocal harmony is the soul of best doo-wop.
Final lines repeat in the limerick formula of Edward Lear.

Twin births (*ibeji*) are strangely endemic to Nigeria.
Baseball's Nolan Ryan struck out 5,714 (!) batters in his career.
Sadness is a common connotation of the plant wisteria.
18th-century polemics were the addressed by the pamphleteer.

Apostasy—conversion from Islam to Christianity—
is a fatal offense, punishable by death in the Sudan.
Actual innocence is *demanded* in any plea of insanity.
Red is held a taboo color for men's clothing in Japan.

Aldous Huxley declared the greatest modern invention
was not the railroad, not the airplane, but Scotch tape.
Teamsters never addressed a Republican Convention.
Fallen out of common use is a tall building fire escape.

The Harlem River is actually a strait, not a river.
Thomas More in *Utopia* approves two slaves per household.
Pleasure, not fear, conventionally describes a "quiver."
Steroid medications are able to be made from bread mold.

TRUISMS II

No job description exists for First Lady of the President.
There is no evidence pirates hoarded treasure in buried chests.
Backward leaning (falling inflection) is the grave accent.
Feathers, alone, exclusively constitute all tree sparrow nests.

The Bronx: no other NYC borough is designated by "the."
The majority of 18th-century novels were written by women.
A universal American response for clarification is "Huh?"
The smallest detectable sensation felt is technically a limen.

Garlic, ginger, oregano, and clove are all natural antibiotics.
Virtue is the vital, crucial precondition to mystical experience.
One third of world's entire population live in the solar tropics.
A distinct aspect of curiosity lingers in all morbid prurience.

During his 56-game hitting streak, 223 official at-bats,
slugger Joe DiMaggio struck out only a mere five times.
J. F. Kennedy's bare head ended the style of wearing hats.
There are 118 ridges on the edges of all American dimes.

Germany signed the Treaty of Versailles with 19 minutes left
in a dictated, pre-ordained, signed-or-be-invaded ultimatum.
Pollinating plants by bees stealing nectar defines a legal theft.
Banned in the EU as a possible carcinogen is all petrolatum.

A cogent rejoinder has always been late to the dance.
Throwing an apple at someone meant love in ancient Greece.
The seasonal act of moving cattle to graze is transhumance.
A pregnant woman at weddings is bad luck for the Vietnamese.

A youngster's favorite go-to chess piece is the knight.
A mustard look with a waxen finish heralds seasickness.
A bay is a bend is a basin is an inlet is a recess is a bight.
"Only 144,000 go to heaven" say the Jehovah's Witness.

The cream on Twinkies is merely vegetable shortening.
The French verb *blesser* means to hurt, to injure, to offend.
The Maldives is considered a paradise for snorkeling.
To ask directions for many males constitutes a vilipend.

Kant: "Thinking is a means of reaching intuition."
Canaan, the "Promised Land," was stolen by the Hebrews.
A lack of purpose of amendment negates contrition.
Atoms of diatomic elements forever come in pairs, twos.

Poland, which did not exist at the beginning of World War I, was created partly out of what had been Germany's Prussia.
The only natural number neither prime nor composite is #1.
Brownish silk, alone, comes from the oriental moth, tussar.

A group of jellyfish is widely referred to as a "smack."
Speaking in tongues as utterance is always unintelligible.
The "house" edge is actually less than 1% in blackjack.
Strong religious belief in a juror is generally unacceptable.

Novelist Kenneth Roberts favorite reading was cookbooks.
No presidential candidate from Connecticut has ever generated enthusiasm.
Murders are frequently occasioned by stopping at overlooks.
The world cure for any and all wounds, ancient and modern, is a cataplasm.

TRUISMS II

The Haitian Creole language is missing both q and x.
Jam is made with fruit, but jelly from fruit juice.
In an Indian accent, consonant sounds are retroflexed.
Men overwhelmingly prefer a female masseuse.

The most popular meat across the world is goat.
Si replaces *oui* in French to answer a question in the negative.
Any flattened third or seventh becomes a blue note.
Nothing, more than simple silence, inflames the argumentative.

Cast-iron, crystal, wood are not dishwasher-safe,
nor is plastic, copper, knives, or aluminum anything.
Condescension is involved in anything vouchsafed.
Vile it is for *couples* to purchase an engagement ring.

Democritus was suspected of being insane,
Aristarchus threatened with an indictment for impiety,
Plato's circular discourse judged basically inane,
and Socrates, condemned, was murdered by society.

Any action, actualizing a single possibility, assaults
to kill other options among which it had to choose,
while each commitment entails a number of defaults,
among which are numbered endless alternate cues.

Plato's Socratic Dialogues are basically all aporetic.
Nothing irks a batter more than a checked swing called a strike.
Sucking lemon slices/lemon water is a natural emetic.
A dam has water on both sides—on one side it is called a dike.

Shy people are invariably people who are lonely.
Stalin knew about the Atomic Bomb before Truman did.
Fashionistas strive for style exclusively: *yours only*.
The "sniper rule"—last seconds—is a standard wily bid.

Thumb protection is paramount in any boxing glove.
There are 59 beads in all Roman Catholic rosaries.
Joe DiMaggio signed baseballs with one dot above
and one below the last *i*, to guard against forgeries.

A tiger's roar can be heard as far as two miles away.
Chloral hydrate is what mystery writers call a "Mickey Finn."
Bisques are free turns for weak players in croquet.
A full fifteen percent of every human's body eight is skin.

The world's most dangerous job is being a fisherman,
state all surveys; test pilots officially come in second.
The personification of France and liberty is *Marianne*.
Arrest awaits a street walker in the act of any beckon.

Astronauts, risk averse, never think in terms of adventure:
"I loathe danger," said the first moon-man Neil Armstrong.
A bread slice (as a plate) served as the medieval trencher.
There should never be slit in material in any worn sarong.

Third Reich emigres helped the U.S.A. reach the moon.
Stravinsky owed his career to the ballet master Diaghilev.
Mozart wrote the definitive "Concerto in B♭" for bassoon.
A practicing Christian was Russia's Mikhail Gorbachev.

TRUISMS II

Homer in his epics invariably referred to Greece as Achaea.
To avoid reading to your children is distinctly child neglect.
All foods containing poppy seeds are banned in South Korea.
The soul—our spiritual nexus—is the will and the intellect.

The grille design of all Toyota Prius automobiles—
headlights on down—shows an angry Japanese face.
Worth more than $2,000 a pound are all glass eels.
White holes (unlike black holes) *spit out* light in space.

Space suits at NASA are all designed to operate in a
-250 degree F to a +310 degree F temperature range.
No one's a loser unless feeling rebuked by a winner.
Amsterdam is the world's first/oldest stock exchange.

Never place a pig on it back: its bellyfat will suffocate it.
Southern women all prefer White Lily self-rising flour.
A sleuth to solve a crime must first mentally duplicate it.
Steaming it conserves the most nutrients in cauliflower.

Ian Fleming, who died at 56, smoked 77 cigarettes a day.
Green cabbage juice relieves the pain of stomach ulcers.
To sing, declared St. Augustine, is the best way to pray.
Bass love nothing more than to nip mayflies or "sulphurs."

Cowardice is (sadly) not a punishable crime.
Connoisseurship is an eloquent way of saying "opinion."
Weaker poets rely on the facile "eye-rhyme."
Santa Fe is a city perfused with the scent of the pinyon.

No photos exist of astronaut Neil Armstrong on the Moon.
Orchestra conductors are easily unsettled, furiously jealous.
The 1918 flu epidemic put an end to the public spittoon.
A new convert to any faith/religion tends to be overzealous.

Conductor L. Stokowski, half Irish, faked a Slavonic accent.
Pianist Olga Samaroff was Texas-born Lucie Hickenlooper.
"Change your mind": what John the Baptist meant by *repent*.
Only a fog that's yellow is technically called a "pea souper."

God, oddly, smote the people of Ashtod with hemorrhoids.
Professional sportscasters should *call* a game, not try to *sell* it.
Modern tabloids flourish by way of trivial, invented factoids.
Police need submission of a rowdy crowd in order to quell it.

On the planet Mercury, a day is twice as long as a year.
Memorialists, peculiarly, never unwrap left floral tributes.
There are 13 suicides in the plays of William Shakespeare.
Acting from duty over love is among the worst substitutes.

You cannot travel by yourself—never alone—in Tibet.
No rain existed until Noah's time: streams watered plants.
Detrimental to all marine life is the indiscriminate gillnet.
Cayenne pepper is the extreme of all repellants to all ants.

At launch, NASA rockets are all aimed to the east,
partly for a boost from the Earth's 915 mph rotation
and in case the flight should go awry, in part at least,
to soar over the ocean away from human habitation.

TRUISMS II

The air that we breathe consists of about 78% nitrogen,
21% oxygen, 1% argon, and 1/3 % of carbon dioxide.
Map mechanisms are inborn in the brain of each pigeon.
Mammalian urine comprises the fertilizer carbamide.

Rhodium is officially a more valuable metal than gold.
An ounce of faith is worth more than all written theology.
Jimmy Durante would eat no candy if it was not cold.
No filibuster is not also a textbook exercise is battology.

Jonas Salk who ended polio never won the Nobel Prize.
Blessed are all the innocents whom the world ignores.
The Rayleigh scattering phenomenon causes blue skies.
Pueblo housing (*kivas*) were constructed without doors.

Architectural Digest never shows people in its articles.
Mahler's *Das Lied von der Erde* was an ode of self-consolation.
Two neutrons and two protons compose alpha particles.
Ancient Romans reclining to eat was a social act of accubation.

Impermanence in anything raises its quotient of beauty.
Neil Armstrong first touched the Moon with his left foot.
Singapore, Hong Kong, Switzerland levy no customs duty.
The Prodigal Son, from humility, returned home barefoot.

The world should have pity for a one-dream man.
Germaine Greer dismissed the Bible as a "silly book."
Guessing wisely is the secret of the game fan-tan.
Lumberjacks handling logs use a peavey or cant hook.

Psychiatry: huge fees, secular confession, no absolution.
Conductor Herbert von Karajan had a controversial Nazi past.
No one was more satirical than the ancient satirist Lucian.
Luke 15 has often been called "The Gospel of the Outcasts."

"Buzz Aldrin" took Holy Communion on the Moon
—kept secret from the public as a private relevance—
the wine and the host to the astronaut a special boon:
the first food eaten there were eucharistic elements.

Nothing is more bogus than tales of "The Other Side."
Slovenian does not use articles such as "a" and "the."
The "Rat Pack" referred to every loser as a "clyde."
Women in years past wore a bandeau instead of a bra.

A damp wood exists that literally glows in the dark:
there are 113 or more species of bioluminescent fungi.
The world's very first drunk was Noah, he of the Ark.
Strabismus is often the cause of reading with one eye.

Salzburg, Austria virtually exists to merchandize Mozart:
ties, scarves, dolls, books, umbrellas, sweets, key chains.
Most schematic processes are represented by a flow chart.
Male babies are said to cause women harsher labor pains.

An elite EB-1 program, issuing green cards arbitrarily
for those of "extraordinary ability," is utterly corrupt.
Food prices are much cheaper in a military commissary.
Cancer is a sign of high risk in a dilated pancreatic duct.

TRUISMS II

George Orwell defined sport as a surrogate for war.
The spirit of inquiry is an act of "experience stretching."
New Yorkers and Jerseyites instead of beach say "shore."
A sense of relief is the comfort of most Yiddish kvetching.

E-cigarettes, with flavor names like "grape slushie"
and "strawberry cotton candy," seduces kids to smoke.
No Hollywood blather is not extravagant and plushy.
In the UK mainly the old or eccentric qualify as a "bloke"

Maria Cebotari was Adolf Hitler's favorite soprano.
Drinking turmeric milk can lower high cholesterol.
Filipino street slang for any male American is a *kano*.
Sissies were sent off at PT to kick a medicine ball.

The oboe sets the standard for tuning in an orchestra.
To see Christianity as a tame faith is a total anomaly.
For bathing and sleeping Jews needn't wear a yarmulke.
Three-quarters of sea creatures have bioluminescent capability.

Every German region has its own recipe for liverwurst.
Torturing a human being for any reason is a diabolical act.
Truly heartfelt prayers are neither formulaic nor rehearsed.
18th-century polemics were all issued by treatise and tract.

Robert Frost's poems follow the *Via Negativa*
and his skewed attempts at theology concealed
a depression that, in attempts to seek a reliever,
in many a squeezed stanza loss itself congealed.

Nutella is made almost entirely palm oil and sugar—
it is less than 12% hazelnuts, with a trace of cocoa.
Julia Child disdained the use of a pressure cooker.
Still primitive are the Warao Indians of the Orinoco.

Elie Wiesel claimed Christianity was solely based on suffering.
The grubbiest buildings in colleges are inhabited by geologists.
More common in boys than in girls is the condition of stuttering
No scholar or sage could match Shakespeare as anthropologist.

Harrow rarely beats Eton in their cricket matches.
German *mädchen* always carry their beer trays high.
On the upper lid, not the lower, are more eyelashes.
A tempo direction equivalent to "very" is *assai*.

We tend to fall in love to create a space for belonging.
Not to know is bad, but not to wish to know is worse.
Seeing or hearing a yawn can actually cause yawning.
A Rolls Royce Phantom B12 is the most expensive hearse.

Whomever seeks to give light must also endure burning.
Goddard Lieberson of Columbia Records signed his letters "God."
Libido in women is raised, it's said, by the act of churning.
After Bach's *St. Matthew Passion*, it is traditional not to applaud.

It is the blue suit that anchors a gentleman's wardrobe.
Add salt meat before, not after cooking, for better flavors.
An organism that needs no oxygen to live is an anaerobe.
The Portuguese and the British led the world as slavers.

TRUISMS II

A salad in presentation always looks better piled high.
Roasted bone marrow proves in cookery there is perfection.
Fuel and water are roughly about the same price in Dubai.
Autopsies are on the deceased, on the live it is vivisection.

Enid Blyton, the famous children's author, hated children.
Green vegetables boiled in salted water stay much greener.
Bram Stoker said Dracula was inspired by Walt Whitman.
Only the way one behaves toward others defines *demeanor*.

Lesser quality chocolate contains emulsifiers and oils
which include coconut and palm, compromising taste.
Distilled water for its purity never needs to be boiled.
A virus "Fifth Disease" gives a child a reddened face.

The Trumps never released Melania's immigration records
or attempted to identify the attorney(s) who represented her.
The Samurai's *katana* of feudal Japan is the king of swords.
Israel alone has banned the use in fashion of all animal fur.

Never clean or wash a cast iron skillet with detergent: it can
also break, if dropped, and may crack if set hot in cold water.
At its peak, 5 million *northerners* joined the Ku Klux Klan.
Mao Zedong can't be topped for numbers in human slaughter.

Among creature features, one's unique to humans—the chin.
The Internet is controlled by only 14 people with seven keys.
Shape-shifting signalizes the major power of a mythic djinn,
There is a weird fluting music in a bad asthmatic's wheeze.

A fetus at the age of three months acquires fingerprints.
Braising liquid should come halfway up the side of meat.
Jesus reproved the venal Pharisees that they tithed mint.
Gluten is determined highest in spelt and durum wheat.

It is nearly impossible to become a citizen in the UAE.
The African continent spreads through all four hemispheres.
Trust or promise ("*treow*") is the linguistic root of tree.
Fall foliage beauty peaks in the Massachusetts Berkshires.

Racing pigeons are the world's most expensive birds.
William Blake claimed to have seen God at the age of four.
Toki Pona is a constructed language with only 120 words.
No fabled coin is more mythic than the Portuguese *moidore*.

A single confetti piece is formally known as a confetto.
J. D. Salinger drank his own urine and spoke in tongues.
A Tuscan diminutive of the name Guiseppe is Geppetto.
Left longs are smaller (for heart space) than right lungs.

Washington Irving, of *Rip van Winkle*, was a bad insomniac.
The Library of Congress published braille copies of *Playboy*.
Jesus's first public encounter was meeting a mad demoniac.
Few words, even inarticulateness, graces the movie cowboy.

Frank Morris, who escaped Alcatraz, had a high 133 IQ.
Cops rarely ticket a car with a pro-police window sticker.
During Asian quakes, people run into groves of bamboo.
Anthony Trollope saw "mutilated grandeur" in every vicar.

TRUISMS II

Protestants are ill at ease, often offended by crucifixes.
All weathermen dearly yearn to be called meteorologists.
A feature on all insects is their legs always come in sixes.
Experts in the study of ferns are botanical pteridologists.

Thomas Jefferson, Charles Dickens, Winston Churchill,
Henry Wadsworth Longfellow, Ernest M. Hemingway,
Virginia Woolf, Vladimir Nabokov, and Lewis Carroll
all wrote standing up, which gave them perfect leeway.

Mercy and compassion, alone, can render an injustice just.
"Be more Irish than Harvard!" (Robert Frost in 1960 to JFK.)
Corruption strikes at the heart of every discretionary trust.
Moisture and humidity are the natural enemy of all parquet.

Revolutionaries, after seizing power with new slogans,
almost always rapidly adopt techniques of the old regime.
In Japan, samurai held much less power than shoguns.
Christian angelology places cherubim second to seraphim.

A hunting rule—seek base of the ear for a side shot,
and just off-center, between the eyes, for a frontal.
Rear quarter left is an automobile's main blind spot.
J.S. Bach was undisputed master of the contrapuntal.

Simple people call supper what society calls dinner.
A Malapertness of Peddlers: a perfect collective noun.
Every starting tightrope walker is always a beginner.
Bilirubin is the pigment in feces that makes it brown.

People who fear the number 666 specifically
suffer from hexakosioihexekontahexaphobia.
Banking was conceived (and deals) in iniquity.
Vaudeville's Ben Turpin embodied esotropia.

Most football concussions take place during kickoffs.
Everyone has his own picture of the Supreme Being.
It was ancient Persians who cultivated the first pilafs.
Windows to one's overall health is found in peeing.

There is a lake in Webster, Massachusetts, 2½ miles wide,
"Chargoggagoggmanchaoggagoggchaubunaguhgamaugg,"
stating in Nipmuc, "You fish on your side, I fish on my side,
and nobody fish in the middle"—a perfectly balancing eclogue.

The Thalidomide drug of the 1950s causing birth defects
is now, FDA approved, selling under the name *Thalomid*.
After his Hajj, all racial strife was abjured by Malcolm X.
A legally binding contract is involved by any winning bid.

The St. Louis Browns on MLB were perpetual cellar dwellers.
W. B. Yeats, warm to aristos and peasants, loathed the middle
    class.
The client's *mind* psychologizes its fate, not the fortune tellers'.
The extreme nerve agent VX is considered the deadliest fatal gas.

Young Winston Churchill's disastrous errors at Gallipoli
have never been forgotten in New Zealand and Australia.
James Joyce never set foot in Ireland after the age of 30.
A schizophrenics' odd word repetition is called echolalia.

TRUISMS II

Hands in prayer formation seem to give devotion flight.
Rod McKuen and Maya Angelou dance the "Poetaster Waltz."
"Dewey" is a nickname given to anyone named Dwight.
Omar Khayyam said but a hair divides what is true and false.

Shameful dislike of Quakers, any Jews, the Scots, all blacks
is a theme of Charles Lamb's essay "Imperfect Sympathies."
The texture of gummy candies is the result of carnauba wax.
Only seven plays are extant of Aeschylus's seventy tragedies.

Nothing is more outmoded than last year's slang.
Mark Twain was first to submit a novel written on a typewriter.
Southern anger at Reconstruction created the chain gang.
Adding a trace of blue to white paint strangely makes it whiter.

Australian aborigines are not and never were Negroes—
all of them are of Indo-European and/or Eurasian origin.
Both Armenia and Azerbaijan are active and eternal foes.
The spirit of evil and strife in Zoroastrianism is Ahriman.

Amount refers to quantity in bulk, *number* to things counted.
Men in general tend to be averse to Jane Austen's novel *Emma*.
Avoid cheap diving gear, cut-rate surgery, brakes discounted.
Lustful desires are said to be associated with a dental diastema.

A single line in Rupert Brooke's poem "The Great Lover,"
"the rough male kiss of blankets," is an icon among gays.
Elevator chat—no serious information—is strictly claver,
Quakers refer to the "Fourth Day" instead of Wednesdays.

Every strong-bonding Akhal Teke is a "one-rider" horse.
The authorship of the book of Hebrews remains a mystery.
Shakers, linking it to original sin, avoid sexual intercourse.
Aristotle in *Politics* accepts slavery, condemns democracy.

Put off by it, Abe Lincoln called the timorous act
of cravenly highlighting mainly the number of *missing*
in any "killed, wounded, and missing" list in fact
was an example of "darky arithmetic"—unforgiving!

The word *fuck* can be used as a conjunctive adverb:
"I chose to walk the old road; fuck, I decided not to."
A *vegetable*—of the Polygonaceae family—is rhubarb.
The prime Masters (golf) sandwich is cheese/pimeneto.

Hitler despised the novel *All Quiet on the Western Front*.
A boomerang predates the aerodynamics of an airplane.
Forever is not in the conversation when discussing a shunt.
Ecclesiastes says the pursuit of pleasure for itself is insane.

The Kennedy family had no so-called Boston accents:
theirs was a mix of Irish, fake posh, haws, and hems,
honks, squawks, brays, and oddly strained vocal kents
—no one in Massachusetts ever quite spoke like them.

The book of James is the bossiest book in the Bible,
where 61 imperatives are crammed into 108 verses,
which means that nearly 2.6% of the words, a tidal
wave, fills a text of imperative verbs and coercives.

TRUISMS II

Chilean poet Pablo Neruda always wrote in green ink.
Leo is considered the most powerful sign of the zodiac.
The color yellow is involved in anything salmon pink.
Madly confounding to open is the inflexible blisterpack.

An asthmatic's wheeze can sound like an oboe or flute.
Prime Minister Anthony Eden was badly addicted to "speed."
Mainly Irish immigrants migrated to Montana's Butte.
It is a scandal Pontius Pilate is named in the Nicene Creed.

The Republic of Haiti has always been a hopeless ochlocracy.
Jorge Luis Borges began writing advertisements, for yogurt.
Pretentiousness and feigning are both vile forms of hypocrisy.
Selfishly to hog something exclusively, in slang, is "to bogart."

All experience ever is, is frankly confirmation in the end.
Hemingway and Hart Crane, suicides both, were born July 21, 1899.
Southern girls have a "gentleman caller," not a boyfriend.
Both male and female reproductive organs are found in a single pine.

Elbert Hubbard, who wrote of the *Titanic* in 1912,
drowned in 1915 on the torpedoed ship *Lusitania*.
The need to search in implied in the verb to delve.
Nail-biting is an obsessive form of phaneromania.

In the vitriolic tirade of Matthew 23, Jesus angrily attacks
deceitful human hogs for their worse than animal desires.
Gummy bears take a shine by way of carnauba leaf wax.
Wishes, desires, and images are all unconscious signifiers.

Cowardice is never better portrayed than in *Lord Jim*.
Sums of money requiring only two words must be written out.
Presbyterians always sing *all* the verses in every hymn.
The early morning hours are by far best time to fish for trout.

Samuel Butler's novel *Erewhon* (1872), all about mankind
being enslaved by machines, predates AI by a full 150 years.
A person's major growth step: refusing by peers to be defined.
Altruism is the perpetual grace and signature of volunteeers.

In the U.S. William Pierce's *The Turner Diaries*
is fully banned—not a single copy can be bought.
People tend to listen with eyes glancing sideways.
The hardest knot to undo is the "constrictor knot."

The weakest passport in the world is Afghanistan's.
Impact is now universally used improperly for *effect*.
Proceeding is, ironically, the goal of marriage banns.
Socrates by his wife Xanthippe was badly henpecked.

Of adverbial causes of clause (*before, for, since, as*),
in terms of correctness, almost everyone is ignorant.
No prisoner was ever put to death at prison Alcatraz.
Reflections emerge when thoughts are most itinerant.

Grilled kangaroo tails are a rare delicacy in Australia.
Clinomania is the compulsive need to stay all day in bed.
No schoolboy's locker can be beat for paraphernalia.
Sancho Panza to his ass: "All sorrows are less with bread."

Lust and asceticism are part of the same destitution.
"Time to consider truth"—an infinitive as an adjective.
Politically skewed talk shows define noise pollution.
Depression is ever heightened by the overly ruminative.

Queen Elizabeth I's hands are the key to the portrait
in Virginia Woolf's biographical 1928 novel *Orlando*.
Chinese sign language is almost impossible to interpret.
Rex Harrison sang songs in *My Fair Lady* via parlando.

No one under six feet is a hero in a novel.
All young women with high energy succeed.
The hypocrite suitor always tends to grovel.
Marriage plots turn on ins and outs of greed.

In his Epistle to the Galatians 1:11–2:14, St. Paul
publicly taxed St. Peter with spiritual dishonesty.
Good fortune is ever associated with a birth en caul.
Nothing is as unpalatable as a political autobiography.

The total capacity of *Titanic's* 20 lifeboats: 1,178 souls;
if each had been filled, 1,023 would have been left to die.
Jesus's name is never mentioned in the Dead Sea Scrolls.
Priests of Israel must belong by law to the tribe of Levi.

Other people's hobbies are always deemed ridiculous.
Too long a sacrifice can create a stone of the heart.
Peru's scary highways are the world's most vertiginous.
No one was more cantankerous than René Descartes.

Stores sell goods at, say, $78.99, adding the 99 cents
since fools may pay anything *but not a dollar more!*
To avoid defacing a landscape, employ a sunk fence
Truth always becomes propaganda in a state of war.

Comic repartee is the job of a minstrel show endman.
Two girlfriends ever exist who do not like your boyfriend.
Joseph Conrad, Ukraine born, spoke/acted like a Frenchman.
Railroad ballast is the most common use for hornblende.

The Gibson Girl had the slender lines of a "fragile lady"
with the bust and hips and hair of a "voluptuous woman."
Any land of bucolic innocence is always called Arcady.
Socrates thought death the highest blessing for a human.

There is overt racism in Gilbert's "The Bab Ballads."
The living ignore the dead, just as coal laughs at ashes.
Regional accents have been detected in quacks of mallards.
A soporific exists in the taking of blackstrap molasses.

Where love and need coincide, there is sustaining joy.
Prime Minister Anthony Eden was badly addicted to "speed."
The Slinky was initially devised as a tool, and not a toy.
Only 27 percent of the inhabitants in South Sudan can read.

Teenage passion is close to martyrdom, love for what
Marcel Proust described as *"la jeunesse féroce et légère.*
An oak's defense against parasitic wasps is a gallnut.
Illegal in the British Isles are any kinds of trap or snare.

TRUISMS II

In 1995 Donald Trump was forced to sell the posh Plaza
—a real estate *mogul?—at a huge loss of $83 million!*
Unrecognized as a de jure part of an extant country is Gaza.
The so-called *figa* is considered good luck to a Brazilian.

Abraham Lincoln, during his Gettysburg Address,
was applauded by the crowd at six different intervals.
Scorpions under ultraviolet light will phosphoresce.
Integration in calculus is an act of computing integrals.

Romantic poetry is that of autumn, childhood, past.
Edgar Allan Poe stated Richard Horne's epic, *Orion*,
was "superior even to John Milton's *Paradise Lost.*"
No one knows the true etymology of the word Zion.

"Retreat is an advance in a reverse direction"—!—
declared Fabius Maximus Cunctator ("The Delayer")
Making flint knives is the main aborigine obsession.
George Washington at age seventeen was a surveyor.

All great novels are at first insurmountably unsaleable.
It is only sad music heard that one describes as "beautiful."
The East Face/East Ridge of Mt. Everest is unscalable.
That the expanding universe has no center is irrefutable.

No one hated her own character more than Edith Wharton
for crass Undine Spragg in her *The Custom of the Country*.
It is corrugated fiberboard that makes any carton a carton.
All those who are unable to dance judge the floor slippery.

Jericho is considered the most ancient city of all
of which history has any evidence: ca. 11, 000 B.C.
Jewelry, pins, and casts are not allowed in volleyball.
Paraguay and Argentinian governments never agree.

Aleuromancy is divination by rolled balls of flour.
The common poorwill is the only bird that hibernates.
A Baltic personality, unempathetic, is basically dour.
The heat of the burning sun in Mali never moderates.

Nullity for Irish writer Samuel Beckett was a muse.
Sails do not flap, they "flog," but flags indeed do flap.
Feigning love just to marry money is the oldest ruse.
A human is able to bend a leg when missing a kneecap,

Corn displays an even number of rows on each ear.
President Joe Biden needs to open his mouth to listen.
Nothing doesn't loom for inmates of perpetual fear.
A tittle of pleasure resides in the fright of any frisson.

Fingernails grow faster on a person's dominant hand.
None of Saki's ephebe don't delight in a feral aspect.
Gamblers hold cards right to left, ever tightly fanned.
Few streets in the Dakotas are diagonal or transect.

Louisiana has the lowest utility rates in the USA.
Tickling to a degree requires an element of surprise.
Haste is the perpetual downside of sexual foreplay.
Tears shed by a rightful heir is laughter in disguise.

Corrosion is the simple reason that guns are blued.
Inability to draw leads many painters to abstraction.
Smugness always shows a face of froggy beatitude,
a soft wide grin of cocky, complacent satisfaction.

Octopus blood—of copper, not iron—is light blue.
Loveable is an aspect of character, *adorable* of looks.
Corfiotes is the proper name for the natives of Corfu.
The "Codex Leicester" is the costliest of all books.

Sticker prices on U.S. automobiles are always variable.
Cleopatra had pure Macedonian ancestry, not Egyptian.
The Musuo of south China are resolutely unmarriable.
Quantum computers are a potential threat to encryption.

Blue lights in Holland = transgender women sex workers.
In Holy Writ, #32 signifies God's covenant with humanity.
State jobs almost automatically manufacture born shirkers.
Scatology is basically the ongoing subtext of all profanity.

Humans acquired the AIDS from a chimpanzee host
from vaccines in Stanleyville in the Belgian Congo.
A vertical tie in a roof truss is called the "queen post."
The small drum is on the dominant side of bongo.

St. Paul's Ephesians, one of the "Captivity Epistles,"
is generally held to be greatest of all of his letters.
A relaxed parasympathetic type constantly whistles.
No debt collector isn't more intractable than debtors.

All union smokers loyally bought only Raleigh tobacco.
The east side of any hurricane is potentially tornadic.
The largest flower (*Rafflesia Arnoldiis*) exists in Borneo.
Eighty-five percent of taste regarding food is osmatic.

All good writing is an assault on cliché.
Written by a goy, Philip Roth's work would be anti-Semitic.
A hazardous technique in climbing to self-belay.
Rhythm in much Homeric verse often depends on the enclitic.

In Roman education, the *Aeneid* had to be memorized.
The Gay Divorce, irking censors, became *The Gay Divorcee*.
No biography sells better than one that is *un*authorized
A furtive euphemism for gay is "He's a friend of Dorothy."

In all of Jesus's parables, a priest appears only once,
negatively, to ignore the victim the Samaritan assists.
Guilt often accompanies winning of a jackpot bunce.
Few political conventioneers are not plain jingoists.

Physicians—lest disaster occur—must never abbreviate
IU (mistaken for IV or number 10, easily garbled vision)
U (unit); MS (can mean morphine *or* magnesium sulfate);
Q.O.D.; @; Cc; or X.O (a trailing zero is an imprecision).

Savage TV talk show host Joe Pyne's most common insult was
"Take your teeth out, put 'em in backwards, and bite your throat."
The full leek (not white alone) must be used in true vichyssoise.
Cuckolds in the Pieter Bruegel's paintings all wore a blue coat.

TRUISMS II

Vorarephilia is the fantastical paraphilia of a cannibal.
Legend] is that gold is buried in the Superstition Mountains.
Napoleon cited as his mentor the Carthaginian, Hannibal.
An Islamic paradise is inconceivable without fountains.

Crossword puzzles oddly use *oner* to mean a unique person.
Heroic roles in opera ideally must be held by a *heldentenor*.
True guardians of the Scottish Highlands is clan MacPherson.
Lovers often kiss the fleshly base of the thumb, the thenar.

Lady Edwina Mountbatten, of the British Royal family,
who slept with any man, was a virtual nymphomaniac.
"Sheng" is a hybrid slang of both English and Swahili.
Wales, a home nation, is unrepresented in the Union Jack.

The Bayeux Tapestry images are not woven into the cloth.
Forever is the occupational disease of all accordion players.
For Biblical anger, it is often said someone "waxed wroth."
Ancient Troy was discovered under 9 archeological layers.

Folks in showbiz are not out of work but are "At Liberty."
A Reuben Sandwich should always be served on rye bread.
Toscanini refused to eat any food that came from the sea.
January 1st is the common birthday of every thoroughbred.

The first step in the creation of any meal is wise shopping.
Knowing God is more important than knowing *about* God.
A felony is committed by illegal telephone eavesdropping.
The drink traditionally is five parts water, one part Pernod.

D minor is definitively the saddest of all musical keys.
"Go west, young man!" said Horace Greeley, who stayed east.
A working week in the Middle East begins on Sundays
Only after 25 years are U.S. classified documents released.

"Gee" orders a horse or mule to turn left, "haw" to go left.
All groups, factions etc. succumb to oligarchic tendencies.
Government benefits are the prime target for identity theft.
Three kisses are standard hospitality greeting for a Lebanese.

The restaurant "21" has always had secret, private wine cellars.
Saul Steinberg, who often drew them, was addicted to breakfasts.
The tip of the blade spins faster than the hub in all propellers.
Having dress pleats too wide have caused Amish to be outcasts.

We often forsake—betray—half of ourselves to mimic others.
The list of closing credits in movies have replaced "The End."
Rare is a fable where deviousness is not a trait of stepbrothers.
No good comes to those in Shakespeare's plays given to lend.

Both love and hate in fact occupy the same brain region.
Showbusiness people all presume to know each other.
The most trusted of all was Julius Caesar's Tenth Legion.
In the book of Job, peace sits in wind called a "souther."

Obadiah Masterson was Skye's full name in *Guys and Dolls*.
Theologian Paul Tillich had a vast pornography collection.
Virtually all fish live that spill over the torrent of Niagara Falls.
The left knee is used before a King (not God) in genuflection.

TRUISMS II

An augmented 4th, or Tritonus, is called "the devil's chord."
Somalia is the largest producer on the planet of frankincense.
The "kick flip" is the most difficult move on a skateboard.
AIPAC sets no money limit to Congress in lobbying expense.

Mouthwash used *after* brushing destroys any good fluoride.
The word playwright (artificer) has no link with the word *write*.
The discriminated in Gaza live a life of complete apartheid.
Yang (masculine) of *yin* and *yang* in China is the color white.

Jesus performed no miracles in Nazareth, his hometown,
since he found honor, faith and trust in him lacking there.
Any American folk dance in duple meter is a "hoe down."
Considered to be an actual caste is the Venetian gondolier.

The front legs of a hyena are longer than its back legs.
A French cop is an *agent de police*. (*Gendarmes* are national.)
Only thieves who are safecrackers are technically "yeggs."
Curiously enough, inflammable is a synonym of flammable.

Papal absolutism, an 11th-century system of rule, must go
to preserve the community of faith in the Catholic Church.
"Why, I oughtta . . ." was the catchphrase of the Stooges Moe.
The standard veneer of pulp and plywood is usually birch.

The dish *truite au bleu* is savagely cooked, boiled live to curl.
Damon Runyon, the "definitive" New Yorker, was born in Kansas.
The shrill, wailing sound of a bagpipe is denominated a *skirl*.
A tonsure—to appear "God's fool"—was adopted by St. Francis.

The original name for volleyball was "mintonette."
Sniffing a person's cheek is a kiss with the Vietnamese.
A single gamble that links two wagers is a parlay bet.
No dictatorship can function without its secret police.

The giraffe, ungainly, is the only mammal unable to swim.
Apple juice, inexpensive, predominates in every juice blend.
Vigor is energy, whereas enthusiasm and ebullience is vim.
Only to wander in a specified direction can a walker *wend*.

"Nelson's dandruff" in modern Navy slang is table salt.
Mark Rothko demanded low lighting when exhibiting his art.
Marry anyone, *anyone*, but never one who is never at fault.
It is ineffective with sequential categories to use a pie chart.

Investigative hypnosis by police has proven fully bogus.
Antonio Gaudi's buildings had no straight lines or sharp corners.
Brides always carry—the "wedding flower"—stephanotis.
The Know Nothing party, nativists to a one, hated all foreigners.

Execution, without spectators, does not fully answer its purpose.
Code-breaker Alan Turing was arguably the greatest WWII hero.
The "Stars and Stripes" played is an emergency alert at a circus.
As the key placeholder number, math is inconceivable with zero.

A privilege of the Royal Navy is they can remain seated
—by tradition—while drinking to the sovereign's health.
All American houses to the British are badly overheated.
Condom removal without a partner's consent is "stealth."

TRUISMS II

To understand a dataset's central tendency, use a quartile.
Feminists hate the transformation of Shakespeare's Kate.
The copula "is" (as, for example, in "Aristotle is mortal")
is not the same "is" of identity (as in "Twice four is eight."

An around the world sail involves 30,140 nautical miles.
Billionaires are the primary gallery guests at any vernissage.
It is illegal to bleach flour in the EU and the British Isles.
Any touching a woman's breast is illegal during a message.

In 2022, undocumented households paid $35.1 billion in taxes,
$21.5 in Federal and $13.6 billion in state/local taxes. Welfare?
Illegal workers pay $13 billion into Social Security—it waxes—
through payroll deductions, while ineligible for benefits. Fair?

Kant insisted that all noumenal reality is unknowable.
By trophallaxis, ants exchange food by vomit or defecation.
Carrots and radishes, for roots, indoors are ungrowable.
In 2024 Mexicans comprised less than 50% of U.S. immigration.

Love needs separation, a certain distance, to preserve it.
"To kiss the gunner's daughter" was to be whipped in a ship.
Every lottery ticket buyer is convinced that he deserves it.
Worse for you—toxic, lead, etc.—is any cigarette filter tip.

Cancer fund solicitations, a perpetual grab bag, never ends.
The CEO of the Jimmy Fund (cancer) makes $1,434,148 a year!
A high school girl is always ready with her *next* best friends.
The tastiest venison is a grilled backstrap of a whitetail deer.

Memory is a mental scrapbook that is never sorted out.
Among plural marriage cults, offspring are supposititious.
College admissions highly rate the fact an Eagle Scout.
There exists in simple ambition much of the avaricious.

Judy Garland was never nominated an Oscar for *Wizard of Oz*.
Vicuna wool is the finest and rarest natural fiber in the world.
Scottish delinquents were beaten (on the buttocks) with a tawse.
"Banana shots," or *trivela* (Pt.), in soccer are kicks that curl.

Squid are believed to be much more intelligent than dogs.
Mrs. Rudd was the prime tart in James Boswell's randy life.
The strongest purchase decisions are made from catalogues,
visual, tactile, choices, no rush, facts to read without strife.

With the advent of his "floating rectangles" theme, Rothko
ceased titling paintings he then identified by number and year.
The softest water on earth is, in Japan, to be found in Kyoto.
Sassafras, now banned by the FDA, made the best root beer.

Jehovah's Witnesses hold a special contempt for the Trinity.
To expect the National Debt be cut is to await the Neat Desk Fairy.
A Jew was never appointed to the faculty at Yale until 1943.
No one more than Willa Cather better evoked the Midwest
    prairie.

John in Revelation (2:13) identifies the city of Pergamum
(modern Bergama, Turkey) as "where Satan has his throne."
Two phalanges (the only digit) comprise the human thumb.
Not a cake nor a biscuit nor a pastry nor a bread is a scone.

TRUISMS II

One desire in being wanted finds ecstasy in being dominated.
Unconscious bias is far more prevalent than conscious prejudice.
Heat must reach 1,400 degrees F. for a body to be cremated.
Wit in the poems of e. e. cummings is located in the parenthesis.

"Baby Boomers" (1946–1964) were AWOL in the 1960s.
Skipping a day's work is a standard state worker's perk
The Roma people consider offensive the racial slur "gypsies."
Proust said that great writers only create a single work.

A current editorial fiat capitalizes Black but not white.
Virtues are not everyday habits; they are character traits.
Magicians rely mainly on the use of hands—"sleight."
Greek *dactylos* (finger) gives us the food word "dates."

Poet Ted Hughes re-shaped dead Sylvia Plath's history
(ripping up diaries, journals, etc.) to hide his own brutality.
The purpose of masked balls is to create sexual mystery.
Blandness less than tolerance denotes the word neutrality.

Have a garrulous or silent spouse? Keep a good library.
No Jewish wedding plays *Lohengrin*'s "Wedding March."
Henry Thoreau's favorite nature treat was the huckleberry.
Tapioca flour can serve just as well on shirts as starch.

Moby-Dick touts whale steaks yet never describes the taste.
A characteristic of bores is that they're deaf and never listen.
Governments usually benefit when its currency is debased.
"The sun's origin" is the translation of Nippon and Nihon.

Rockland is considered the lobster capital of Maine.
Every clothespin is worthless without a great spring.
All forms of life possess a soul, according to a Jain.
No true evidence supports the validity of "superstring."

While at the *Rapture*, Jesus will return *for* His saints.
although He will not in fact descend to Earth, whereas
at the *Second Coming*, He will return *with* His saints,
as a prelude to his earthly reign, to all a judgement pass.

The limit of ready gunpowder on ships at sea—initially—
explains a 21-gun salute, now the international standard.
Growth based on debt is unsustainable, done artificially.
Chasing prey in shallow waters explains whales stranded.

The name *Sarah* is banned in Morocco; in Saudi Arabia
so is *Linda*, as is *George* in Portugal and *Wolf* in Spain;
Judas in Switzerland; *Qu'ran* in China; *007* in Malaysia,
even *John* in Denmark, where strictest naming laws reign.

Locusts have no king, yet they advance in ranks.
Astronomy grew out of astrology, as chemistry from alchemy.
One man in a firing squad always shoots blanks.
No word in English is less convincing than that of *probably*.

Six thousand people or so have summited Mt. Everest.
Ambergris, waxy lumps, is never found in healthy whales.
Women actually make up more than 70% of therapists.
"Nail-sickness" in old ships was solved by use of trunnels.

TRUISMS II

Asbestos in fibrous deposits grows next to talc like twins.
Wassily Kandinsky sought to create *sound* in his painting.
Born in Braunau, Hitler always called his hometown Linz.
Reflex syncope is the essential cause of women fainting.

Sometimes a person has to tell a lie to convey the truth.
The Laodicean church, smug, was apathetic to Christ's words.
Lou Gehrig often had chats in German with Babe Ruth.
Omne trium perfectum: excellence, it is said, comes in thirds.

Poison is considered women's primary murder weapon.
Logic was not a part of Wittgenstein's life but the whole of it.
The French educational system has long suppressed Breton.
Macho existentialism: the aim of the Abstract Impressionist.

Tallulah Bankhead, who was constitutionally incapable
of discretion, never kept a secret and had a compulsion
just as often to make up secrets—in a drive inescapable—
in order *not* to keep them, loving any attendant revulsion.

Lotteries are a tax on people who are bad at math.
Cheese is always in spectacular conversation with wine.
A city constantly reprehended in the Bible is Gath.
Gobbledygook is the essential prose of Gertrude Stein.

When boasters loudly say, "You can't make this stuff up!"
the laughable truth by far, in fact, is that *anyone* can do so.
The arrival of Spring in Alaska is referred to as "break up."
A direction in music for humor is invariably *capriccioso.*

Demographic studies are a subset of economics.
Andy Warhol purposely lied in every interview he gave.
The trickle-down theory animated Reaganomics.
Total sequestration is a requirement in a Papal conclave.

The middle of the 8th and middle of the 4th centuries B.C.
was the most important in the history of human thought:
Buddha, Confucius, Zoroaster, all of Greek philosophy,
and all the prophetical books the Old Testament wrought.

Elon Musk's essential ambition is to colonize Mars.
Suicide attempts by adolescent girls triple that of boys.
Not one leaf is chemically treated in the making of cigars.
A distinct "*sshhhh*" is audible under all white noise.

The triumphalism of feminist rhetoric is male.
Afghani food is basically multiple iterations of kabobs.
For downwind use, always employ a large sail.
Bumfodder for most American pioneers were corncobs.

Eastern European wedding bands are worn on the right hand,
Mount Horeb is, curiously, the same as Mount Sinai.
Jews wear wedding rings on the index finger of the right hand.
English is the most common language spoken in Dubai.

China, xenophobic, refuses to take in immigrants.
Nuclear energy is key to reversing climate change.
What revives a boxer is ammonia—smelling salts.
Kuwaiti Dinar is top currency in foreign exchange.

TRUISMS II

Famous for its *Chinatown* is Japan's Yokohama.
Mansaf is considered the national dish of Jordan.
Mayonnaise is despised by Pres. Barack Obama.
Innocence is never signified by any issued pardon.

All who believe in psychokinesis, *raise my hand!*
Otto Weininger held sexual desire inimical to greatness.
Sardines, tuna, and anchovies all taste better canned.
Force of rotation configures every planet's oblateness.

Fate implies inevitability; destiny one achieves by will.
All helmets during World War I were made of leather.
Nothing can match peacocks for an eerie, piercing shrill.
Fuel, thatch, fodder, ropes, medicine: all uses of heather.

The English never drink sherry before the evening,
avoid reading novels in the morning, orderly queue
to board a bus, take tea at 3 and 4 p.m., convening,
apologize if *you* bump into *them*, and always make do.

It is much easier to wish people dead than to kill them.
Every French person feels obliged to explain the USA.
A frontline defense of bacteria and viruses is phlegm.
Marriage proposals are traditionally made on a leap day.

A curse afflicts those with only half a talent.
Donald Trump made $300,000 endorsing the Holy Bible.
"T'garns'l" is sailor slang for the top gallant.
A small byte in nerdly computer speak is called a "nybble."

"Star-Spangled Banner" lyrics consists solely of questions.
A coffin's a box for corpses, a casket for anything precious.
A major tribulation for narcissists is uninvited suggestions.
Cucurbits, coconuts, cucumbers are all curiously monecious.

There is no authoritative version of *Hamlet*, sadly.
with radical differences between the First Quarto (1603)
(often called the "Bad Quarto," transcribed badly,
the Second Quarto (1605), and the First Folio (1623).

Qom, the holy Shiite city in Iran, is not as holy as Mashhad.
10-year-old girls—"tweens"—are obsessive about cliques.
An overly air-conditioned workplace can bring on Raynaud's.
The most crucial key to human facial symmetry is its cheeks.

Americans constantly, like, when they are speaking, like,
robotically, like, keep interjecting, like, the word like. *Why?*
Hans Daunekar is the 10-year-old hero of "The Dutch Dyke."
Although handsome, Pres. John F. Kennedy had a wall eye.

The definitive Palestinian dish is *msakhan*, a round
flatbread, doughier than pita, glistening with olive oil.
Bred for hunting in packs is the sociable foxhound.
The Amish quilt pattern most favored is the quatrefoil.

A typhoon is as frequent in Taiwan as snow in Buffalo.
Each digit in a U.S. zip code has its own specific function.
Sweet or wild marjoram is a culinary version of oregano.
Contrition, deeper, is not merely regret, like compunction.

TRUISMS II

Young William Faulkner enrolled briefly at Ole Miss
in 1919, received a D in English, often skipped classes,
as an applicant by a college literary society was dissed,
and after three semesters dropped out with no passes.

People shapeshift constantly, trying on various personae.
No character ever died on stage in ancient Greek drama.
Stowage capacity (for tannins, acidity) is high with cabernet.
Shot, Mahatma Gandhi's last words were "*Rama, Rama!*"

Smoking toad is the uppermost climax in psychedelics.
Rhyme without rhythm is a martini without a lemon twist.
Protestants find inappropriate any veneration of relics.
Philemaphobia is the odd fear of kissing and being kissed.

Although we are told that Jonah preached to Nineveh,
we have no record whatsoever of the words he used.
In the UK, negative connotations link to the word *clever*.
Gin when agitated loses crispness as it is badly bruised.

No one seems superior walking into a public toilet.
That no one else is you precisely defines your power.
Overheating Hollandaise sauce will promptly spoil it.
No one suddenly summoned by Stalin didn't cower.

The very earliest undisputed inhabitants of all America
descendants from Asia, were people known as Clovis,
roughly 12,000 years ago, who vanished like chimerica,
possibly by a sudden asteroid impact—without notice.

Only Psalm 86—it alone—is technically called a "prayer."
The Tour de France (*Grand Départ*) doesn't start in France.
Being hired help or a family member confuses an *au pair*.
St. Paul at times made decisions after he fell into a trance.

No complete Bible can be said to be older than the 9th-c A.D.
Judy Garland's "If I Love Again" dwarfs Lee Wiley's version.
Butter is far less shelf-stable at room-temperature than ghee.
After 1935, the endonym Iranian replaced the identity Persian.

South African cookery, with *bobotie, sosotie*, and such,
has been strongly influenced Malay and Javanese cuisine.
Bad traffic snarls cause motorists to drive riding a clutch.
Teeth do not exist in whales whose jaws feature baleen.

One glacier ice crystal can grow as big as a baseball.
We never learn if Jesus and Pontius Pilate spoke Greek or Latin.
It is hydraulic lock that causes a car in water to stall.
Monks never wear soft fabrics, velvet, poplin, fleece, silk, or satin.

"No young man who aspired to be a serious writer
would ever consent to be being published by a house,
which kept its offices west of Fifth Avenue," inciter
Truman Capote once perorated in a typical grouse.

Bolla Soave, white, fruity, was Frank Sinatra's favorite wine.
St. Luke, not to impugn Rome, blamed the Jews for Jesus's death.
Pity is at bottom a vice, despite its attitude to appear benign.
It is strictly taboo in theaters for actors to utter the word
    Macbeth.

TRUISMS II

Malachi is Hebrew for "messenger"—not a proper name—
and the author of that Scriptural book remains anonymous.
The world famous generally excoriate the virtues of fame.
Communal and confraternity types fear being autonomous.

Writer John Gardner, sober, in a *Washington Post* interview
claimed he was the greatest master of prose since Chaucer.
An hexagonal hole alone is found in the head of Allen screw.
In the 18th-century, coffee was largely drunk from a saucer.

The Biblical term *Selah* used in Psalms means a "lifting up."
and may refer both to either voices or musical instruments.
Cattle, avoiding its high toxicity, will never eat a buttercup.
Making anyone unduly wait rates high on a list of insolence.

Most inventions of the Shakers were never patented—
to them taking out a patent smacked of selfishness.
Devon Island in Canada is completely uninhabited.
Citizens fight not to feel their vote's ineffectiveness.

Donald Trump never sat face to face with the fact of himself.
Sunday morning radio programs in general are all abysmal.
Only that money gained by deceit and/or dishonesty is pelf.
Asthma can bring on a type of coughing that is paroxysmal.

Qiviut, musk ox underhair, is eight times warmer than wool.
Shakers believe Original Sin—Adam on Eve—is intercourse.
If an "*indulto*" (pardon) is granted, then life is spared a bull.
Even the Vatican—with the Swiss Guard—has a police force.

The Trapp Family, escaping Austria, all fled to Italy by train,
not over to Switzerland on foot as seen in *The Sound of Music*.
Petrichor, an oil of plants, gives a fresh, earthy smell to rain.
Avoiding psychiatrists is the healthiest psychotherapeutic.

There is a rank, ammoniacal smell to a goat.
The U.S. mint produces no paper currency,
only metal coins alone and never a banknote.
Bank not on anyone "self-employed currently."

Marion Crawford, a gentle, loving governess,
on Princess Elizabeth and Meg wrote a book,
which Royalty scorned with icy unforgiveness,
snubbing for life, with never a word or look.

Never offer alcohol to warm a person up.
A jellyfish sting can be thwarted by vinegar.
Lithium was in the original mix of Seven-Up.
Painters roughed out frescoes with sinoper.

The emotion of feeling jealousy is never admitted.
Each English county has its own style of thatching.
No novelty hats at Royal Ascot are ever permitted.
21 days is standard for an egg of a chicken hatching.

The oldest language in all western Europe is Basque.
Decadence basically informs molecular gastronomy.
A Shaker belief: "Work is worship whatever the task."
Only in fantasy can exist a true socialist economy.

TRUISMS II

The oldest inhabited house in the British Isles
is dark, sinister, ghost-haunted Glamis Castle.
Outsiders in the Mormon religion are "Gentiles."
The most overused 1960s noun/verb was "hassle."

Waves approach the shore of a beach by threes.
Curtseying involves bending the left knee to bow.
Sweet wine only should be drunk with bleu cheese.
Unique as to pattern is a individual's eyebrow.

There are 300 clocks to wind in Buckingham Palace.
An ISBN number—13—may use hyphens or spaces.
While the penis is an object, symbolic is the plallus.
In 1959, NASA invented the wires used in braces.

Shakespeare mentions no balcony in *Romeo and Juliet*.
The most preferred xenotransplantation animal is a pig.
The shortest of all (12 letters) is the Rotokas alphabet.
A lightning shaft, in any direction, is described a "twig."

Fortiter Feliciter Fideliter

About the Author

Alexander Theroux, who lives in West Barnstable, Massachusetts, has taught at Harvard, MIT, Yale and at the University of Virginia. He is the author of four highly regarded novels, *Three Wogs* (1972) *Darconville's Cat* (1981), *An Adultery* (1987), and *Laura Warholic* (2007), as well as four volumes of poetry and several books of nonfiction.